Moving Image Knowledge and Access
The BUFVC Handbook

Fourth Edition

Editors: Cathy Grant and Luke McKernan

British Universities Film & Video Council

British Universities Film & Video Council
77 Wells Street, London W1T 3QJ
Tel:: 0 7393 1500 Fax: 020 7393 1555
E-mail: ask@bufvc.ac.uk

First published 1991 as *The BUFVC Handbook for Film & Television in Education 1991/92*
Second edition 1995 as *Film and Television in Education: The Handbook of the British Universities Film & Video Council*
Third edition 2001 as *The BUFVC Handbook*
Fourth edition 2007

ISBN 978-0901299-77-2

Cover design by Graeme Campbell Design
Typesetting by Gem Graphics
Printed in Great Britain by Latimer Trend and Company

MOVING IMAGE KNOWLEDGE AND ACCESS

The British Universities Film & Video Council (BUFVC) promotes the production, study and use of **moving image** and **sound** for teaching, learning and research. We provide **access** to television programmes under licence, we are a centre of **specialist knowledge** and expertise, we make available significant **content** across **all subject disciplines**, we provide **advice** and **training**. We support the use of moving image and sound as an integrated and rewarding part of the **learning experience**.

CONTENTS

Introduction   vi

About the BUFVC
Publications   7
Learning on Screen   11
Membership of the BUFVC   11
BUFVC contacts   13

Articles
Sixty years of the BUFVC – *Luke McKernan*   14
ERA Plus – *Andrew Yeates*   19
A world in your ear: radio archives and education – *Seán Street*   23
Moving images and sound: inclusive and accessible – *Alistair McNaught*   29
Video, education and the new funding agenda: building new values –   34
    Peter B. Kaufman

Directory
Archives   43
Awards   47
Blogs   53
Broadcasting   56
Courses and training   103
Discussion lists   108
Distributors   112
Festivals   122
HE Academy subject centres   131
Media legislation and reports   137
Organisations – UK   157
Organisations – international   191
Podcasting   198
Regional Support Centres   203
University audio-visual centres   205
Web sites   225

Index   237

INTRODUCTION

This is the fourth edition of the British Universities Film & Video Council's Handbook, which was first published in 1991. The Handbook has always aimed to deliver a valuable guide for teachers, librarians, producers, service providers, and anyone using audio-visual media in higher education. This edition bears a title which expresses the BUFVC's on-going mission in its sixtieth year of operation, *Moving Image Knowledge and Access*. We aim to know all that needs to be known about moving image and sound for use in higher education and research: the resources, the issues, the technologies, and the contacts. We aim to be an access point to such knowledge, and to the audio-visual content itself, either provided by ourselves or through partnerships which we have brokered. Sixty years after the BUFVC was first established as a representative body and a central source of information for UK universities, our field of work has grown considerably. Improving access to broadcast content and the startling rise in the delivery of all kinds of video content online are just two developments which bring a greater need for evaluation, curation, reliable description and critical review. In 2008, the BUFVC has an increasing role to fulfill.

This latest edition of *The BUFVC Handbook* is expected to be the first in what will be developed as an annual publication. This is an added benefit for staff in BUFVC Member Institutions, and a reflection of a rapidly-changing media landscape. Each edition of the Handbook has seen some alteration in the kinds of information provided. While traditional listings information for Organisations, Distributors and University Audio-visual Centres remain, new categories such as Blogs and Podcasting have appeared. Other listings, such as Education Officers in Television, regrettably are now obsolete.

It is our intention to develop a complementary electronic database of this and additional Directory information, regularly updated, and accessible online to staff and students in BUFVC Member Institutions. This database will complement and augment our existing core datasets, such as HERMES (audio-visual materials in current distribution), the Moving Image Gateway and the Researcher's Guide Online, with the aim of eventually integrating BUFVC datasets and making them accessible through a single search interface.

The articles that precede the main Directory section are an important feature. These take us from Luke McKernan's account of the foundation of the BUFVC in 1948, when 16mm film was the medium of choice, through to Peter B. Kaufman's astonishing vision, just a few years hence, when 'all the media ever created in the world' may be carried on a piece of equipment the size of an iPod. Andrew Yeates describes the possibilities for increased, online access to off-air recordings for educational institutions through the ERA Plus licence, while Alistair McNaught of TechDis describes the creative ways in which moving images and sound may be used to increase accessibility and inclusion. The BUFVC is increasingly engaged in initiatives to improve access and use of radio and audio recordings in higher education, and Seán Street's inspiring article on the potential of radio archives ought to heighten our perception of this neglected field.

We hope that this latest edition of our Handbook will be of value to BUFVC Members and anyone working with moving image and related media across the Higher Education sector. We welcome any feedback.

Murray Weston
Chief Executive
BUFVC

Credits

This book was compiled by the BUFVC Information Service: Sergio Angelini, Cathy Grant, Luke McKernan and Marianne Open. Our grateful thanks go to all of them for their hard work and attention to detail. Whilst every care has been taken to ensure the accuracy of the information in this Handbook, if errors are found, or if there is information that you may wish to see in a future edition, please contact the editors at library@bufvc.ac.uk.

All photographs were taken by Nick Townend and Luke McKernan for the BUFVC.

Note

Entries in the individual sections of the Directory are listed alphabetically by title, except for *University Audio-Visual Centres*, where they are listed alphabetically by university (i.e. University of Manchester files under M); *HE Academy Subject Centres*, where they are listed by subject; and *Media Legislation and Reports*, where they are listed chronologically.

Off-Air Recording Back-up Service

We offer a television recording back-up service for UK educational institutions with an Educational Recording Agency (ERA) licence. A member institution can request videocassettes or burned CD/DVD copies of missed programmes broadcast since June 1998. The BUFVC is one of the few bodies in Britain holding a letter of agreement with the ERA permitting the post-transmission supply of copies of UK television programmes under Section 35 of the Copyright, Designs and Patents Act 1988.

Our Off-Air Television Recording Back-Up Service currently records BBC1, BBC2, BBC3, BBC4, ITV1, Channel 4 and Five. We have retained recordings from 1998 and can call on other collections to locate a requested programme as far back as 1990. We have recorded over 300,000 hours since 1998, with 44,000 hours now being added every year. Users can elect to receive their programmes in a variety of formats; burned CD copies with compressed files in QuickTime and Windows Media variants, or the more popular VHS and DVD options.

BUFVC member representatives may now2 order copies of programmes via TRILT. Simply find the programme record in the TRILT database (see below) and the system will carry across all the details. Representatives can see at a glance the programmes that have already been requested and track their progress on the system.

TRILT – Television and Radio Index for Learning and Teaching
Web: http://www.trilt.ac.uk

TRILT delivers advance information on programmes and an e-mail alert service. It is an essential tool for all audio-visual librarians and for those wishing to identify and order specific programme content from our Off-Air Television Recording Back-Up Service.

Unlike other online electronic programme guides, TRILT retains the programme data long term, creating an archive of broadcast information growing by more than a million records each year. With comprehensive data from 2001 and selected data from 1995 to 2001, TRILT can be used to research a topic, find programme repeats, locate a specific missed programme, or plan viewing and recording up to ten days in advance.

TRILT database entries indicate which programmes are available from our Off-Air Television Recording Back-Up Service. Selected programme entries are 'enhanced' with additional information, such as longer descriptions, contributor details, production credits, links to relevant web sites, tie-in books and keywords.

TRILT is accessible only to staff and students in subscribing BUFVC member institutions. To check the current membership status of your institution please telephone 020 7393 1500 or e-mail ask@bufvc.ac.uk. It is possible also to test TRILT with four weeks of data in our open access demonstration version (http://demo.trilt.ac.uk).

HERMES

Web: http://www.bufvc.ac.uk/hermes

Hermes catalogues some 30,000 audio-visual programmes selected for their usefulness in higher and further education. It covers films, videotapes, DVDs, sound recordings and other media, accessible by title, production company, personality, date and subject, and gives full content and distribution details. It also contains records of BUFVC library holdings.

Moving Image Gateway (MIG)

Web: http://www.bufvc.ac.uk/gateway

The Moving Image Gateway connects you to 1,000 reviewed sites around the Internet which deliver valuable moving image, sound and related content online. It is fully searchable by subject discipline, and now includes references to podcasting and video podcasting sources.

Researcher's Guide Online (RGO)

Web: http://www.bufvc.ac.uk/rgo

The RGO is an authoritative guide to accessible film, television and radio archives in the UK. It is complemented by our long-established printed reference work, *The Researcher's Guide: Film, Television, Radio and Related Documentation Collections in the UK.*

British Universities Newsreel Database (BUND)

Web: http://www.bufvc.ac.uk/newsreels

The BUND is the world's leading resource for the study of cinema newsreels. The BUND offers a fully searchable database of 180,000 newsreel and cinemagazine stories, 80,000 digitised production documents and a wealth of contextual resources including audio interviews, bibliographies and links to over 40,000 downloadable film clips of British Pathe newsreels.

An International Database of Shakespeare on Film, Television and Radio

Web: http://www.bufvc.ac.uk/shakespeare

We are currently developing an international database of Shakespeare on film, television and radio programmes, from 1898 to the present day, with funding from the Arts and Humanities Research Council. The full database will be published in summer 2008, although a preliminary version with 2,000 records has been made available.

BUFVC manages three television and radio research databases on behalf of Bournemouth University:

The TV Times Project (TVTiP)

Web: http://www.bufvc.ac.uk/itvdata

TVTiP provides unique online access to the programme listings of the London edition of the *TVTimes* from September 1955 to March 1985. Available without charge via Athens to all UK higher and further education institutions and subscribing BUFVC members.

This Week

Web: http://www.bufvc.ac.uk/itvdata

THIS WEEK was a leading ITV current affairs series from 1956-1992. This database offers detailed information, including programme descriptions and personnel. Available without charge via Athens to all UK higher and further education institutions and subscribing BUFVC members.

The Radio Research Database (RRDb)

Web: http://www.bufvc.ac.uk/databases/rrdb.html

The RRDb aims to carry a record of all current radio-centred academic research in the UK, to assist all those researchers working in the new discipline of Radio Studies. The database is funded by the Radio Academy and managed by the Radio Studies Network.

Information Service

Web: http://www.bufvc.ac.uk/services

At the heart of the BUFVC's work is our specialist Information Service. The reference library holds over 4,000 books, and ninety journal runs, with current catalogues from over 800 British and overseas distributors of audio-visual materials. We also hold an extensive archive of historical film catalogues, documenting educational and training programmes no longer in distribution. Our collection of journals and magazines includes every issue of the *Radio Times* since March 1991 when it began listing all terrestrial television channels; over twenty years of *American Cinematographer*; *Screen Digest* since 1972; thirty years of *Monthly Film Bulletin*; and every issue, including supplements, of *Sight and Sound*. Information Service staff handle a wide variety of enquiries from university lecturers, television researchers, teachers and health professionals and members of the public on audio-visual materials for teaching and learning.

The Information Service and Library is available free of charge to members. Visitors are advised to make an appointment in advance.

Special collections

Web: http://www.bufvc.ac.uk/services/specialcollections.html

BUFVC holds a number of unique book and documentation collections of great value in moving image history and research:

- *Bert Baker book collection* – relating to television and media studies
- *British Movietone News newsreel documents* – complete set of commentary scripts (1929-1979) and photocopied set of Newsreel Association of Great Britain and Ireland papers
- *British National Film and Video Catalogue documentation* – selection of papers and index cards
- *British Pathe newsreel documents* – entire surviving paper collection for British Pathe newsreels and cinemagazines
- *Brook Associates programme data* – production material on three historical television series: THE WINDSORS (1994), THE LAST EUROPEANS (1995) and THE CHURCHILLS (1995)
- *Channel 4 press releases* – complete set of press releases, November 1982 to June 2002
- *Clem Adelman collection* – cine films, audio tapes, transcripts and slides from Professor Adelman's researches into teacher-pupil relations, 1970-76
- *David Buckingham collection* – papers covering interviews with primary school children on their television viewing habits 1989-1991 for the project 'The Development of Television Literacy in Middle Childhood and Adolescence'
- *David Samuelson papers* – papers of Movietone newsreel cameraman
- *Margaret Leahy photograph album* – belonged to winner of a newsreel competition in 1922 to star in a Hollywood feature film
- *Mark Lewisohn television papers* – collection of television and radio press releases
- *Norman Fisher collection* – newsreel cameraman's photographic collection, diaries and other memorabilia
- *Norman Roper collection* – newsreel cameraman and editor's photographs, news clippings, address books, posters and equipment
- *Reg Sutton memoirs* – newsreel sound engineer's memoirs
- *Reuters Television newsreel documentation* – substantial collection of original documents, such as shot lists, dope sheets and commentary scripts, for Gaumont-British, Paramount and Universal newsreels
- *Scientific Film Association* – paper archive of the Scientific Film Association and papers of Stanley Bowler, relating to the International Scientific Film Association.
- *Shell Film Unit papers* – collection of documentary film scripts
- *Slade Film History Register* – register of documents relating to film of value to historians, originally collated under Professor Thorold Dickinson.

Courses

Web: http://www.bufvc.ac.uk/courses

The BUFVC runs regular one-day courses on topics relating to the use of moving images in learning, teaching and research.

Current and forthcoming BUFVC courses include:

- *Authoring Streaming Media for the World Wide Web*
- *Copyright Clearance for Print, Broadcast & Multimedia Production*
- *Data Projectors for Education*
- *Encoding Digital Video – Introduction*
- *Encoding Digital Video – Advanced*
- *Finding and Using Audio-Visual Media in Further & Higher Education*
- *Introduction to Streaming: From Production to Delivery*
- *Shooting with HDV (High Definition Video)*
- *Streaming and Handheld Technologies to Support Students with Disabilities*
- *Video in Flash*

Facilities and room hire

Web: http://www.bufvc.ac.uk/facilities

We have a 25-seat seminar room with high quality video/data projection facilities. Our primary connection to JANET runs at 10 mbps, so live online moving image demonstrations can be offered. Our offline viewing facilities include a 16mm (six-plate) Steenbeck viewing table, and the facility to transfer 16mm film archive recordings to video. There are also video copying facilities for various formats and standards. High quality videoconferencing facilities are planned for the end of 2007.

Film and video distribution

Web: http://www.bufvc.ac.uk/services/distribution

The BUFVC distributes and makes available for sale a number of specialist titles. Classic titles include Sir Lawrence Bragg's famous study of the properties of bubbles on the surface of a liquid, BUBBLE MODEL OF A METAL (1954); Professor Stanley Milgram's controversial experiments on obedience to authority, OBEDIENCE (1969); John Lowenthal's documentary on a notorious Cold War case, THE TRIALS OF ALGER HISS (1980); and the thematic compilations of British newsreels produced by the InterUniversity History Film Consortium. The full list with prices is available on our online distribution catalogue or via the HERMES database.

Consultancy

Web: http://www.bufvc.ac.uk/consultancy

We provide specialist consultancy services capable of addressing a wide range of issues relating to the provision of academic support services using moving image and sound. Drawing upon specialist practitioners within the Council's membership, we provide assistance in fields including copyright clearance, encoding, cataloguing, metadata construction, archiving and many others.

RESEARCHER'S

Researcher's Guide to British Newsreels

Second edition

Film and Tele

RESEARCHER'S GUIDE TO BRITISH

YESTERDAY'S NEWS

Virgilio Tosi CINEMA BEFORE CINEMA

FILMING HISTORY THE M

THE RESEARCHER'S GU

RESEARCHER'S GUIDE TO BRITISH F

THE RESEARCH

PUBLICATIONS

Web: http://www.bufvc.ac.uk/publications

Our magazine *Viewfinder* is published four times a year and is delivered to subscribing BUFVC member institutions. This popular publication brings you up-to-date on the production, study and use of film, television and related media for higher education and research, and includes subject listings of recent video and audio titles.

Current BUFVC book publications:

The Researcher's Guide: Film, Television, Radio and Related Documentation Collections in the UK

Sergio Angelini (ed.)

This 2006 edition of *The Researcher's Guide: Film, Television, Radio & Related Documentation Collections in the UK* has been completely revised and updated. Known as the film researcher's 'bible' and first published in 1981, this seventh edition now has details for over 640 audio-visual collections from the United Kingdom and Ireland. It features national and regional film and television archives as well as stockshot libraries and collections held by local authorities, museums, institutions of further and higher education, industrial companies and private individuals. *The Researcher's Guide* is now available for the first time in a new compact format. It also includes two dozen new illustrations and is fully indexed.

> 2006. pbk. 232 pages. ISBN 0 901299 76 6. Price £19.99 (£15.99 to BUFVC members). UK delivery included; £5.00 postage and packing elsewhere.

Cinema Before Cinema: The Origins of Scientific Cinematography (First English Edition)

Virgilio Tosi (translated by Sergio Angelini)

This classic history of early film and photography, first published in 1984, describes the scientific impulses behind sequence photographers such as Eadweard Muybridge and E.J. Marey, whose work led directly to the birth of cinema. Now entitled *Cinema Before Cinema: The Origins of Scientific Cinematography*, the book has been updated to include recent research in the field. The BUFVC is the distributor of the English-language version of the film series THE ORIGINS OF SCIENTIFIC CINEMATOGRAPHY, which Tosi produced over 1990-1993 to complement his written researches. The BUFVC has produced a DVD edition of the films, to mark the publication of the English edition of the book (see below).

> 2005. pbk. 248pp. ISBN 0-901299-75-8. Price £29.99 (£25.00 to BUFVC members). UK delivery included; £5.00 postage and packing elsewhere.

About the BUFVC

The Origins of Scientific Cinematography

Virgilio Tosi's classic documentary series has been made available on DVD in English for the first time. The films complement Tosi's book *Cinema Before Cinema* (also published by the BUFVC), using archive film and original equipment to show how cinematography had its origins not in the music hall or the fairground, but in the laboratory, as scientists of the 19th and early 20th centuries attempted to find new ways of seeing and measuring the natural world. Subjects covered include Jules Janssen's 'photographic revolver' (1873-4), Eadweard Muybridge's development of serial photography of human and animal locomotion (1878-87); Étienne-Jules Marey's 'photographic gun' (1882), and his models of the Chronophotographe (1882-93); technical advancements of scientific cinematography between 1883 and 1914 in different countries; and a compilation of sequences from twenty scientific films, made between 1895 and 1911.

> 2005. 97 mins, col/bw, in English. Region 0. Available in PAL or NTSC formats. Classification: E (Exempt). Price: £49.99 (£39.00 to BUFVC members) inc. postage and packing.

Yesterday's News: The British Cinema Newsreel Reader

Luke McKernan (ed.)

This reader brings together over forty key texts on the British news-reels, from their silent beginnings to their revival as the ingredient of television documentaries. The texts come from trade papers, memoirs, parliamentary debates, newspapers articles, publicity brochures, film reviews and academic essays past and present. The reader documents how the newsreels were produced, how they were received, and the controversies they inspired through the conflicting demands of news and entertainment. It covers filming of two World Wars, from the invasion of Belgium to the liberation of Belsen; the Spanish Civil War; the rise of television; and enduring arguments over censorship, propaganda and political bias in the news. It documents their organisation, the cameramen's experiences, and the overlooked role of women in the newsreels. It covers the academic interest they have aroused, with classic studies and the best of research taking place today.

> 2002. pbk. 330pp. ISBN 0 901299 73 1. Price £39.00 (£29.00 to BUFVC members), UK delivery included; £5.00 postage and packing elsewhere.

Filming History: The Memoirs of John Turner, Newsreel Cameraman

John Turner

John Turner worked as a cameraman for *Gaumont-British News* between 1937 and 1952. As a war correspondent he was attached to the Royal Navy and filmed in the UK, North Sea, Mediterranean, Italy, North Africa, north west Europe and the Far East. In peace time he filmed many classic news stories, and was in India at the time of independence and Gandhi's assassination. In 1952 he became the royal rota cameraman for the Newsreel Association, filming the royal Commonwealth tours and numerous exclusive royal events. Between 1962 and 1970 he became production manager and then news editor for *Pathe News*. *Filming History* will be of importance to social, cultural and political historians, university courses on media and communication studies, and anyone interested in the history of British film and the important part played in that history by the newsreels.

2001, pbk, 256pp, ISBN 0 901299 72 3. Price: £35.00, including UK p&p. BUFVC member's rate: £29.00, UK delivery included; £5.00 postage and packing elsewhere.

Film and Television Collections in Europe: the MAP-TV Guide
Daniela Kirchner (ed.)
An indispensable guide to 1,900 film and television archives in over forty European countries from the Atlantic to the Urals. Includes large and well known national film archives, television companies, newsreel and stock-shot libraries, as well as many small and lesser known collections held by regional and local authorities, museums, business and industry, and private individuals.

1995. hbk. 671pp. ISBN 1 85713 015 4. Price £75.00 (£67.50 BUFVC members) + £5.50 postage and packing UK, + £9.50 postage and packing elsewhere.

'The Story of the Century!': An International Newsfilm Conference
Clyde Jeavons, Jane Mercer and Daniela Kirchner (eds.)
The papers, presentations and proceedings of an international conference held at the National Film Theatre, London, between 2 and 4 October 1996, which brought together cameramen, editors, producers, film and television researchers and academics from many countries to celebrate 100 years of news on film and television. The book provides a lively insight into the world of the newsfilm – one of the century's most powerful forms of journalism. With its mix of formal papers, presentations and discussions, the material will inform and entertain everyone interested in news on film and television.

1998. pbk. 170pp. ISBN 0 901299 69 3. Price £15.00 + £2.50 postage and packing UK, + £9.50 postage and packing elsewhere.

British Universities Newsreel Project
The CD-ROM of the British Universities Newsreel Project database was published in March 2000, and contains details of almost 160,000 British cinema newsreel stories. Between 1910 and 1979 the newsreels, released twice a week in British cinemas, gave millions their picture of national and world events. They have now preserved an invaluable record of life and news in the twentieth century. Based on the data contained in original newsreel issue sheets, the BUNP CD-ROM contains full text and keyword search facilities, allows users to see the order in which stories were presented in each reel,

and contains other details such as footage lengths, cameramen's credits, and regional variations to content.

The CD-ROM comes with a detailed booklet giving a short history of the British cinema newsreel. For film researchers, archivists, historians and students of news media, the BUNP database CD-ROM is an indispensable tool.

2005, CD-ROM. Suitable both for PC and Apple Macintosh systems. £95.00 including VAT and p&p. £65.00 to all BUFVC subscriber researchers and Member institutions including VAT and p&p. *Note:* The CD-ROM does not include the digitised documents and additional data for cinemagazines added to the online database since 2000.

LEARNING ON SCREEN

Conference

Learning on Screen is an annual conference organised by the British Universities Film & Video Council since the BUFVC merged with the Society for Screen-Based Learning in 2004.

Learning on Screen is for those developing and using moving image and sound content in learning, teaching and research. It brings together producers, courseware creators, e-learning specialists, media librarians, academic service providers, lecturers, researchers and staff developers.

Increasing quantities of moving image and sound content are now available on demand from broadcasters and national online services, and educational establishments are rapidly taking up use of these resources in their own virtual learning environments to deliver bespoke courses.

Other Learning on Screen events, such as one-day conferences, seminars and workshops, are also organised. See the Learning on Screen web site for details: http://www.bufvc.ac.uk/learningonscreen.

Awards

The Learning on Screen Awards celebrate excellence in the production of effective learning material which employs moving pictures, sound and graphics. Such learning material might be delivered as physical media, or online, or via broadcast media – or a combination of all three. The competition is open to all-comers involved at any level in the fields of production, publishing, broadcasting, education and research.

For information on upcoming Learning on Screen events, the Awards, or to join the mailing list, visit the Learning on Screen web site at http://www.bufvc.ac.uk/learningonscreen or e-mail learningonscreen@bufvc.ac.uk.

MEMBERSHIP OF THE BUFVC

Members of the BUFVC enjoy a range of benefits, from access to off-air recordings to discounts on publications, courses and conferences.

Voting rights

Representatives of Ordinary Member institutions carry voting rights to determine the management and conduct of the Council.

Off-Air Television Recording Back-up Service

Licensed Ordinary Member institutions can order copies of programmes from BBC1, BBC2, BBC3, BBC4, ITV1, Channel 4 and Five from June 1998 (and earlier where possible). These are available in DVD and VHS, or as burned CD copies with compressed files in QuickTime or Windows Media Player formats.

About the BUFVC

Television and Radio Index for Learning and Teaching (TRILT)

This database is only available to staff and students in BUFVC Member institutions. It holds over eight million records, and members can order copies of off-air recordings direct from the database.

Other databases

The TV Times and This Week databases are available to BUFVC Members and UK higher education users with an Athens password only. Other BUFVC databases including Hermes, Moving Image Gateway and the British Universities Newsreel Database, do not require access authentication.

Technical services

Members enjoy discounts on BUFVC technical services, including viewing, copying and encoding facilities.

Information Service

Members have full use of our Information Service, which will answer queries by e-mail, telephone, letter, fax or in person. Members also have access to the BUFVC book library and special collections.

Courses and Events

Staff in BUFVC Member institutions obtain discounts on registration charges for all BUFVC courses and events.

Publications

The BUFVC's quarterly magazine *Viewfinder* magazine is only available to BUFVC Members, and is supplied without further charge. One free copy of each new BUFVC book publication is supplied to institutional Members, with discounts on all other purchases.

We are constantly working to add new services and resources for the benefit of BUFVC members.

Applications for membership should be accompanied by a formal letter addressed to the Director of the BUFVC. Applications will be considered by the Executive Committee of the Council before acceptance.

For further information, including details of current rates and an application form, visit http://www.bufvc.ac.uk/membership.

77 Wells Street, London W1T 3QJ
☎ 020 7393 1500 **Fax:** 020 7393 1555
E-mail: ask@bufvc.ac.uk Web: http://www.bufvc.ac.uk

BUFVC staff (as of October 2007)

- Murray Weston – Chief Executive 020 7393 1505 murray@bufvc.ac.uk
- Geoffrey O'Brien – Assistant Director – Finance & Administration
  020 7393 1503 geoff@bufvc.ac.uk (*To retire December 2007*)
- Nick Townend – Assistant Director – Online Projects & Services
  020 7393 1510 nick@bufvc.ac.uk
- Sergio Angelini – Library and Database Manager 020 7393 1506
  sergio@bufvc.ac.uk
- Lotfallah Bekhradi – Network and Content Manager 020 7393 1509
  lotfallah@bufvc.ac.uk
- Markeda Cole – Media Assistant 020 7393 1514 markeda@bufvc.ac.uk
- Cathy Grant – Information Officer 020 7393 1507 cathy@bufvc.ac.uk
- Perri Mahmood – Assistant Administrator 020 7393 1519
  perri@bufvc.ac.uk
- Dominic O'Brien – Media and Network Technician 020 7393 1514
  dominic@bufvc.ac.uk
- Marianne Open – TRILT Officer 020 7393 1501 marianne@bufvc.ac.uk
- Nancy Prall – Events Officer / Director's Assistant 020 7393 1512
  nancy@bufvc.ac.uk

David Lean and Gaumont Sound News/Screen Heritage projects

- Linda Kaye – Senior Researcher 020 7393 1518 linda@bufvc.ac.uk

Newsfilm Online

- Lydia Pappas – Senior Cataloguer 020 7393 1511 lydia@bufvc.ac.uk

Shakespeare Project

- Eve-Marie Oesterlen – Broadcast Researcher 020 7393 1502
  evemarie@bufvc.ac.uk
- Olwen Terris – Senior Researcher 020 7393 1502 olwen@bufvc.ac.uk

SIXTY YEARS OF THE BUFVC

Luke McKernan

The British Universities Film & Video Council was first established as the Universities Film Council in February 1948 by a group of university teachers who were pioneering the use of film for higher education and research. The value of film as a research tool had long been recognised in the field of science, but the use and production of films for university work was barely considered. It was common to find 16mm projectors in schools, with libraries of appropriate films on which to call, but few films existed that were felt suitable for teaching at university level, and still less could the interested lecturer find the right production or projection equipment, or simply the information necessary for the support of the use of moving images in higher education.

The original objects of the Council, enshrined in its Articles of Association were as follows:

> The advancement of education in the universities and institutions of university standard in the United Kingdom by the co-ordination and development of the use and study of film and related media, materials and techniques for the purpose of university teaching and research, and in particular:
> to promote:
>> the collection and dissemination of information
>> the distribution
>> the production of films suitable for the above purpose
> to co-operate with universities and similar bodies in other countries for the performance of these objects.

The British Universities Film Council (BUFC), as it soon became, was sustained by a small number of volunteer representatives, who took it upon themselves to identify the needs within higher education, in particular building up a small collection of films which were otherwise hard to locate (often at the recommendation of the Scientific Film Association) and establishing a catalogue of suitable films available for hire. Any film on the catalogue was evaluated by university teachers in terms of its suitability for their work. Originally maintained as a card index, the catalogue was first published in book form in 1960 as *Catalogue of Films for Universities*. Around 1,400 titles were listed.

The Council encouraged the use of film as a research tool. This meant promoting filmmaking skills, as well as the availability of suitable equipment, and a directory of academics using cinematographic techniques was established. The Council also organised conferences and first published its *University Film Journal* in 1953, which became *University Vision* in 1968, folding in 1976. A journal reporting on the Council's activities was established as

BUFC Bulletin in 1950, to be followed by *BUFC Newsletter* in 1967, and then *Viewfinder* in 1987, which continues today as a quarterly journal.

Brynmor Jones

Throughout the first twenty years of its existence, the BUFVC had no permanent secretariat or headquarters. It was sustained by members' subscriptions and a small grant from the British Film Institute. Change began to occur with the publication of the report of the Robbins Committee, *Higher Education*, in 1963, and of the Hale Committee, which investigated university teaching methods. This activity was followed by the Brynmor Jones Committee, which looked specifically at the use of audio-visual materials in university, resulting in its 1965 report *Audio-Visual Aids in Higher Scientific Education* (1965). The BUFC's representations to the Committee were significant, and following the report several audio-visual centres were set up within UK universities. Brynmor Jones also recommended the creation of a national centre for the production and promotion of audio-visual materials in UK higher education. This proved too expensive to realise, but gave impetus to the BUFC requesting a substantial increase in its grant. This was agreed by the Department of Education and Science, and the BUFC subsequently received funding as a grant-in-aid body of the British Film Institute, opening a small office within the BFI in October 1967. A full-time secretary was appointed, and between 1968 and 1975 the Council's staff grew to seven full-time personnel.

Among the significant activities at this time for the Council was the establishment of the Higher Education Film Library in 1971. This was a collection, operated on a not-for-profit basis, for the distribution of specialised films across subject disciplines, which commercial distributors would be unlikely to consider. The catalogue was published in regular editions as *Audio-Visual Materials for Higher Education* from 1972, generated from a computerised database. In 1976 the Council took over the publication of HELPIS (Higher Education Learning Programmes Information Service), a catalogue of audio-visual materials made by higher education institutions, from the National Council for Educational Technology. The Council also was influential in encouraging the use of film as evidence in the field of history, and following some notably successful conferences, in 1974 it took charge of the Slade Film History Register of resources of value for the study of history through film. The acquisition and continual augmentation of the Register led in 1981 to the first edition of the *Researcher's Guide to British Film & Television Collections*, a work which rapidly became established as an essential source for film researchers, and which has now gone through seven editions, with a complementary existence as an online database.

The Council's increased activity at this period was inevitably the reflection of an increased use of audio-visual materials within the higher education sector. The creation of the Open University in 1969 brought together university teaching and broadcasting in a huge advance for the field. The emergence of the videocassette led to the decline of 16mm libraries and a new demand for recordable television output for use in education – something that the law at that time did not permit.

In 1983 the Council moved away from the British Film Institute into separate offices, now funded direct by the Department of Education and Science. It also acknowledged the rise of a new medium by changing its name to the British Universities Film & Video Council (BUFVC). The BUFVC continued its regular activity of publication, conferences and information provision, while developing specialist expertise in the subject of newsreels, data which derived from the Slade Film History Register. Three editions of the *Researcher's Guide to British Newsreels* (1983, 1988, 1993) were published, and a microfiche edition of all known newsreel issue sheets (1984). In 1987 the BUFVC began a selective index of television programmes, the Television Index, which soon built up into an invaluable resource for members, and a timely innovation in view of changes to copyright law which were soon to come into force.

Copyright exceptions

The Copyright, Designs and Patents Act (1988) included some important exceptions which were intended to enable educational institutions to take advantage of technology for the recording of television programmes. From 1989 onwards, universities and schools could legitimately acquire copies of broadcast television and not only show them but make copies of them, for purposes of learning and teaching within an educational setting. The BUFVC saw the opportunity for the creation of an Off-Air Recording Back-up Service, retaining copies of programmes that the universities themselves might not have recorded, under licence from the Educational Recording Agency (ERA). This proved to be immensely important for the BUFVC's future, and it has been the bedrock on which membership of the Council, with all of its associated services, has rested ever since. Initially, programmes were kept for three months, and then the tapes wiped; a revised agreement with the ERA has enabled the BUFVC to retain copies indefinitely, and the archive of recordings which begins in 1998 now amounts to over 300,000 hours of UK terrestrial television.

In 1996, the Council ceased to be directly funded by the DES and was now supported by a grant from the Joint Information Systems Committee (JISC) of the Higher Education Funding Councils, received via the Open University. This ushered in an era where computer networks, electronic databases and digitised content were to be of ever increasing importance for the Council's work. This was demonstrated by the Imagination pilot project for the delivery of moving picture content to universities and colleges online, developed in collaboration with the JISC and the British Film Institute in 1998. More than thirty hours of moving pictures, relevant to study in Medicine, Social History and Film Studies, were selected, predominantly from the National Film and Television Archive, encoded at the University of Manchester, and then delivered to pilot sites for integration with their associated metadata.

In 1995 the BUFVC's commitment to newsreel history took a significant step forward with the British Universities Newsreel Project, funded by the Higher Education Funding Council for England (HEFCE). This four-year project created a database of 160,000 records out of the collection of newsreel issue sheets, and led not only to the publication online of the British Universities Newsreel Database in 2000, but to a succession of major research projects that built upon this internationally significant resource.

Television and radio data

Online delivery of information and moving image content has dominated the BUFVC's work over the past ten years (its first web site was published at the end of 1996). Of the several online databases that have been published since 2000, by far the largest and most significant for future developments is TRILT – the Television and Radio Index for Learning and Teaching. Inspired by the BUFVC's Television Index, and originally a JISC-funded development, TRILT (launched in 2001) exploited the simple idea of retaining electronic programme guide data which was being disposed of by commercial sources. The resultant database covers virtually all UK television and radio since June 2001, with over eight million records added so far, and 3,000 new records being added every single day. Now linked to the booking of television programmes available through the BUFVC's Off-Air Recording Back-up Service, TRILT is well placed to serve the higher education community in a world where post-transmission content may be delivered across networks and distributed across campuses through Virtual Learning Environments. Further complementing this work was the creation of a hard disk-based system for the provision of post-transmission access to UK broadcast television programmes as encoded files, whimsically named Box of Broadcasts, or BoB.

The experience of the Imagination pilot project for the delivery of moving image content across networks was followed by two major encoding projects. In 2001 the BUFVC established the JISC-funded Managing Agent and Advisory Service for moving pictures and sound online (2001-2005), which led to the library of online audio-visual content now managed by the EDINA National Data Centre as Film and Sound Online. In 2004, following an intensive scoping study, the BUFVC was able to build on its expertise in newsfilm by managing a three-year JISC digitisation project to encode and prepare for online delivery 3,000 hours of television news and cinema newsreel content from the collections of ITN and Reuters. This massive project, bigger in scale and weightier in the pressures it put on the Council than any previous project, was completed successfully in 2007 and is planned for release to UK higher and further education through EDINA early in 2008.

Most recently, the BUFVC has undergone significant operational change. In 2004 it merged with the Society for Screen-Based Learning, taking over that organisation's Learning on Screen annual conference and awards. At the end of the academic year 2005-2006 it was agreed that the funding relationship by which core grant monies came via the Open University would come to an end, and the BUFVC would be funded directly by HEFCE under a new 'Related Bodies Funding Agreement' with oversight by the JISC. The BUFVC simultaneously entered a process of strategic options review. This resulted in a new Articles of Association, and revised Objects of the charity (the BUFVC is a limited company of charitable status), which now read:

The advancement of education by promoting the production, study and use of moving image, sound and related media within post-compulsory education and research.

The future for the BUFVC will see an increased commitment to the preparation and delivery of specialist moving image content online, the enhancement and augmentation of its database deliveries, and a growing interest in radio.

Luke McKernan was formerly Head of Information at the BUFVC.
He is now Curator, Moving Images at the British Library.
E-mail: luke.mckernan@bl.uk

ERA PLUS

Andrew Yeates

The Educational Recording Agency Limited (http://www.era.org.uk) is a copyright collecting society created following the passing into law in England and Wales of the 1988 *Copyright, Designs and Patents Act* (CDPA). It was set up in 1989 with a view to operating a certified copyright licensing scheme for educational use of copyright protected material.

ERA licences have now been available for educational establishments for seventeen years. In that time the number of broadcast services from which licensed recordings can be made has increased exponentially. At the same time, the technology has changed almost beyond recognition. The concept of the 'VHS trolley' moving between classrooms has given way to on-line access facilities for students linked to broadband services which would have been almost inconceivable seventeen years ago. The HE sector took the lead in testing ways of harnessing the educational opportunities opened up through the use of new technologies. More recently the deployment and use of information and communications technology (ICT) in education has been recognised by Government as a crucial means of achieving progress in the accessibility of educational resources. In 2005 alone some £252 million was invested in ICT in primary and secondary schools.

ERA has therefore been discussing the ways in which its licensing scheme may be extended to enable students and teachers to access off-air recordings of broadcasts made by or for educational establishments for the non-commercial educational purposes of such establishments, whether the students or teachers are physically on the premises of the educational establishment or not. This sounds simple, but in terms of rights clearance, without ERA taking a positive role, the situation could be very complex. This is because rights owners are generally individually entitled expressly to consent to a third party electronically transmitting files containing their work in ways that they are 'communicated to the public.'

Although the CDPA provisions on which the certified licence scheme is based apply an educational copyright exception to off-air recordings being 'communicated' for educational purposes within the premises of an educational establishment, the exception does not extend to 'communication' beyond the premises of the school, college or university. The thinking behind this reflects how rights owners are developing new business models for licensing the use of content online. The new music download services and subscription audio and video on demand services available through services such as Napster or Lovefilm.com are examples of these.

Steps taken by ERA to date

Since its establishment in 1989, ERA has grown to encompass a uniquely broad membership willing to mandate the agency to represent the copyright works relevant to licensing under section 35 and paragraph 6 of Schedule 2 CDPA. The growth in membership has to a large extent been driven by its efficiency as a copyright licensing agent, and the copyright distributions that can be made through it in an area where individual licensing would prove much more costly and time consuming for rights owners and consumers. In addition the structure provided by the CDPA has helped simplify both the application and the administration of ERA licences by educational establishments of all kinds.

For the benefit of both its members and its licensees, ERA has always attempted to keep the bureaucracy involved in licensing to a minimum, and has supported the issue of blanket licences for schools within the remit of Local (Education) Authorities to help minimise bureaucracy. The agency has therefore tried to build on these benefits when developing the ERA Plus 'add on' licence enabling educational establishments to make the educational recordings covered by the certified scheme available for educational purposes to students and teachers directly connected with the relevant educational establishment via a secure network.

Using the Gowers Review to help facilitate ERA Plus licensing

Although an enormously broad range of rights would be covered by any ERA Plus licence (as mandated by members participating in the certified scheme – see http://www.era.org.uk for details of the current scheme), there is nevertheless a risk that there may be some rights included in the broadcasts of programmes from which the off-air recordings are made, which have not been 'cleared' for the uses envisaged under the add-on licence.

Where section 35 (2) and paragraph 6 (1B) of Schedule 2 apply, licensees do not need to worry about any 'missing' rights unless a separate certified scheme existed. In practice the only other section 35 certified scheme has been that relevant to Open University programmes, which are easily identifiable.

As the law stands, the agency can give no such assurances as regards the 'remote access' rights to be licensed in ERA members' repertoire under the possible ERA Plus licence. On the other hand, the risks to licensees over the 'missing rights' clearances are likely to be low because of the broad spectrum of ERA representation. In any event such risks exist in all areas where there is reliance upon blanket licences from collecting societies. In that context the proposed ERA Plus licence will have a significant value for licensees. However, bearing in mind the broader social benefits which arise from educational copyright licensing, the members of ERA responded to the 2006 Call for Evidence by the Gowers Review of Intellectual Property (the consultation document can be found at http://www.hm-treasury.gov.uk) by outlining possible options which could reduce the 'missing rights' risk for licensees.

ERA suggested that section 35 (1) and paragraph 6 of Schedule 2 might be amended to cover the full scope of the current licence and the ERA Plus licence, enabling such recordings to be accessed from the server of an educational establishment by authorised students across the UK, regardless of whether they are physically on the campus of the school or college. It proposed that one way that this might be done would be to apply the exception for communication of licensed off air recordings:

a) to persons who are connected with the establishment; but
b) for the non commercial private study purposes of such connected persons; when the communication is
c) controlled by the educational establishment so that the identity and use by such connected persons is known.

In this context, it suggested that 'connected persons' might comprise:

individuals who are either currently enrolled to study at an educational establishment (which holds an ERA licence) or who are current members of the academic, research or teaching staff of the educational establishment (whether on a permanent, temporary or contract basis) and who are authorised by the educational establishment to access a secure network where the (ERA) recording has been reproduced.

Extending ERA membership

In an effort to address the possible 'missing rights' issues, regardless of possible change to the scope of section 35, ERA has been in negotiation with a number of additional bodies representing rights linked to films not currently wholly owned by the existing members, to agree the basis upon which they will join and thus make the ERA repertoire even more comprehensive for the purposes of granting both standard and ERA Plus licences.

ERA Plus licence

Following helpful consultation meetings with representatives across all sectors of education, ERA has developed a draft ERA Plus licence. Details can be obtained by contacting the agency at era@era.org.uk. It has been open to licensees to take out an ERA Plus licence from 1 April 2007. Tariffs for ERA Plus licences are linked to payments under current licences, although, for the time being, separate documentation will be needed. For establishments of Higher education the tariff proposed for ERA Plus licences in the year commencing 1 April 2007 is 78 pence per annum per student or full time equivalent (before application of any agreed discounts).

Gowers

In December 2006 the Gowers Review published its recommendations. These included as 'Recommendation 2' that steps should be taken 'to enable educational provisions to cover distance learning and interactive whiteboards by 2008 by amending section 35 ... of the Copyright, Designs and Patents Act 1988.' ERA is hoping that implementation of the recommendation will support the roll out and take up of ERA Plus licences in ways that will benefit both rights owners and educational establishments.

Andrew Yeates *is General Counsel to the Educational Recording Agency.*
E-mail: legal@era.org.uk

A version of this article was originally published in Viewfinder no. 67 (June 2007)

A WORLD IN YOUR EAR: RADIO ARCHIVES AND EDUCATION

Seán Street

Some years ago, as part of a broadcasting oral history initiative in the Media School at Bournemouth University, I conducted a series of recorded interviews with retired BBC staff who had been active in the development of radio during the first half of the twentieth century. Among those I interviewed was the late Dr Desmond Hawkins, a former controller of the BBC's West Region, a moving force in the creation of the Natural History Unit in Bristol, and an active programme maker in pre-war British broadcasting. He recalled the experience of listening to early transmissions during the 1920s from the then British Broadcasting Company: 'I first experienced a Shakespeare play through radio ... and Beethoven – I heard my first quartet not in a concert hall, but in my living room. My parents were not the types to take me to such events *in situ* so to speak, but fortunately I was part of the first generation for whom sound broadcasting provided access to the cultural world beyond the family walls.'[1]

For the young Desmond Hawkins, radio's democratising power was a key to his first response to the medium. For several subsequent generations, prior to the development of television, the same was true, not solely in terms of high art, but crucially in the field of entertainment, music and news. The power of sound to create pictures in the mind, to fuel the imagination or to simply tell stories has remained constant and much vaunted through the years, and through the development of new media. At the same time the death of the medium has frequently been predicted, not least within the first decade of the twenty-first century, when downloading content and new platforms for delivery have forced the industry to consider in which direction it is to reinvent itself this time. One of the beneficiaries in this new world of downloads, podcasts and audio on demand is showing itself to be speech-based radio; the technology which enables listeners to store content on MP3 players also enables them to create and understand the value of their own personal archives. Thus we are coming to a point where the purpose of radio archives needs no explanation or justification; it is 'case proven.'

Radio ballads and new beginnings

When, in 1958, Charles Parker, Ewan MacColl and Peggy Seeger made THE BALLAD OF JOHN AXON, a new form of radio feature blending actuality, location-recorded speech and music, enabled largely by new portable recording technology, it is likely that they saw themselves as programme makers developing radio into fresh fields of making and production. The fact that fifty years on, this and the subsequent seven other *Radio Ballads* would have spawned an annual conference studying their work and methods, as well as a commercial release of every programme in the series, may well not have occurred to them.[2] The fact is, there has emerged over recent years, the new academic phenomenon of 'Radio Studies,' which, coupled with a growing industry awareness of its past, is developing useful work in the exploration how – and why – radio interacts with its audience.

Yet the value of our radio collections exists beyond the confines of the study of the medium for its own sake. Charles Parker left a huge personal archive of tapes, books and papers, now held at Birmingham Central Library. This material is perceived as a living, valuable resource, not just for the study of radio, or the past, but as a modern-day commentary and cultural link in today's mixed society. *Connecting Histories* is a partnership project led by Birmingham City Archives, working with the School of Education at the University of Birmingham, the Sociology Department at the University of Warwick, and the *Black Pasts, Birmingham Futures* group. The mission statement of the project clearly articulates the role of archives as currency rather than history:

> Britain today is commonly portrayed as a multicultural nation. However, the diverse historical experiences which constitute the story of this 'new' Britain are less well known. The history of the West Midlands in the 20th century is central to this story but the stories that make up this history remain largely hidden in archive collections. *Connecting Histories* aims to release the potential of these collections so that connections can be made between the past and the present and thereby encourage debate about our shared identities, our common sense of belonging and our multiple heritages.[3]

The audio material recorded by Parker and his team half a century before this project, is given a new importance here, rediscovered and placed in context to relate to twenty-first century concerns.

Witnesses to history

The pace of change affects us all, we live increasingly in a sort of permanent present; that strange country, the past, where people did things differently, seems increasingly remote. Yet within 100 years we have moved to a point only dreamed of by historians of yesterday; the very existence of broadcasting is still just – only just – within the lifespan of a human being. A man or woman born in 1910 grew into a world where mass media provided a commentary on their life. Imagine reading Pliny the Younger and *hearing* the voice of the Emperor Trajan, or being able to play news reports from the French Revolution… Film, television and sound can do this with modern history; above all, sound, the human voice, concentrates the mind on the *spoken* text. A transcript will give you the sense and meaning, but a recording demonstrates the nuances of speech, the hesitations, the inflections, the thought process and the emotion. A written version of Herb Morrison's famous commentary on the Hindenburg disaster of 6 May 1937 conveys only a fraction of the anguish in Morrison's voice as he strives to describe the experience. Here, the impact of the event is in the sound of the voice as much as in the words themselves.[4]

Within the United Kingdom, we may be aware of two principal sources of audio history, available to varying degrees to public and academic scrutiny, the BBC Sound Archive and the British Library Sound Archive: one, the sound of broadcast history and the other, the broader soundtrack of life, both touching from time to time. Yet there has been, until recently, a neglected and at risk third source, another voice that provides a different angle, an approach to broadcasting as oral/aural history that, because of the pace of change in radio regulation, technology and style, might not at first seem to offer promising potential for the historical and social researcher. UK commercial radio – or 'Independent Local Radio' as it was first titled under the severe regulation of the Independent Broadcasting Authority (IBA) at its birth – did not come into existence – legal existence at least – until 8 October 1973. Compared to other national broadcasting systems, this is highly unusual; look outside of Great Britain, and you will find that most media cultures embraced commercial radio before commercial television, the financing following the developing technology. This has not been the case in Britain, with ITV, born in 1955, coming almost twenty years before its radio equivalent.

Thus we have a relatively short historical span, yet within that period, two vastly differing models of broadcast output. The over-regulation of UK commercial radio, up to the 1990 Broadcasting Act, when companies were released to a certain extent from the public service role they had been forced to play under the IBA, produced as a by-product of commercial aspiration a range of often excellent and largely forgotten speech programming – 'meaningful speech' was the phrase coined by one IBA executive. The changing map of commercial radio – the amalgamation or disappearance of the original companies, the creation of large groups such as GCap, Emap and others – all this might suggest that many of these archives have been lost or destroyed. While in some cases this is true, there have been a number of notable cases where collections have survived, often against the odds. One such archive, the subject of digitisation and cataloguing by the Centre for Broadcasting History Research (CBHR) in the Media School at Bournemouth University, and academic dissemination via the BUFVC web site, is the Felicity Wells Memorial Archive – the IBA/AIRC ILR Programme Sharing Archive, covering programmes on all sorts of subjects, shared between stations from the late 1970s until 1990.

This material is being augmented by other collections; the Wessex Film and Sound Archive in the Hampshire Record Office holds material which is the subject of a similar process – a tripartite collaboration between the County archive, the CBHR at Bournemouth and the BUFVC – to make commercial radio archives from Central Southern England available to researchers of late twentieth-century history and sociology. Here we are able to examine specific aspects of media/audience relationships, taking important historical events as case studies. For example, the Falklands conflict of 1982 affected the whole country in one form or another, but for families of service personnel in cities such as Portsmouth, the impact was visceral. Radio Victory was the Independent Local Radio station serving Portsmouth at the time; the war demanded a re-examination of its role, and the Wessex Archive gives us insight into the pastoral place of local radio within a community in emotional crisis. At the same time it provides a window on national and international history at once unexpectedly intimate, personal and often extremely poignant.

To these collections can be added a third strand from UK commercial radio, the archive of LBC/IRN, the largest and most significant British radio news collection outside of the BBC. LBC (The London Broadcasting Company) was the first legal, land-based commercial radio station in Britain, commencing broadcasting at 6.00 am on 8 October 1973. For nearly the first twenty years of its existence, it was a company linked to Independent Radio News, and the sound archive of those years has been preserved on more than 7,000 reels of quarter-inch tape. Here is the witness of a new strand of broadcaster on the turbulent twilight of a century, including all of the Thatcher years, the destruction of Apartheid and the issue of Northern Ireland. Thanks to funding provided by the Joint Information Systems Committee this invaluable archive will become academically available through a further partnership between BUFVC and the Bournemouth Centre for Broadcasting History Research, turning a collection of boxes of fragile tape, almost forgotten, into a vibrant, accessible witness, available to listen to and reference online to education at every level.[5]

Preserving yesterday

Thus it can be seen that the responsibility of those involved with this work is two-fold. Firstly there is often a process akin to rescue archaeology; the importance of the work has to be established, and the material saved, often involving remedial technical issues. Once preserved, transferred to what is hoped to be a stable medium, the second aspect of such projects takes over – that of making the material available to new and coming generations.

We might, in rediscovering such archives and giving them new life, occasionally pause and reflect on the often remarkable background to the very survival of these newly found collections, consider how fortunate we are that they exist, and that their importance has been recognised. Yet in so doing, we might well run the risk of being complacent about preserving the voices of our present, before they themselves become obscured by the next layer of time. From 2005, Ofcom has been periodically licensing a new strand of broadcasting in the form of Community Radio stations. Here is society speaking to itself at local and ethnic level, catching always a moment in time, a snapshot of existence. What would Parker, MacColl and Seeger have made of such material? More importantly, where does – where will – that material go? Some stations may keep local archives, but Community Broadcasting is by its very nature volunteer based, chronically short of cash and resources, and born into a world where the pace of reflecting today through media at every level moves us too quickly beyond yesterday. We have a unique, one-off opportunity to help these new stations to themselves help future generations understand what the very word 'community' meant at the start of the twenty-first century. Yet to do so, some form of national, overarching archive strategy needs to be established as a matter of urgency; we cannot keep everything of course, but we should be aware of the importance of this new resource at the time of its genesis. It will be a tragedy if, despite the apparent lessons learned from the preservation and cataloguing of past collections, we find ourselves in a similar – or worse – position in ten or twenty or fifty years time, when today's audio voices are silent and lost.

As we have seen through the example of Birmingham's *Connecting Histories* project, past and present can hold a vital dialogue together. Perhaps crucially, we have now at our disposal a new use of technology which potentially by its very existence provides the platform for a personal archive. The growth of downloadable programmes – podcasts – has been pushing us towards a redefinition of what we mean by radio, and an awareness that an audio archive, be it institutional or personal, is a device whereby we take sound content and make it available 'on demand,' when and where we want to access it. Every MP3 player owner is his or her own archivist. This being the case, the public perception of audio preservation is growing, providing a major opportunity in education for the use of voices from our past – local, national and international – to talk to us of *their* present. It also provides us with a developing technology which is revolutionising the means by which those voices talk to our students.

The title of this article was chosen with some thought; it reflects a radio programme which until May 2007 was a regular part of the BBC Radio 4 schedule, a magazine of audio from all over the world, reflecting specific topics of common interest. Such insights matter; it is sad that such a programme should cease, yet notwithstanding that, the world is whispering in our ear from all sorts of other sources. Now the technology exists which enables students not simply to quote from a written text, but to include an *audio* quotation within an electronic essay, the voice of the historian, the poet or the scientist themselves. We have moved here from a 'push' media culture, where the broadcaster sends the content to the listener when the scheduler decides, to a 'pull' initiative, with the listener in control of 'when and how ...' It is the very accessibility of recorded sound, stripped of visual distractions, which makes this all the more exciting – and that of course is the very stuff of which old-fashioned radio has always been made. The turning of pages augmented by a murmur of voices is the gift of accessible audio archives. Let us ensure that the understanding of the importance of these things, manifest in the preservation and transfer of knowledge from existing sound archives, continues to inform our strategy for the ongoing development of future resources, as and when they become available.

Seán Street *is Director, the Centre for Broadcasting History Research, the Media School, Bournemouth University.*
E-mail: sstreet@bournemouth.ac.uk

Notes

1 Video Oral History Archive, Centre for Broadcasting History Research, the Media School, Bournemouth University, http://media.bournemouth.ac.uk/research/cbhr.html.

2 The complete *Radio Ballads* were issued as a series of individual CDs by Topic Records in 1999.

3 http://www.connectinghistories.org.uk, accessed June 2007.

4 The complete Hindenburg broadcast, including an interview with Morrison, conducted the day after the event, was issued on a CD entitled THE AVIATORS (Pavilion Records PAST CD 9760) 1991.

5 The digitisation, cataloguing and dissemination of these collections is part of an on-going partnership between the Centre for Broadcasting History Research and the BUFVC, with the objective of making material available for academic use through online access on the BUFVC web site.

MOVING IMAGES AND SOUND: INCLUSIVE AND ACCESSIBLE

Alistair McNaught

For many learners who struggle with text-based content, the use of alternative media is welcome. Moving images can add significant value to learning materials, especially if the user can independently start, stop and replay the clip. For science-related subjects, moving images can portray processes where the speed or scale of the process is outside normal human cognition. In arts subjects they can portray pathos, atmosphere and a whole host of other visual subtleties. Similarly, audio resources provide many benefits for users. MP3 files are highly portable and the learner can be listening to them on a bus or in the local supermarket, but the benefit of listening to content goes beyond multi-tasking. Content in audio form may require less concentration and is more perceivable to people with print-related disabilities or poor literacy skills.

However, substituting traditional text-based resources with moving images/ sound may disadvantage some learners. The extent of their disadvantage may be negligible or significant depending on several factors. These include:

- the learning objectives of the exercise
- the nature of the video/audio
- whether the video/audio enhances or replaces existing resource
- whether accessibility considerations have been built into the production of the alternative resource.

This article explores the use of sound and moving images to maximise the benefits and minimise the barriers. Good practices provide benefits well beyond the target group. For example, captions on a video clip benefit people with a hearing impairment but they also benefit:

- people working in a noisy environment
- people working on a PC with no soundcard
- people with limited English skills for whom the caption provides a simple summary of fast or complex speech.

Ways of using moving images and sound

Moving images and audio resources are, intrinsically, accessibility aids for many users, adding value to the learning experience in many ways. The list below has been adapted from the TASI web site at
http://www.tasi.ac.uk/advice/using/use-examples.html.

Moving images can be used:

- to illustrate concepts and to show examples
- to inspire discussion of a topic, looking at multiple aspects and contexts

29

- to teach diagnosis and treatment
- to stimulate students writing, enhancing creative and language skills
- to encourage team work and foster collaboration and the sharing of learning experiences
- to encourage critical thinking skills
- to illustrate case studies
- to enhance communication skills (e.g. decoding the message from a photograph, video clip or sound clip)
- to document an event and analyse practice
- to assess student knowledge, understanding and observational skills
- to introduce unpopular topics (within a subject discipline) in a novel and, perhaps, more exciting way than a straightforward lecture/ tutorial.

In a similar vein, the TechDis web site has information on using sound effectively in the Creation of Learning Materials section of its web site at http://www.techdis.ac.uk/index.php?p=9_7. This includes using sound in the following ways:

- as a pronunciation aid
- providing a narrated version of text
- providing additional content via sound
- as a class stimulus
- as an individual stimulus
- within assessment – e.g. multi-choice and drag and drop etc.

As tutors expand their repertoire of teaching approaches, they become more skilled at adapting the learning experience to the needs of the learners, whatever their accessibility/inclusion needs. The accessibility of the learning experience is due in part to the nature of the resources – a deaf learner will struggle to make sense of a podcast – but the pedagogical approach is also a significant element of accessibility. Very few resources are universally accessible. Equally, very few resources are 'inaccessible' – everything is accessible to someone. The next section explores how accessibility considerations vary with context.

Is it accessible?

Accessibility is an area where it is very easy to focus upon minority requirements and miss the whole point of the teaching and learning experience. The question 'Is it accessible?' makes no sense without a clear context. The following considerations are an important part of the context in which accessibility is situated:

The context of delivery and support mechanisms in place – a resource being used with an unknown learner group via remote delivery needs higher standards of technical accessibility than a resource used in blended teaching with a tutor and support workers in place.

The longevity of the resource – a high-profile resource that is expected to be reused on many occasions needs higher standards of technical accessibility than a resource with a very short shelf-life.

The reach of the resource – a resource that will be used with many different groups needs a higher standard of technical accessibility than one which has been created for a very specific context (e.g. fieldwork videos from an archaeology summer school).

The technical expertise of the content creator – it is a reasonable expectation that full time developers should produce materials to higher standards of technical accessibility than teaching staff with limited technical skills.

Small changes can make big differences to many learners and there is much to be gained by many staff making modest accessibility improvements. In an ideal world, every resource would have high levels of technical accessibility. However, experience shows that institutions that adopt very rigorous accessibility policies towards digital resources tend to have very few resources online, disadvantaging far more disabled learners in the process. However, while it can be difficult and time consuming to make all resources equally accessible to all users, it takes very little to add significant accessibility benefits to resources. The guidance below shows a range of different ways in which accessibility value can be added to moving images and audio resources respectively.

Adding value to moving images

It has become increasingly simple to make short video clips for inclusion on web sites and learning platforms. Many digital still cameras come with the facility to create short bursts of video. It is easy to edit such clips using free software like Windows Movie Maker. Video clips can be excellent tools for inclusive learning but some processes cannot be videoed and are more effectively visualised using animation – based on PowerPoint, animated GIF files or Flash platforms (such as the excellent – and free – Wink software).

Visualisations can add considerable value for a wide range of accessibility needs but may present barriers to others. These barriers can be reduced using the following approaches:

Quality imagery – the value added by moving images will depend on the choice of images used. If lighting levels are low, resolution is poor or contrast is limited less value will be added for all learners, particularly those with visual impairments. Likewise, it is important to consider colour choices and contrasts when creating an animation.

Appropriate narration – videos of fieldwork or practical work can suffer from poor sound quality or distracting background noise. Using free software such as Windows Movie Maker it is possible to add appropriate audio narrative after shooting. An effective narrative on a video clip or Flash animation can make the difference between the resource being accessible or inaccessible to a visually impaired learner. It also adds significant value for users without disabilities.

Effective text descriptions – there are alternative ways of providing text descriptions of a video or animation. Different methods are appropriate in different circumstances.

Scene description – where the scene forms a significant part of the learning experience a text description can be provided for each scene. For example, a video where interviewees describe their quality of life may contain significant visual material in the scene (litter, graffiti). A simple text-based scene description – e.g. introductory text before the link to the video – would add value significantly for visually impaired learners.

Subtitling/captions – subtitling can be used to capture spoken narrative for deaf learners. If using subtitling in this way it is important to realise that sign language users are less fluent in written English than would normally be expected (it is their second language). Consequently it may be more effective for subtitles to capture a summary of the spoken content rather than every word. Subtitling can also be used to clarify and draw attention to processes on the screen – for example 'The sulphuric acid is slowly added to the beaker. Note the safety precautions used.'

Signalling alternatives – some visualisations provide such rich learning experiences to a sighted learner that a 'screen reader accessible' version is a poor substitute – often requiring complex screen navigation for very little benefit. A 'text only version' may contain the relevant content description but is a poor substitute for an engaging interactive experience.

In these circumstances there is a compelling argument for effective signalling of (i) accessibility difficulties and (ii) off-line substitutes. For example, an interactive 3D visualisation of a weather system may be highly engaging for a sighted user but the time taken to adapt the screen version for a blind user may be better used in constructing a tactile version made of cardboard and cotton wool. Where spatial relationships are concerned, signalling alternative approaches can result in a much better user experience than spending development time struggling to make something technically accessible but still utterly unusable. The latter may conform to the letter of accessibility standards but certainly undermines the spirit.

Adding value to audio based resources

With the advent of cheap voice recorders, MP3 players and free audio software (such as Audacity) it has become much easier to use audio-based resources. These can include recordings of fieldwork/practical observations, summaries of discussions or arguments and interviews or audio presenta-tions. Audio resources are an assistive technology for many learners, especially those with print difficulties or those with visual problems. Even learners with hearing difficulties can benefit from audio resources online because they can at least adjust the volume and play back bits they missed – something they cannot do in a lecture theatre or classroom.

Nevertheless, all learners (particularly deaf learners) will benefit from the simple value-added techniques below:

Description of purpose – different recordings have different purposes and a short description of the purpose will make a significant difference to the focus the user gives the task. For example, in a recorded interview, is the objective to find specific information? Or to recognise rhetorical devices? To analyse group dynamics? A clear context will help the learner tune their listening and alert a disabled learner to concepts they may need to access in alternative ways.

Transcription of content – whether the transcript needs to be a word-for-word script or a summary description will depend on the learning objectives. A word-for-word explanation will help learners who want to cut and paste information into their assignment but a précis of the content may be better in other circumstances. Again, the learning objectives must be very clear – a summary of complex arguments is a reasonable adjustment for learners with accessibility needs … unless the learning objective is to summarise complex dialogue!

Controllability and navigation – audio is of most use if (i) the user knows it is there and (ii) it is possible to pause it while reflecting or taking notes. Embedded audio in Word documents may not always be accessible to an inexperienced screen reader user. If there is any doubt with your user group, use a hyperlink to a separate MP3 file. The issue of controllability is more uncertain because it depends on the media player installed on the user's system. In general a user with particular needs will have found a player that suits their needs but this may not be available on the institution's learning platform. The best practice is to alert users that audio may play differently on different systems and give them the opportunity to raise any specific problems this might cause.

Conclusion

Moving images and sound add considerable value for learners, including many disabled learners. They may provide barriers for some users but these barriers can be reduced in a variety of ways, many of which require little additional time or expertise. TechDis encourages innovative and creative approaches to accessibility and offers advice and guidance at http://www.techdis.ac.uk – particularly under the Key Topics and Resources and references (publications) sections.

Alistair McNaught *is Senior Advisor, TechDis, the JISC-funded Advisory Service for the fields of accessibility and inclusion.*
E-mail: Alistair@techdis.ac.uk

VIDEO, EDUCATION AND THE NEW FUNDING AGENDA: BUILDING NEW VALUE

Peter B. Kaufman

Moving-image media are the primary source of information in the world today. The only blood shed in the so-called bloodless or velvet revolutions in Central and Eastern Europe and Russia in the 1989-1991 period was lost at the foot of the television towers in Bucharest, Vilnius, and Moscow, as people struggled for control of what the Polish fantasist Tadeusz Konwicki used to call the giant hypodermic needle that shot narcotic lies into the East bloc body politic. The fact that screen-based media are central to the daily lives of billions on our planet may be anti-intellectual and out of vogue (in their influential and in many ways path-breaking book, *The Social Life of Information*, John Seeley Brown and Paul Duguid ignore television as a source of information), but the medium is here to stay nonetheless.[1]

What then is the future of the use of moving images in education, scholarship, and research? What should be the funding agenda for government agencies, foundations, and others (corporate underwriters, commercial investors, venture capitalists) interested in education moving forward? At a minimum, we in the field should be thinking about what we should put on the millions of screens that university students look at each day, and what we should do with the colossal archives of audio-visual material that we already have.

Trends

As we define a new research, funding, and action agenda, we need to consider four trends:

1. Public expectations and skills regarding moving images are rising
The demand for video is huge. More than 100 million videos are watched on YouTube every day. Fox Interactive, Yahoo, Google/YouTube, Viacom, etc. now stream over seven billion videos per month. BitTorrent is the number-one file format on the Internet.

The tools in our hands now for producing video are proliferating:

- http://www.apple.com/ilife/imovie
- http://www.adobe.com/products/premiere
- http://www.pinnaclesys.com/PublicSite/us/Home
- http://www.jumpcut.com ('Be good to your video')
- http://grouper.com ('Watch. Share. Create')
- http://www.eyespot.com ('Moviemaking for all of us')
- http://www.videoegg.com ('People-powered media')

There are 150 plus new tools and resources besides these for video sharing, video hosting, v-logging, video search and organisation – in a video-dominated world, the means of production.

Our moving image heritage is being digitised:

- http://videoactive.wordpress.com
- http://mic.imtc.gatech.edu
- http://newsfilm.bufvc.ac.uk
- http://www.wgbh.org/resources/archives
- http://video.google.com/nara.html
- http://www.archive.org/details/opensource_movies

One way to look at this trend is as resource materials for our work ahead.

Personal storage and portability are accelerating exponentially. Over the past twenty-five years computer processing performance has gone up x 3,500, computer memory prices has gone down x 45,000, and computer disk storage prices have gone down x 3.6 million.

Over the next thirteen years, an iPod or a device its size will be able to hold:

- a year's worth of video (8,760 hours) by 2012 (five years from now)
- all the commercial music ever created by 2015 (eight years), and
- *all the content ever created (in all media) by 2020* (thirteen years)

By the time my children are in college, in other words, they will be able to carry all the media ever created in the world on an iPod around their necks.[2]

2. Culture, education and the academy are linking their assets

In addition, we have to understand the momentum in scholarship to link resources and technologies, collections and artifacts, through a common cyber-infrastructure – moving images are part of it. Librarians speak increasingly today of building the 'global digital library.' Museum curators speak of 'heading toward a kind of digital global museum.'[3] And beyond linking these assets, there is an effort among the vanguard in education and scholarship to render them – and moving images, new and old, among them – more relevant and sustainable. In the field of scholarship, those active at the intersection of computing and publishing now appreciate what one leading scholar and digital activist, Michael Jensen at the National Academies, calls the 'new metrics of authority' for scholarship in the digital age.[4] This is something that community members working with video should take account of.

How are we going to make sense and value out of our content in a universe of hundreds of billions of screens or pages of content, where tens, sometimes hundreds, of thousands of these pages are similar if not virtually identical? Publishers and producers, we are told, need to start understanding about new business models – models built on foundations deeper and more fascinating than Google's value proposition and PageRank system of today. Citing the

Web 2.0 'authority models,' represented by Digg, Delicious, Slashbdot, Flickr, YouTube, MySpace, Facebook, and Wikipedia, Jensen tells us that the answer is by 'competing in computability' – by helping that content be understood by the machines that will be reading it. That is, the answer lies in working to make our content feedable into, and findable by, all the automated computer-assisted systems that make decisions to pre-select, pre-cluster, and prepare material in search; while at the same time seeing that we attend very closely to the individual user's actions, wants, needs, and historic interests, and adapt to them. Our prestige as publishers and the prestige of peer reviewers and other commentators still count in everything we do, of course. But authority, online, is now computable by the following much richer and extended list of metrics, which the machines are using in their calculations:

- the percentage of a document quoted in other documents
- raw links to the document
- valued links, in which the values of the linker and all his/her other links are also considered
- obvious attention: discussions in blogspace, comments in posts, re-clarification, and continued discussion
- nature of the language in comments: positive, negative, interconnective, expanded, clarified, reinterpreted
- quality of the context: what else is on the site that holds the document, and what is *its* authority status?
- percentage of phrases that are valued by a disciplinary community
- quality of author's institutional affiliations
- significance of author's other work
- amount of author's participation in other valued projects, as commentator, editor, etc.
- reference network: the significance rating of all the texts the author has touched, viewed, read
- length of time a document has existed
- inclusion of a document in lists of 'best of,' in syllabi, indexes, and other human-selected distillations
- types of tags assigned to it, the terms used, the authority of the taggers, the authority of the tagging system.

The preconditions for success in 'Authority 3.0,' Jensen says, include increasing the digital availability of our media for indexing; increasing the digital availability of our media for referencing, quoting, linking, tagging; and improving the metadata which we provide that identifies the media, categorises it, con-textualises it, summarises it, and perhaps provides key phrases/images/and sounds from it – and doing all this while allowing others to enrich that media with their own comments, tags, and contextualising elements. This is the number one thing that we can do as publishers – as educators – to increase the value of our content.

3. Commercial investors are in the neighbourhood

A third trend we must take account of is a kind of dialectical double-helix kind of a thing, involving the transformation of online content.

The first strand of that change is that all of us, in almost every act in which we engage on a computer, have become producers or co-producers of screen-based media, of screen-based advertiser-supported media. Every book our institutions scan, every newsreel we digitise, every image we post online, every blog post, every e-mail, will be today or become tomorrow a piece of the monetisable cosmos for Google, Microsoft, Apple, Adobe, Cisco, and Amazon. It is no coincidence that at the same time Jensen is outlining these criteria, Wall Street investment banks, consulting companies, and management and strategy firms are paying attention to exactly the same trends – and the way that commercial companies such as Google, MySpace, and Facebook are helping to define them.

Analysts like Gartner who cover the media tell us that too much choice can actually be detrimental, leading to lower user satisfaction (Gartner calls this 'consumer vertigo'); that rendering our content searchable, or what Jensen might call computably competitive, is as good if not a better investment of resources than making more content available. They tell us that paid search – the business of some of our new business partners – is a \$15 billion business that has grown at an eighty-eight percent compounded annual growth rate since 2002. They tell us that in three years twenty-five percent of online music store transactions will be driven directly from consumer to consumer taste-sharing applications such as playlist publishing and ranking tools built into online music stores. They tell us that user-generated content now accounts for thirteen percent of total Internet traffic in the United States, up from 0–1 percent in 2004.[5]

The second strand is that more formerly commercial content is becoming available online – for free. Analysts have noted that more and more companies seem to be acting in ways that are completely counter-intuitive to those of us with any classical education in business or economics. This is called the economics of open content.[6] There is a subset of courses in business schools now being developed around this theme – a kind of mash where people study the benefits of open source projects, collaborative projects that mobilise whole communities of people without paying, and the business models (rather successful ones at that) of drugs and pornography, where it makes good financial sense to give certain things away for free to draw in the community, even as you expect to sell those things or things related to them later.

To observers trained in classical business behaviour before the Internet, some of these decisions – Steve Jobs' call to the music industry in February 2007 to abandon digital rights management (not that surprising, perhaps given that he makes most of his money on hardware); but then EMI's decision to abandon digital rights management; Warner Music now doing the same, putting its albums up online; Amazon's decision in May 2007 to sell EMI's music and music from 12,000 independent record companies without DRM (venture capital firms are betting that half of all recorded music in the catalogues of EMI, Universal, Sony BMG and Warner will be available for sale without DRM by this Christmas); publishers putting PDFs of books online for free even before their sale dates; journal publishers embracing open access; universities like MIT putting all of their courses online in so-called open courseware – seem like acts out of a psychedelic novel, as though these music companies are taking too many drugs with their acts. (As Jimi Hendrix wrote in 1967, 'If a six/Turns out to be a nine/I don't mind/I don't mind.')

The economics of open content need to be better understood by all of us, especially by institutions who have so much content and who are committed by their charters to provide content to people who want it. Chris Anderson, the editor of *Wired Magazine* and the author who introduced the Long Tail analysis, is writing his next book on the subject. The title of the book, tentatively, is *Free*, and his publisher Hyperion, which is part of Disney, intends to give the book away ... free.[7]

4. Distribution options are proliferating
Fourth and finally, it is important for us to recognise that distribution options for moving images are proliferating. There are over fifty new start-ups in the web-video world, including YouTube, Joost, MySpace, Veoh, Democracy, and Daily Motion.

There are scores of ways to watch free television online legally and thousands of opportunities to do it illegally. No piece of film or television is now impossible, technologically, to see, if it is in digital form. The video, as they used to say about the truth, is out there.

Some media enterprises consider all distributors possible allies in the business or mission. In the spring of 2007, Viacom announced to the world the establishment of the 'CBS interactive audience network.' This 'network' (in the original sense of this word) was established by a 'network' (in the television sense of the word) to stitch together content deals with a variety of online distributors including AOL, Microsoft, CNET Networks, Comcast, Joost, Bebo, Brightcove, Netvibes, Sling Media and Veoh – Google being absent, as Viacom had already started suing its subsidiary YouTube for copyright infringement. In June 2007, CBS announced that it was beginning 'phase two' of the audience network by signing agreements with social network application providers, allowing users, in short, to incorporate CBS-provided clips to their blogs, wikis, widgets and community pages. These new partners include Automattic, Clearspring, DAVE Networks, Goowy Media, meebo, MeeVee, Musestorm, Ning, RockYou!, Slide, VideoEgg, Voxant, and vSocial, amongst others.

Looking ahead

At a 2007 conference at Columbia University on video, education, and open content, the question was posed what public broadcasting would – could – look like if it were built anew today. Not remade, but *made*, explicitly, for education.[8] We know what a newly designed audio-visual archive might look like. The National AudioVisual Conservation Center is just being finished outside of Washington, designed by librarians for librarians around workflow from the loading dock to the refrigerator, with $250 million of funding as part of the Library of Congress. What if we could create a new studio for educators; a new laboratory for educational video technologists; and a new network – again broadly, loosely defined – that favours education?

At major universities – in the United States and the United Kingdom – video production capabilities and talents abound. At Columbia University, for example, there are television studios that are part of the Columbia University Video Network (designed for distance education and headquartered at the School of Engineering and Applied Sciences); at Columbia University Television, the campus television station; among the most modern university production facilities in the world at the School of Journalism, the Center for Biomedical Communication at Columbia Medical School, and the Center for New Media Teaching and Learning. Video assets also are being produced outside of these formal studios but no less professionally daily and throughout the campus – from the Earth Institute, to the Business School, to the Law School and Teachers' College – all for use in the classroom and more generally for teaching and learning. Imagine taking the assets and expertise at this university – just one example – and linking them up with other institutions – Royal Holloway, for example, or Sheffield. Imagine establishing a production network to effect positive change by making educational video productions with, say, the University of California Berkeley's Educational Technology Services and Multimedia Research Center; MIT's Academic Media Production Services;

Yale's world-class Center for Media and Instructional Innovation; and many others.[9]

With core support from the William and Flora Hewlett Foundation, Intelligent Television is now establishing just such an initiative, meant to connect the production facilities at a range of higher education institutions in a distributed production environment. This Open Education Video Studio, as it is called, will cost-effectively produce educational video for university needs and make it broadly available. It will evaluate the use of such video in teaching and learning and help support new tools – editing, annotation, search, summarisation – for more cost-efficient video production and distribution worldwide. It will also sponsor intensive meetings for educators, technologists, video producers, and other stakeholders who together will help to articulate a sustainability plan for the Studio's productions and research and development projects. These productions will cover, among other subjects: *Alzheimer's disease*; *American Foreign Policy: A Visual History*; *The History of Harlem*; *A History of the American Labor Movement*; *A Visual History of Literacy*.

In its second year, 2008-2009, the Studio will work to organise new multi-institutional collaborations into a distributed educational video production network, and help establish a new educational video commons to help better define best practices in video preservation and access.

Summary

Video is central to the daily lives of many people. It is becoming even more central each day. Educators and cultural stewards need to take control of their futures in this context by recognising that they, too, are producers of screen-based media. The opportunity exists now to have stewards of moving image collections get excited about the future and, as this essay suggests:

- compete in computability;
- compete in the marketability of our computability competitiveness, as Wall Street might suggest; and
- build a creative partnership network analogous to the one that Viacom and others are establishing for their own commercial reasons.

All of us, in so doing, would be able to connect to our users everywhere where they are they are beside a screen and speaker. At that point, we as a community will be well on our way to making our e-resources in moving images more useful, more sustainable, and more valuable over the near and long term.

Peter B. Kaufman *is president and executive producer of Intelligent Television* (http://www.intelligenttelevision.com) *in New York*.
E-mail: pbk@intelligenttv.com

Notes

[1] John Seeley Brown and Paul Duguid, *The Social Life of Information* (Boston: Harvard Business School Press, 2000).

[2] See Peter B. Kaufman, 'Video, Education, and Open Content: Notes Toward a New Research and Action Agenda,' *First Monday* 12, No. 4 (April 2007), at: http://www.firstmonday.org/issues/issue12_4/kaufman/index.html.

[3] Deanna Marcum, 'The Sum of the Parts: Turning Digital Library Initiatives into a Great Whole,' keynote address to the Joint Conference on Digital Libraries, Denver, 8 June 2005; Ben Williams, lead librarian at the Field Museum, quoted in James Gorman, 'In Virtual Museums, An Archive of the World,' *New York Times*, 12 January 2003. See also: *Our Cultural Commonwealth: The Report of the American Council of Learned Societies Commission on Cyberinfrastructure for the Humanities and Social Sciences* (New York: American Council of Learned Societies, 2006).

[4] Michael Jensen, 'The New Metrics of Scholarly Authority,' *Chronicle of Higher Education*, June 2007, available at: http://chronicle.com/free/v53/i41/41b00601.htm.

[5] Spencer Wang, Shub Mukherjee, Stefan Anninger, 'A Longer Look at the Long Tail,' (New York: Bear Stearns Equity Research, June 2007); and Mike McGuire and Derek Slater, 'Consumer Taste Sharing is Driving the Online Music Business and Democratizing Culture,' (Cambridge: Gartner/Harvard University Berkman Center for Internet and Society, 13 December 2005).

[6] Intelligent Television recently concluded a year-long investigation of the economics of open content in various media and education environments from textbooks to gaming: http://www.intelligenttelevision.com/research.htm.

[7] http://www.thelongtail.com.

[8] http://opencontent.ccnmtl.columbia.edu.

[9] For inspiration, see: Neal Gabler, *Walt Disney: The Triumph of the American Imagination* (New York: Alfred A. Knopf, 2006); Neal Gabler, *An Empire of Their Own: How the Jews Invented Hollywood* (New York: Crown Publishers, 1988); and Thomas Schatz, *The Genius of the System: Hollywood Filmmaking in the Studio Era* (New York: Pantheon Books, 1988).

The BUFVC maintains the Researcher's Guide Online (http://www.bufvc.ac.uk/rgo), a directory of over 655 moving image and radio collections in the UK and Ireland. The archives listed here are all those in the public sector, whose interests are represented by the Film Archive Forum (http://www.bufvc.ac.uk/faf), of which the BUFVC is an Observer member. A number of these archives are based in Higher Education institutions.

BFI National Archive

J. Paul Getty Conservation Centre, Kingshill Way, Berkhamsted, Hertfordshire HP4 3TP
☎ 01442 876 301 **Fax:** 01442 289 112
London office: 21 Stephen Street, London W1T 1LN
☎ 020 7255 1444
Web: http://www.bfi.org.uk/archive
The BFI National Archive is one of the world's greatest collections of film and television. The majority of the collection is British material but it also features internationally significant holdings from around the world. It also collects films which feature key British actors and the work of British directors. There is a wealth of material of every genre from silent newsreels to CinemaScope epics, from home movies to avant-garde experiments, from classic documentaries to vintage television, from advertisements to 3-D films, soap opera to football. The archive contains more than 50,000 fiction films, over 100,000 non-fiction titles and around 625,000 television programmes.

East Anglian Film Archive

The Archive Centre, Martineau Lane, Norwich NR1 2DQ
☎ 01603 592 664 **Fax:** 01603 458 553
E-mail: eafa@uea.ac.uk Web: http://www.uea.ac.uk/eafa
The East Anglian Film Archive collection comprises over 60,000 films and videos. The collection includes a large amount of non-fiction material, such as documentaries, television productions, family and personal films, home videos, newsreels, educational films, travelogues, films produced by municipalities, councils and government sponsored, as well as advertising films, dramas and an increasing number of feature films. The archive is owned by the University of East Anglia and is part of the School of Film and Television Studies in the faculty of Arts and Humanities. The archive operates from The Archive Centre and at the University of East Anglia campus, both in Norwich.

Imperial War Museum Film and Video Archive

Lambeth Road, London SE1 6HZ
☎ 020 7416 5291/2 (commercial users)
☎ 020 7416 5293/4 (non-commercial users) **Fax:** 020 7416 5299
E-mail: film@iwm.org.uk
Web: http://collections.iwm.org.uk/server/show/nav.00g004
The Imperial War Museum's Film and Video Archive is one of the foremost archives in the UK providing rich illustrations for military and social history from throughout the twentieth century. The archive holds some 120 million feet of film and 6,500 hours of video tape. A large proportion of material has been transferred to the Museum from the Services and other public bodies as the Archive is the official repository for such public record films.

London's Screen Archives: The Regional Network

E-mail: screen.archives@mlalondon.org.uk
Web: http://www.filmlondon.org.uk/screenarchives
London's Screen Archives is a new regional network supporting organisations in London that hold collections of moving image material. It helps researchers and the public find these collections and tries to ensure the preservation of important material made in or about the city.

Media Archive for Central England

I Salisbury Road, University of Leicester, Leicester LE1 7RQ
☎ 0116 252 5066
E-mail: macearchive@le.ac.uk Web: http://www.macearchive.org
The archive was established in 2000 as the English regional moving image archive covering the East and West Midlands. The archive exists both to collect and to be a point of reference and information about all aspects of the life, culture and history of the East and West Midlands as reflected in the moving image media. The collections of film, videotape and digital media span the entire era of moving image production from the mid-1890s to the present day and are constantly growing. The archive is located within the University of Leicester.

National Screen and Sound Archive of Wales

National Library of Wales, Aberystwyth SY23 3BU
☎ 01970 632 828 **Fax:** 01970 632 544
E-mail: agssc@llgc.org.uk Web: http://screenandsound.llgc.org.uk/index.htm
The National Screen and Sound Archive of Wales is responsible for safeguarding and celebrating Wales' rich audio-visual heritage. The collection encompasses over 5.5m feet of film, over 250,000 hours of video, over 200,000 hours of sound recordings, and thousands of tapes, records and compact discs.

North West Film Archive

Manchester Metropolitan University,
Minshull House, 47-49 Chorlton Street, Manchester M1 3EU
☎ 0161 247 3097 **Fax:** 0161 247 3098
E-mail: n.w.filmarchive@mmu.ac.uk Web: http://www.nwfa.mmu.ac.uk
The North West Film Archive is the professionally recognised home for moving images made in or about Cheshire, Cumbria, Greater Manchester, Lancashire and Merseyside. It is located within Manchester Metropolitan University.

Northern Region Film and Television Archive

c/o Tyne and Wear Archives Service, Blandford House, Blandford Square, Newcastle-upon-Tyne NE1 4JA
☎ 0191 277 2250 **Fax:** 0191 230 2614
Web: http://www.nrfta.org.uk
The NRFTA is the public-sector moving image archive serving County Durham, Northumberland, Tees Valley and Tyne and Wear. The NRFTA operates from two sites: at the University of Teesside in Middlesbrough, at which most of the staff and approximately half the collection are located, and at Tyne and Wear Archives Service in Newcastle.

Scottish Screen Archive

National Library of Scotland, 39-41 Montrose Avenue, Hillington Park, Glasgow G5 4LA
☎ 0845 366 4600 **Fax:** 0845 366 4601
E-mail: ssaenquiries@nls.uk Web: http://www.nls.uk/ssa
The Scottish Screen Archive was set up in 1976 to find, protect and provide access to Scotland's moving image heritage. From 1 April 2007, it has been part of the Collections Department at the National Library of Scotland.

Screen Archive South East

University of Brighton, Grand Parade, Brighton BN2 0JY
☎ 01273 643 213 **Fax:** 01273 643 214
E-mail: screenarchive@brighton.ac.uk
Web: http://www.brighton.ac.uk/screenarchive/
Screen Archive South East is a public sector moving image archive serving the South East of England. Established in 1992 at the University of Brighton as the South East Film & Video Archive, the function of this regional screen archive is to locate, collect, preserve, provide access to and promote screen material related to the South East and of general relevance to screen history.

South West Film and Television Archive

Melville Building, Royal William Yard, Stonehouse, Plymouth PL1 3RP
☎ 01752 202 650 **Fax:** 01752 205 025
E-mail: info@tswfta.co.uk Web: http://www.tswfta.co.uk
SWFTA is the public regional film archive for the South West of England. Its holdings are from 1898 to the present day and its core collections are the Television South West Film and Video Library (which includes all Channel 3 material for the area from 1961 to 1992) and the BBC South West Film Collection (dating from 1961 onward). In addition to the core collections the archive also holds many other amateur and professional collections.

Wessex Film and Sound Archive

Hampshire Record Office, Sussex Street, Winchester SO23 8TH
☎ 01962 847 742 **Fax:** 01962 878 681
Web: http://www.hants.gov.uk/record-office/film
The Wessex Film and Sound Archive was set up in 1988, funded by Hampshire County Council through Hampshire Archives Trust, a registered charity. It serves not just Hampshire, where it is based, but Central Southern England, including Berkshire and the Isle of Wight.

Yorkshire Film Archive

York St John University, Lord Mayor's Walk, York YO31 7EX
☎ 01904 876 550 **Fax:** 01904 876552
E-mail: yfa@yorksj.ac.uk Web: http://www.yorkshirefilmarchive.com
The Yorkshire Film Archive is the public access film archive for Yorkshire and the Humber. It holds over 14,000 items of film and video tape, dating from the earliest days of film making in the 1880s to the present day. It is based in York at the Fountains Learning Centre, York St John University.

learning on
screen conference & awa

See and discuss the latest
moving image work – film,
vision and online delivery –
ucation and research

ces:
/ Culture Online

oduction and Delivery:
of Broadcasts, Circle
ing Teachers

AWARDS

A selection of regular film, television and video production awards, predominantly offered in the UK, as well as awards for writing on film and television themes.

BAF Awards

Web: http://www.nationalmediamuseum.org.uk/baf/2007/submit.asp
Held annually as part of the Bradford Animation Festival, BAF awards cover the following categories: student films, professional films, independent films, commercials, music videos, television series, films for children, films produced by children, and films produced using computer games software.

BBC4 World Cinema Awards

Web: http://www.bbc.co.uk/bbcfour/cinema/worldcinema/award2007.shtml
An annual prize celebrating the best in foreign language filmmaking. A panel of judges chooses the winner from a shortlist of six films nominated by the UK's leading critics, film-school heads and festival directors.

Betting on Shorts

Web: http://www.bettingonshorts.com
BoSs is a short-film contest held annually at the Institute of Contemporary, Arts, London since 2004. Each year submissions are invited on a particular theme – in the past these have been 'playtime', 'vacancy' and 'mad or bad.' The festival is competitive and the audience is invited to bet on which film will win.

BFFS Film Society of the Year Awards

Web: http://www.bffs.org.uk/awards.html
Each year in February, the British Federation of Film Societies invites film societies to submit applications for the prestigious Film Society of the Year Awards. Categories are The Engholm Prize for Film Society of the Year; Best film programming; Best programme; Best marketing and publicity; Best Web site; Community award; Best new society; Best student society; The Charles Roebuck Cup, for an individual contribution to the BFFS.

British Academy of Film and Television Arts (BAFTA)

195 Piccadilly, London W1J 9LN
☎ 020 7734 0022 **Fax:** 020 7734 1792
E-mail: info@bafta.org Web: http://www.bafta.org
One of the principal functions of the British Academy of Film & Television Arts is to identify and reward excellence in the art forms of the moving image. It achieves this objective by bestowing awards on those practitioners who have excelled in their chosen field of expertise. In 1947, the Academy granted three awards. Today, more than one hundred awards are bestowed annually in the fields of film, television and video games.

British Animation Awards (BAA)

Web: http://www.britishanimationawards.com
The British Animation Awards covers all aspects of the UK animation scene, from student work to commercials, children's entertainment, short and experimental art films, music videos, new technologies, script-writing and craftsmanship. BAA is held every two years, most recently in 2006. The awards themselves are unique artworks (e.g. a drawing, painting, cel, collage, sculpture

etc) created specially for the occasion by a leading international or UK animation artist. The 'BAAs' are exhibited for a month at the Animation Art Gallery in central London.

British Archaeological Awards
Web: http://www.britarch.ac.uk/awards
The biennial British Archaeological Awards are a showcase for the best in British archaeology. Established in 1976 they have grown to encompass fourteen awards covering every aspect of archaeology. Among these are awards for the best Broadcast television/radio programme, and the best ICT project (web site, CD-ROM, etc). These awards are sponsored by Channel 4 and are administered by the BUFVC/CBA Committee for Audiovisual Education (CAVE).

British Independent Film Awards
Web: http://www.bifa.org.uk
Created in 1998 and organised by Raindance, the British Independent Film Awards set out to celebrate merit and achievement in independently funded British filmmaking, to honour new talent, and to promote British films and filmmaking to a wider public.

British Interactive Media Association (BIMA) Awards
Web: http://www.bima.co.uk/the-bimas
An annual competition looking for outstanding interactive projects in a range of categories including integrated campaign, interactive advertising, interactive television, mobile game, mobile, microsite, Web site, community web site or campaign, outstanding achievement in accessibility, education and training, government and information, children, entertainment, arts and culture, etc.

Broadcast Awards
Web: http://www.broadcastnow.co.uk/awards
Annual awards rewarding excellence in television programme making.

Broadcast Digital Channel Awards
Web: http://www.broadcastnow.co.uk/dcawards
Founded in 2004, the Broadcast Digital Channel Awards feature thirteen categories highlighting the rapid growth and success of the digital platform. The categories include Best Factual Channel, Best Use of Interactive, Best News Channel, Best Specialist Channel and Best Online Community Site.

Commonwealth Broadcasting Association Awards
Web: http://www.cba.org.uk/awards
Annual awards for television and radio programmes from the Commonwealth. Entries may be in any language but television programmes should have English subtitles and foreign-language radio programmes must be accompanied by a text in English explaining the concept of the programme and its impact.

Descartes Prize for Science Communication
Web: http://ec.europa.eu/research/descartes
Launched in 2004, the Descartes Prize for Communication is an annual competition open to science communication initiatives across Europe. The competition is open to individuals and organisations that have achieved outstanding results in science communication, and have won prizes from European and/or national organisations.

Ethnographic Film Awards
Web: http://www.raifilmfest.org.uk
This biennial competition is part of the international film festival sponsored by the Royal Anthropological Institute covering films on social, cultural and biological anthropology or archaeology.

Exposures National Student Film Awards
Web: http://www.exposuresfilmfestival.co.uk
Part of the Exposures Festival held in Bristol, the awards are open to student-produced films in the categories drama, documentary, experimental and animation.

First Light Movies Awards
Web: http://www.firstlightmovies.com/awards
Founded in 2001, First Light Movies funds and offers training to 5-18 year-olds throughout the UK in writing, acting, shooting, lighting, directing, and producing films. Each year First Light holds a competition to choose the best film in each of nine categories and the awards are presented at a ceremony in the West End attended by stars and film industry executives.

FOCAL Awards
Web: http://www.focalint.org/focalawards.htm
The annual FOCAL Awards recognise productions which have used library archive and stock footage in an imaginative and innovative way and to acknowledge the work of key services involved with preservation and restoration, plus those archives and individuals who have served the industry well.

The FREDDIE Awards
Web: http://www.thefreddies.com
MediMedia's International Health & Medical Media Awards are open to health and medical videos, DVDs, CD-ROMs or web sites that address health or medical issues for consumers or health care professionals.

Grierson Awards
Web: http://www.griersontrust.org
The Grierson Awards commemorate the pioneering Scottish documentary filmmaker John Grierson. The awards, held in November each year, recognise and celebrate the best documentary filmmaking from Britain and abroad.

Iamhist Prize for a Work in Media and History
Web: http://www.iamhist.org
Biennial prize awarded for the book, radio or television programme or series, film, DVD, CD-ROM, or URL making the best contribution on the subject of media and history to have been published or shown in the preceding two years. The prize is worth $1000. The prize was awarded for the first time in 2007.

Imperial War Museum Student Film Awards
Web: http://london.iwm.org.uk/server/show/ConWebDoc.2310
Since 2000 the IWM has held an annual competition for students who have made films and videos incorporating archive film from the Museum's collection or about its subject matter. The awards have three categories: Best Documentary; Best Creative Response to the Subject of War; Winner of the Audience Poll.

International Visual Communication Association (IVCA) Awards

Web: http://www.ivca.org/award-schemes/ivca-awards.html
Annual awards, held in London in Spring each year, which reward effective business communication in corporate video, live events, interactive media projects, business television and web sites.

John Brabourne Awards

Web: http://www.ctbf.co.uk/johnbrabourneawards
The John Brabourne Awards are a stepping stone for young people driven to further their experiences and careers in all aspects of film and television. The CTBF awards provide cash sums of between £1,000 and £5,000 to assist with training, equipment, or the costs of travel, rent, bills or childcare. The Sponsored awards are cash sums and/or access to training, work experience, equipment or materials of a value of £1,000 to £5,000.

Kraszna-Krausz Awards

Web: http://www.editor.net/k-k
The Kraszna-Krausz Awards recognise publications about film, television and photography. Independent panels of judges select winners in all these categories and now do this annually instead of, as in the past, giving awards in alternate years to books about the still image and the moving image. The Awards are open to entries world-wide and in all languages.

Learning on Screen

Web: http://www.bufvc.ac.uk/learningonscreen
The Learning on Screen Awards celebrate excellence in the production of effective learning material which employs moving pictures, sound and graphics. Such learning material might be delivered as physical media, or online, or via broadcast media – or a combination of all three. The competition is open to all-comers involved at any level in the fields of production, publishing, broadcasting, education and research.

Panda Awards

Web: http://www.wildscreenfestival.org
Held as part of the biennial Wildscreen Festival, the Panda Awards are the world's most prestigious awards for films about the natural world. Leading filmmakers from all over the world enter for the twenty Panda Award Categories, covering subjects as diverse as Animal Behaviour, Campaigning and Earth Sciences and skills such as Cinematography, Editing, Music, Sound and Script.

Projection Box Essay Award

Web: http://www.pbawards.co.uk
The aims of this annual award are to encourage new research and new thinking into any historical, artistic or technical aspect of projected and moving images up to 1915; and to promote engaging, accessible, and imaginative work. The first prize of £250 is for an essay of between 5,000 and 8,000 words (including notes).

Scottish Students on Screen

Web: http://www.baftascotland.co.uk/ScottishStudentsonScreen.htm
Annual competition designed to be a platform for the screen talent in Scotland's colleges and universities. Organised by BAFTA Scotland.

Sony Radio Academy Awards

Web: http://www.radioawards.org
Founded in 1983, the Sony Radio Academy Awards seek to recognise the very best of the UK radio industry, nationally, regionally and locally. Over the years the awards have set out to recognise the creative talents of journalists, writers, producers, performers and broadcasters, covering the wealth of UK radio output from speech and drama through to news, comedy and music.

Student Radio Awards

Web: http://www.studentradio.org.uk
Held as part of the Student Radio Association conference.

BLOGS

A blog (the word is short for weblog) is a web site which adds information chrono-logically in the form of posts, to which others can add comments. Blogs are used both as personal diaries and as commentaries on particular topics. All come with RSS (Really Simple Syndication) feeds allowing users to subscribe to favourite blogs and receive regular posts. All list posts by categories, which build up into subject-classified archives of information. A growing number of blogs contain information of relevance to the study and use of motion pictures in UK higher education. The blogs listed below are some of those that the BUFVC has found useful as information sources.

There are dedicated blog search engines for pursuing particular topics, such as Technorati (http://www.technorati.com) and Google Blog Search (http://blogsearch.google.com). For those interested in setting up a blog, the BBC provided a good introductory guide (http://www.bbc.co.uk/webwise), while some of the popular (and free) programmes for setting up a blog include Blogger (http://www.blogger.com), LiveJournal (http://www.livejournal.com) and Wordpress (http://www.wordpress.com).

AHDS Blog
Web: http://blogs.ahds.ac.uk
Digital resource news from the Arts and Humanities Data Service (AHDS).

Alternative Film Guide
Web: http://www.altfg.com/blog
A guide to alternative films around the world, with reviews, news and commentary.

BBC Blog Network
Web: http://www.bbc.co.uk/blogs
The 'home' for the wide range of blogs from across the entire BBC output. The blogs cover individual television and radio programmes, news, sport, local and international communities, and the views of editors and senior staff.

BioethicsBytes
Web: http://bioethicsbytes.wordpress.com
Blog from the University of Leicester, bringing together information on multimedia resources to assist in the teaching of bioethics, with an emphasis on television programming.

The Bioscope
Web: http://bioscopic.wordpress.com
News and information on early and silent cinema, with an emphasis on research resources.

The Center for Independent Documentary
Web: http://documentaries.wordpress.com
Not-for-profit American organisation collaborating with independent documentary filmmakers; a useful source of information on American documentary filmmaking in general.

DAVA – Digital Audiovisual Archiving
Web: http://av-archive.blogspot.com
A blog focused on the digital transformation and preservation of audio-visual materials.

David Bordwell
Web: http://www.davidbordwell.net/blog
Exceptional blog from one of the world's leading film theorists, providing wide-ranging observations on film art in an accessible and thought-provoking style.

Digital Ethnography
Web: http://mediatedcultures.net/ksudigg
Blog from a working group of Kansas State University Students and faculty exploring the possibilities of digital ethnography. Includes ongoing projects investigating the YouTube phenomenon.

The Documentary Blog
Web: http://www.thedocumentaryblog.com
Enthusiastic and informative reports on the latest documentary film releases, with background features looking at documentaries thematically.

Information Aesthetics
Web: http://infosthetics.com
Blog on the visualisation of information, exploring the symbiotic relationship between creative design and the field of information visualisation.

JISC Digitisation Blog
Web: http://involve.jisc.ac.uk/wpmu/digitisation
The latest news on the JISC Digitisation programme, which includes major audio-visual collections including Newsfilm Online, Archival Sound Recordings, InView: Moving Images in the Public Sphere, and the London Broadcasting Company/Independent Radio News Archive.

Media Resources Center
Web: http://blogs.lib.berkeley.edu/mrc.php
Latest information from the excellent Media Resources Center at the University of California, Berkeley, which maintains one of the best online resources guides available for film, video and broadcast references sources.

Michael Geist
Web: http://www.michaelgeist.ca
Well-presented blog on technology law from Dr Michael Geist, Canada Research Chair of Internet and E-commerce Law at the University of Ottawa. There is a multimedia section, with video and audio content of radio and television events in which he has taken part, plus podcasts.

Organ Grinder
Web: http://blogs.guardian.co.uk/organgrinder
News, discussion and opinion from *The Guardian* newspaper's Media section.

Prelinger Library Blog
Web: http://prelingerlibrary.blogspot.com
Reports from the Prelinger Library, putting public domain materials online through the Internet Archive (http://www.archive.org) and commenting on open access issues.

ResearchBuzz
Web: http://www.researchbuzz.org
Handy information source on the world of Internet research, reporting on search engines, new data managing software, browser technology, large compendiums of information, Web directories etc.

Restoration Tips & Notes
Web: http://www.richardhess.com/notes
Detailed advice, in blog format, on the restoration, repair and mastering of audio formats.

Stephen's Web
Web: http://downes.ca
Personal site, with blogging features, of Stephen Downes of the National Research Council, Canada, investigating online learning, content syndication and new media.

Street Anatomy
Web: http://www.streetanatomy.com/blog
The past, present and future of medical visualisation.

The TASI Lightbox
Web: http://www.tasi.ac.uk/blog
News and views on digital imaging from the Technical Advisory Service for Images.

Television Archiving
Web: http://www.archival.tv
Jeff Ubois' well-informed blog covering online video and the future of broadcasting.

Trace the Noble Dust
Web: http://www.bardcentral.com/blog
News and discussion on the latest audio-visual Shakespeare productions, maintained by the Canadian specialist retailer Poor Yorick.

Video Active
Web: http://www.videoactive.eu
The aim of the European-funded Video Active is to create access to television archives across Europe. The site is in the form of a blog, and reports on the progress of the project, which began in September 2006, and includes presentations, workplans, and news.

Vlogdir
Web: http://www.vlogdir.com
A directory of video blogs, offering options to browse the latest blogs, most popular blogs, or a random selection. Videobloggers can submit their own vlogs and vodcasts.

BROADCASTING

The UK television and radio channels listed in this section are all of those covered by the BUFVC's database the Television and Radio Index for Learning and Teaching (TRILT) since June 2001. They are categorised as follows, then listed alphabetically within in each section:
A. Television channel recorded by the BUFVC
B. Other television channels listed on TRILT
C. Radio stations listed on TRILT (by region and nation)

The channels covered in TRILT include terrestrial, digital, cable and satellite television (with regional variations), national and local radio stations, Asian-language, Irish, Scottish Gaelic and Welsh channels and programmes. Virtually all of the British television and radio channels broadcast over this period are included. All channels that are still active on TRILT have dates of coverage, contact information and a brief description. Those channels that are no longer active on TRILT have varying levels of information; if the channel is still broadcasting, contact details are included where possible. In many cases channels have changed names since 2001. For consistency, all channels are listed under their current name, even if they appear in TRILT under their former name. Further information on all channels can be found in our channel profiles database: http://www.trilt.ac.uk.

TELEVISION CHANNELS RECORDED BY THE BUFVC

BBC1
Television Centre, Wood Lane, London W12 7RJ
☎ 020 8743 8000
Web: http://www.bbc.co.uk/bbcone
BBC1 is a terrestrial channel available to all UK viewers. It is also available on cable, satellite and digital television. It has a diverse programming policy encompassing all genres. Most programmes are shown over the entire country but there are occasional regional opt-outs and local news and weather reports. The BUFVC records the London broadcasts of this channel. TRILT coverage: Selective from July 1995, and comprehensive from June 2001 to date.

BBC2
Television Centre, Wood Lane, London W12 7RJ
☎ 020 8743 8000
Web: http://www.bbc.co.uk/bbctwo
BBC2 is a terrestrial channel available to all UK viewers. It is also available on digital, cable and satellite platforms. Most programmes are shown over the entire country but there are occasional regional opt-outs and local news and weather reports. The BUFVC records the London broadcasts of this channel. TRILT coverage: Selective from July 1995, and comprehensive from June 2001 to date.

BBC3

Television Centre, Wood Lane, London W12 7RJ
☎ 020 8743 8000
E-mail: bbcthreefeedback@bbc.co.uk Web: http://www.bbc.co.uk/bbcthree
BBC3 is a digital television channel and is a re-branding of BBC Choice. BBC3 is a general entertainment channel aimed at young adults. TRILT coverage: February 2003 to date.

BBC4

Television Centre, Wood Lane, London W12 7RJ
☎ 020 8743 8000
Web: http://www.bbc.co.uk/bbcfour
BBC4 is a digital television channel and is a re-branding of BBC Knowledge. It shows a mix of documentaries, dramas and foreign language films. TRILT coverage: March 2002 to date.

ITV1 London (weekday)

101 St Martin's Lane, London WC2N 4AZ
☎ 020 7240 4000 **Fax:** 020 7615 1775
Web: http://www.itvlocal.com/london
Available on digital, cable and satellite as well as terrestrially, Carlton is the ITV franchise covering London and the southeast from 6 am on Monday morning to 6 pm on Friday evening, with LWT broadcasting over the weekend period. Carlton and LWT were both re-branded ITV1 London in 2002, although they remain separate franchises. TRILT coverage: June 2001 to date.

ITV1 London (weekend)

The London Television Centre, Upper Ground, London SE1 9LT
☎ 020 7620 1620 **Fax:** 020 7261 1290
Web: http://www.itvlocal.com/london
London Weekend Television is the joint ITV1 franchise holder for the London region, along with Carlton. LWT broadcasts from early evening Friday to 6 am on Monday morning. LWT and Carlton were both re-branded as ITV1 London in 2002. TRILT coverage: June 2001 to date.

Channel 4

124 Horseferry Road, London SW1P 2TX
☎ 020 7396 4444 **Fax:** 020 7306 8366
Web: http://www.channel4.com
Channel 4 is a terrestrial channel available to all UK viewers. It is a general entertainment channel that is popular with younger viewers and is also strong on documentaries. TRILT coverage: Selective from July 1995, and comprehensive from June 2001 to date.

Five

22 Long Acre, London WC2E 9LY
☎ 0845 705 0505
E-mail: customerservices@five.tv Web: http://www.five.tv
Five, formerly known as Channel 5, is a terrestrial television channel available in the UK. It began broadcasting at 6.00pm on 30 March 1997. It aims to provide general light entertainment, with a mix of films, sport, quiz shows, soap operas and documentaries. TRILT coverage: Selective from March 1997, and comprehensive from June 2001 to date.

OTHER TELEVISION CHANNELS LISTED ON TRILT

ABC1
Building 12, 2nd Floor, 566 Chiswick High Road London W4 5AN
☎ 0870 880 7080
E-mail: feedback@abc1tv.co.uk Web: http://www.abc1tv.co.uk
Available on Freeview, as well as digital and cable platforms, ABC1 is part of the Disney Corporation. TRILT coverage: 31 March 2006 to date.

Adult Channel
Aquis House, Station Road, Hayes, Middlesex UB3 4DX
☎ 020 8581 7000 **Fax:** 020 8581 7007
Web: http://www.adultchannel.co.uk
The Adult Channel broadcasts adult entertainment that is permissible within British law. Available on pay-per-view basis on cable, satellite and digital. TRILT coverage: June 2001 to date.

Adventure One
Shepherds Building East, 3rd Floor, Richmond Way, London W14 0DQ
☎ 020 7751 7700 **Fax:** 020 7751 7698
E-mail: natgeoweb@bskyb.com Web: http://www.natgeochannel.co.uk
Part of the National Geographic Channel, it broadcasts a wide range of programmes, including documentaries on natural history and extreme sports. TRILT coverage: June 2001 to date.

Anglia See **ITV1 Anglia**

Animal Planet
Discovery House, Chiswick Park, Building 2, 566 Chiswick High Road, London W4 5YB
☎ 020 8811 3000 **Fax:** 020 8811 3100
E-mail: mail_us@discovery-europe.com Web: http://www.animalplanet.co.uk
The Animal Planet channel is affiliated with the Discovery Channel and shows wildlife programmes. It is only available to cable, digital and satellite viewers and it is split into digital and analogue versions. TRILT coverage: June 2001 to date.

Animal Planet Analogue See **Animal Planet**

Artsworld See **SkyArts**

ARY Digital
ARY Digital UK Ltd, 65 North Acton Road, Park Royal, London NW10 6PJ
☎ 020 8838 9400 **Fax:** 020 8838 1440
Web: http://www.arydigital.tv
ARY Digital, formerly known as the Pakistani Channel, is available on cable, digital and satellite platforms. TRILT continues to carry listings for the channel under the old name, Pakistani Channel. TRILT coverage: June 2001 to date.

Asia 1 TV
An Asian-language cable, satellite and digital channel. No longer active on TRILT.

Asia1Net
An Asian-language cable, satellite and digital channel. No longer active on TRILT.

AsiaNet
Asianet (Europe) Ltd, 344 High Street North, Manor Park, London E12 6PH
☎ 020 85866511 **Fax:** 020 85866517
E-mail: website@asianetworld.tv Web: http://www.asianetuk.com
An Asian-language cable, satellite and digital channel. No longer active on TRILT.

Bangla TV
150 High Street, Stratford, London E15 2NE
☎ 0870 005 6778 **Fax:** 02085362751
E-mail: info@banglatv.co.uk Web: http://www.banglatv.co.uk
A Bengali-language channel cable, satellite and digital channel. No longer active on TRILT.

BBC Choice See **BBC Three**

BBC Knowledge See **BBC Four**

BBC News 24
Television Centre, Wood Lane, London W12 7RJ
The BBC's 24-hour news service is available on digital, cable and satellite and, for a limited period each night, terrestrial BBC1. TRILT coverage: June 2001 to date.

BBC Parliament
MC3 C3, The Media Centre, Media Village, 201 Wood Lane, London W12 7TQ
☎ 020 8008 1923
Web: http://news.bbc.co.uk/1/hi/programmes/bbc_parliament
The BBC's broadcasts of the UK parliament are available on digital, cable and satellite television. TRILT coverage: June 2001 to date.

BBC1 See **Television channels recorded by the BUFVC**

BBC1 East
The Forum, Millennium Plain, Norwich NR2 1BH
☎ 01603 619331
E-mail: look.east@bbc.co.uk Web: http://www.bbc.co.uk/lookeast
Most BBC1 programmes are shown in all regions but there are occasional regional opt-outs and local news and weather reports. TRILT coverage: June 2001 to date.

BBC1 London
PO Box 94.9, Marylebone High St. London W1A 6FL
☎ 020 7224 2424
E-mail: yourlondon@bbc.co.uk Web: http://www.bbc.co.uk/london
TRILT coverage: June 2001 to date.

BBC1 London and South East See **BBC1 London** and **BBC1 South East**

59

BBC1 Midlands
London Road, Nottingham NG2 4UU
☎ 0115 955 0500 **Fax:** 0115 902 1984
E-mail: emt@bbc.co.uk Web: http://www.bbc.co.uk/eastmidlandstoday
TRILT coverage: June 2001 to date.

BBC1 North
2 St Peter's Square, Leeds LS9 8AH
☎ 0113 244 1188
E-mail: look.north@bbc.co.uk
Web: http://www.bbc.co.uk/looknorthyorkslincs
TRILT coverage: June 2001 to date.

BBC1 North East
Broadcasting Centre, Barrack Rd, Newcastle upon Tyne NE99 2NE
☎ 0191 232 1313
E-mail: look.north.comment@bbc.co.uk
Web: http://www.bbc.co.uk/looknorthnecumbria
TRILT coverage: June 2001 to date.

BBC1 North West
New Broadcasting House, Oxford Road, Manchester M60 1SJ
Telephone 0161 200 2020
E-mail: nwt@bbc.co.uk Web: http://www.bbc.co.uk/northwesttonight
TRILT coverage: June 2001 to date.

BBC1 Northern Ireland
Broadcasting House, Ormeau Avenue, Belfast BT2 8HQ
☎ 028 9033 8000
E-mail: bbcni.feedback@bbc.co.uk
Web: http://www.bbc.co.uk/northernireland
TRILT coverage: June 2001 to date.

BBC1 Scotland
BBC Scotland, 40 Pacific Quay, Glasgow G51 1BA
☎ 0141 422 6000
E-mail: enquiries.scot@bbc.co.uk Web: http://www.bbc.co.uk/scotland
TRILT coverage: June 2001 to date.

BBC1 South
Broadcasting House, 10 Havelock Road, Southampton SO14 7PU
☎ 023 8022 6201
E-mail: south.today@bbc.co.uk Web: http://www.bbc.co.uk/southtoday
TRILT coverage: June 2001 to date.

BBC1 South East
The Great Hall, Mount Pleasant Road, Tunbridge Wells TN1 1QQ
☎ 01892 670000
E-mail: southeasttoday@bbc.co.uk
Web: http://www.bbc.co.uk/southeasttoday
TRILT coverage: June 2001 to date.

BBC1 South West

Broadcasting House, Seymour Road, Plymouth PL3 5BD
☎ 01752 229 201
E-mail: spotlight@bbc.co.uk Web: http://www.bbc.co.uk/spotlight
TRILT coverage: June 2001 to date.

BBC1 Wales

BBC Broadcasting House, Llandaff, Cardiff CF5 2YQ
☎ 02920 322000 **Fax:** 02920 555960
E-mail: feedback.wales@bbc.co.uk Web: http://www.bbc.co.uk/wales
TRILT coverage: June 2001 to date.

BBC1 West

Broadcasting House, Whiteladies Road, Bristol BS8 2LR
☎ 0117 973 2211
E-mail: pointswest@bbc.co.uk Web: http://www.bbc.co.uk/pointswest
TRILT coverage: June 2001 to date.

BBC2 See **Television channels recorded by the BUFVC**

BBC2 East

The Forum, Millennium Plain, Norwich NR2 1BH
☎ 01603 619331
E-mail: look.east@bbc.co.uk Web: http://www.bbc.co.uk/lookeast
Most BBC2 programmes are shown in all regions but there are occasional regional opt-outs and local news and weather reports. TRILT coverage: June 2001 to date.

BBC2 London

PO Box 94.9, Marylebone High St. London W1A 6FL
☎ 020 7224 2424
E-mail: yourlondon@bbc.co.uk Web: http://www.bbc.co.uk/london
TRILT coverage: June 2001 to date.

BBC2 Midlands

London Road, Nottingham NG2 4UU
☎ 0115 955 0500 **Fax:** 0115 902 1984
E-mail: emt@bbc.co.uk Web: http://www.bbc.co.uk/eastmidlandstoday
TRILT coverage: June 2001 to date.

BBC2 North

2 St Peter's Square, Leeds LS9 8AH
☎ 0113 244 1188
E-mail: look.north@bbc.co.uk
Web: http://www.bbc.co.uk/looknorthyorkslincs
TRILT coverage: June 2001 to date.

BBC2 North East

Broadcasting Centre, Barrack Rd, Newcastle upon Tyne NE99 2NE
☎ 0191 232 1313
E-mail: look.north.comment@bbc.co.uk
Web: http://www.bbc.co.uk/looknorthnecumbria
TRILT coverage: June 2001 to date.

BBC2 North West

New Broadcasting House, Oxford Road, Manchester M60 1SJ
Telephone 0161 200 2020
E-mail: nwt@bbc.co.uk Web: http://www.bbc.co.uk/northwesttonight
TRILT coverage: June 2001 to date.

BBC2 Northern Ireland

Broadcasting House, Ormeau Avenue, Belfast BT2 8HQ
☎ 028 9033 8000
E-mail: bbcni.feedback@bbc.co.uk
Web: http://www.bbc.co.uk/northernireland
TRILT coverage: June 2001 to date.

BBC2 Scotland

BBC Scotland, 40 Pacific Quay, Glasgow G51 1BA
☎ 0141 422 6000
E-mail: enquiries.scot@bbc.co.uk Web: http://www.bbc.co.uk/scotland
TRILT coverage: June 2001 to date.

BBC2 South

Broadcasting House, 10 Havelock Road, Southampton SO14 7PU
☎ 023 8022 6201
E-mail: south.today@bbc.co.uk Web: http://www.bbc.co.uk/southtoday
TRILT coverage: June 2001 to date.

BBC2 South East

The Great Hall, Mount Pleasant Road, Tunbridge Wells TN1 1QQ
☎ 01892 670000
E-mail: southeasttoday@bbc.co.uk
Web: http://www.bbc.co.uk/southeasttoday
TRILT coverage: June 2001 to date.

BBC2 South West

Broadcasting House, Seymour Road, Plymouth PL3 5BD
☎ 01752 229 201
E-mail: spotlight@bbc.co.uk Web: http://www.bbc.co.uk/spotlight
TRILT coverage: June 2001 to date.

BBC2 Wales

BBC Broadcasting House, Llandaff, Cardiff CF5 2YQ
☎ 02920 322000 **Fax:** 02920 555960
E-mail: feedback.wales@bbc.co.uk Web: http://www.bbc.co.uk/wales
TRILT coverage: June 2001 to date.

BBC2 West

Broadcasting House, Whiteladies Road, Bristol BS8 2LR
☎ 0117 973 2211
E-mail: pointswest@bbc.co.uk Web: http://www.bbc.co.uk/pointswest
TRILT coverage: June 2001 to date.

Bid TV

sit-up House, 179-181 The Vale, London W3 7RW
☎ 0870 166 6667
Web: http://www.bid.tv
Bid TV is a digital television shopping channel featuring auctions, allowing viewers to bid on a variety of products. TRILT coverage: March 2006 to date.

Biography Channel

Grant Way, Isleworth, Middlesex TW7 5QD
☎ 0870 240 3000
E-mail: contact@thebiographychannel.co.uk
Web: http://www.thebiographychannel.co.uk
The Biography Channel is available on digital, satellite and cable. It shows documentaries about people of note. TRILT coverage: June 2001 to date.

Bloomberg TV

City Gate House, 39-45 Finsbury Square, London EC2A 1PQ
☎ 020 7617 7813 **Fax:** 020 7392 6634
Web: http://www.bloomberg.com/tvradio/tv/tv_index_europe.html
A finance and economics channel operated by Bloomberg LP. It is available on digital, satellite and cable platforms. Different versions of the channel are broadcast in different territories. TRILT coverage: June 2001 to date.

Bollywood 4U (B4U)

B4U Network Europe Ltd, 19 Heather Park Drive, Transputec House, Wembley, Middlesex HA0 1SS
☎ 020 8795 7171 **Fax:** 020 8795 7181
E-mail: enquiries@b4unetwork.com Web: http://www.b4utv.com
Available on digital, B4U concentrates on South Asian films. It also shows star interviews, news and interactive programs. TRILT coverage: June 2001 to date.

Boomerang

TCN at Turner House, 16 Great Marlborough Street, London W1F 7HS
☎ 020 7693 1000
Web: http://www.boomerangtv.co.uk
A children's animation channel, available on cable and satellite. It is part of the Cartoon Network. TRILT coverage: June 2001 to date.

Border See **ITV1 Border**

Bravo

Virgin Media Television, 160 Great Portland Street, London W1W 5QA
☎ 0870 043 4029
E-mail: enquiries@bravo.co.uk Web: http://www.bravo.co.uk
A subscription channel available on analogue and digital cable and satellite, Aimed at male viewers, Bravo shows comedy, horror and action films and erotica. TRILT coverage: June 2001 to date.

Bravo Analogue See **Bravo**

British Eurosport

Eurosport London, 55 Drury Lane, London WC2B 5SQ
☎ 0207 468 7777 **Fax:** 0207 468 0023
E-mail: info@eurosport.com Web: http://www.eurosport-tv.com
Sports channel available on cable, digital terrestrial and satellite. Part of the Eurosport network, which is available in over sixty countries and broadcasts in over 15 European languages. TRILT coverage: June 2001 to date.

Carlton See **ITV1 London** (weekday)

Carlton Central See **ITV1 Carlton Central**

Carlton Cinema

Carlton Cinema was available to cable, digital and satellite viewers until March 2003. It showed films from the 1930s to the present. No longer active on TRILT.

Carlton West Country See ITV1 Carlton West Country

Cartoon Network

Turner House, 16 Great Marlborough Street, London W1F 7HS
☎ 020 7693 1000 **Fax:** 020 7693 1001
Web: http://www.cartoonnetwork.co.uk
Unsurprisingly this channel is devoted to cartoons. In the UK the channel is available on cable, satellite and digital television. TRILT coverage: June 2001 to date.

Cartoon Network Satellite

Satellite version of Cartoon Network. See **Cartoon Network** for full details.

CBBC

Television Centre, Wood Lane, London W12 7RJ
☎ 020 8743 8000
E-mail: cbbc.online@bbc.co.uk Web: http://www.bbc.co.uk/cbbc
CBBC is a channel from the BBC, available on Freeview, cable and digital satellite platforms. The channel broadcasts from 7 am to 7 pm daily and is aimed at children aged eight to twelve. TRILT coverage: April 2003 to date.

CBeebies

MC3 C3, The Media Centre, Media Village, 201 Wood Lane, London W12 7TQ
☎ 020 8743 8000
Web: http://www.bbc.co.uk/cbeebies
CBeebies is a channel from the BBC, available on Freeview, cable and digital satellite platforms. The channel broadcasts from 7 am to 7 pm daily and is aimed at children under the age of six. TRILT coverage: April 2003 to date.

Challenge

Virgin Media Television, 160 Great Portland Street, London W1W 5QA
☎ 0870 043 4030
E-mail: enquiries@challenge.co.uk Web: http://www.challenge.co.uk
Challenge is available to digital, cable and satellite viewers. Its programming consists mainly of game shows and quizzes. Both analogue and digital versions are available. TRILT coverage: June 2001 to date.

Challenge Analogue See Challenge

Channel

Television Centre, St Helier, Jersey JE1 3ZD
☎ 01534 816816 **Fax:** 01534 816777
E-mail: broadcast@channeltv.co.uk
Based in Jersey with offices in Guernsey, Channel TV operates the ITV1 franchise area covering the Channel Islands. It is the smallest ITV company and produces local programmes as well as taking ITV network programmes. TRILT coverage: June 2001 to date.

Channel 4 See Television channels recorded by the BUFVC

Channel 5 See Five

Civilisation

Discovery House, Chiswick Park Building 2, 566 Chiswick Park Road, London W4 5YB

☎ 020 8811 3000 **Fax:** 020 8811 3100

Web: http://www.discoverycivilisation.co.uk

Civilisation, formerly known as Discovery Civilisations, is available to digital, cable and satellite customers. Its programming focuses on events and characters that made history and defined cultures. TRILT carries listings for the channel under the old name, Discovery Civilisations. TRILT coverage: June 2001 to date.

CNBC

10 Fleet Place, London EC4M 7QS

☎ 020 7653 9300 **Fax:** 020 7653 9488

Web: http://www.cnbc.com

A US-based business and news channel that is available on cable. TRILT coverage: June 2001 to date.

CNNI

Turner House, 16 Great Marlborough Street, London W1V 7HS

☎ 020 7693 0786 **Fax:** 020 7693 0788

Web: http://edition.cnn.com

News, current affairs and business channel available on cable and satellite. There are different versions for various parts of the globe. The web site carries transcripts of some programmes. TRILT coverage: June 2001 to date.

CNX See **Toonami**

Community Channel

3-7 Euston Centre, Regent's Place, London NW1 3JG

☎ 08708 505500

E-mail: info@communitychannel.org

Web: http://www.communitychannel.org.uk

The Community Channel's slogan is 'TV that gives a damn.' It is available on various digital cable and satellite platforms and runs a limited service on Freeview. TRILT coverage: April 2003 to date.

Discovery

Discovery House, Chiswick Park, Building 2, 566 Chiswick Park Road, London W4 5YB

☎ 020 8811 3000 **Fax:** 020 8811 3100

Web: http://www.discoverychannel.co.uk

The Discovery Channel is only available to cable, digital and satellite viewers. Education, with a scientific or historical slant, is a strong feature of Discovery's programming. Both analogue and digital versions are available. TRILT coverage: June 2001 to date.

Discovery Analogue See **Discovery**

Discovery Civilisations See **Civilisation**

Discovery Health See **Discovery Home & Health**

Discovery Home & Health

Discovery House, Chiswick Park Building 2, 566 Chiswick Park Road, London W4 5YB

☎ 020 8811 3000 **Fax:** 020 8811 3100

Web: http://www.homeandhealthtv.co.uk

Discovery Home & Health is available on cable, satellite and digital television. The channel started life as Discovery Health, but was re-branded in 2005, at which point it became more female-oriented. TRILT continues to carry listings for the channel under the old name, Discovery Health. TRILT coverage: June 2001 to date.

Discovery Home & Leisure See **Discovery Real Time**

Discovery Home & Leisure Analogue See **Discovery Real Time**

Discovery Kids

Discovery House, Chiswick Park Building 2, 566 Chiswick Park Road, London W4 5YB

☎ 020 8811 3000 **Fax:** 020 8811 3100

Web: http://www.discoverychannel.co.uk/kids

A children's channel with an educational slant available on digital cable and satellite. TRILT coverage: June 2001 to date.

Discovery Real Time

Discovery House, Chiswick Park Building 2, 566 Chiswick Park Road, London W4 5YB

☎ 020 8811 3000 **Fax:** 020 8811 3100

Web: http://www.realtimetv.co.uk

Discovery Real Time is available on cable, satellite and digital television. The channel started life as Discovery Home & Leisure, but was re-branded in 2005, at which point it became more male-oriented. TRILT continues to carry listings for the channel under the old name, Discovery Home & Leisure. An analogue version of the channel is also available from some providers. This has the same programming but broadcasts for fewer hours a day. TRILT coverage: June 2001 to date.

Discovery Science See **Science**

Discovery Sci-Trek

Discovery House, Chiswick Park Building 2, 566 Chiswick Park Road, London W4 5YB

☎ 020 8811 3000 **Fax:** 020 8811 3100

One of the Discovery channels, Sci-Trek was available on cable, satellite and digital television. No longer active on TRILT.

Discovery Travel & Adventure See **Travel & Living**

Discovery Wings See **Turbo**

Disney Channel

Walt Disney Company Ltd, Building 12, 2nd Floor, 566 Chiswick High Road London W4 5AN

☎ 08708 80 70 80

E-mail: studio@disneychannel.co.uk

Web: http://www.disney.co.uk/DisneyChannel

Channel aimed at children with both animated and live action programmes. The channel is available on digital, cable and satellite television and includes programmes made by companies other than Disney. TRILT coverage: June 2001 to date.

E4
124 Horseferry Rd, London SW1P 2TX
☎ 020 7396 4444 **Fax:** 020 7396 8368
E-mail: viewerenquiries@channel4.co.uk
Web: http://www.e4.com
E4 is an entertainment channel from Channel Four available on Freeview, digital, cable and satellite. Programming is geared towards young people, and the channel shows a lot of comedy, drama and reality shows. TRILT coverage: June 2001 to date.

E4 + 1
124 Horseferry Road, London SW1P 2TX
E-mail: viewerenquiries@channel4.co.uk Web: http://www.e4.com
E4 + 1 is a time-shift channel, showing the same programmes as E4 one hour later.

Eurosport
Eurosport London, 55 Drury Lane, London WC2B 5SQ
☎ 020 7468 7777 **Fax:** 020 7468 0023
E-mail: info@eurosport.com Web: http://www.eurosport-tv.com
Available on cable, satellite and digital in European countries, Eurosport provides sports coverage, including ones that are less commonly given coverage on terrestrial television. TRILT coverage: June 2001 to date.

Fantasy Channel See Television X

Fantasy Channel Analogue See Television X

FilmFour
124-126 Horseferry Road, London SW1P 2TX
Web: http://www.channel4.com/film
FilmFour is a film channel from Channel 4. It is available on Freeview and digital, satellite and cable platforms. TRILT coverage: April 2003 to date.

Fox Kids
Jetix Europe Limited, Jetix Club, Online and Interactive, Chiswick Park, Building 12, 566 Chiswick High Road, London W4 5AN
Web: http://www.jetix.co.uk
Channel aimed at children, showing both animated and live action programmes. It is available on cable, satellite and digital television. Both analogue and digital versions are available. TRILT coverage: June 2001 to date.

Fox Kids Analogue See Fox Kids

Front Row
Front Row is the name given to a group of pay per view channels showing films on demand on cable television. No longer active on TRILT.

FTN

Virgin Media Television, 160 Great Portland Street, London W1W 5QA
☎ 0870 046 4141
E-mail: enquires@ftn.tv
Web: http://www.virginmediatv.co.uk/our_channels/ftn.php
FTN is a general entertainment channel from Virgin Media, available on Freeview and various digital, cable and satellite platforms. It screens highlights from Trouble, Living, Challenge and Bravo. TRILT coverage: April 2003 to date.

Grampian See **Scottish**

Granada See **ITV1 Granada**

Granada Breeze

Granada Breeze was available on digital, cable and satellite television. It stopped broadcasting in late 2004. It was aimed at women and mostly showed lifestyle, cookery and talk shows. No longer active on TRILT.

Granada Men and Motors See **Men and Motors**

Granada Men and Motors Analogue See **Men and Motors**

Granada Plus

Granada Plus was available on digital, cable and satellite television until late 2004. It showed mainly drama and comedy repeats from ITV. It was available in analogue and digital versions. No longer active on TRILT.

Granada Plus Analogue See **Granada Plus**

Hallmark

234a King's Road, London SW3 5UA
☎ 020 7368 9100 **Fax:** 020 7368 9101
E-mail: info@hallmarkchannel.co.uk Web: http://www.hallmarkchannel.co.uk
Hallmark is available on various digital, cable and satellite platforms. It shows general entertainment programmes and films, with many US imports. TRILT coverage: June 2001 to date.

History

Grant Way, Isleworth, Middlesex TW7 5QD
☎ 0207 705 3000
E-mail: feedback@thehistorychannel.co.uk
Web: http://www.thehistorychannel.co.uk
The History Channel is only available to cable, digital and satellite viewers. Its programming consists of high quality factual material. Both analogue and digital versions are available. TRILT coverage: June 2001 to date.

History Analogue See **History**

HTV Wales See **ITV1 Wales**

HTV West See **ITV1 West of England**

Ideal World

Ideal Home House, Newark Road, Peterborough PE1 5WG
☎ 020 7397 8116/08700 700 802 **Fax:** 08700 700 803
E-mail: customer.services@idealshoppingdirect.co.uk
Web: http://www.idealworld.tv
Ideal World is a digital television shopping channel, allowing viewers to purchase a variety of products. TRILT coverage: March 2006 to date.

TRILT
Television and Radio
Press Information

BBC TV

1998 -

ITV News

ITV News was a 24 hour television news channel available in the UK on digital, cable and satellite platforms. No longer active on TRILT

ITV Sport Channel

Sports channel. No longer active on TRILT.

ITV Sport Plus

Sports channel. No longer active on TRILT.

ITV1 See **Television channels recorded by the BUFVC**

ITV1 Anglia

Anglia House Norwich, Norfolk NR1 3JG
☎ 01603 615151 **Fax:** 01603 631032
E-mail: dutyoffice@itv.com Web: http://www.itvregions.com/anglia
Anglia Television holds the ITV franchise covering the East of England. It produces its own programmes for local broadcast. TRILT coverage: June 2001 to date.

ITV1 Border

The Television Centre, Carlisle CA1 3NT
☎ 01228 525 101 **Fax:** 01228 541 384
E-mail: dutyoffice@itv.com
Border holds the ITV1 franchise for the north of England, southern Scotland and the Isle of Man. Little of its output is networked. TRILT coverage: June 2001 to date.

ITV1 Carlton Central

Central Court, Gas Street, Birmingham B1 2JT
☎ 0121 6439898 **Fax:** 0121 6344898
Web: http://www.itvlocal.com/central
Available on digital, cable and satellite as well as terrestrially, Carlton Central was formed in 1999 when Carlton and Central TV merged. ITV1 Carlton Central covers the Midlands. Sometimes known as ITV1 Central. TRILT coverage: June 2001 to date.

ITV1 Carlton West Country

Langage Science Park, Plymouth PL7 5BQ
☎ 01752 333333 **Fax:** 01752 333444
Web: http://www.itvregions.com/westcountry
Available on digital, cable and satellite as well as terrestrially, ITV1 Carlton West Country is the ITV franchise for the South West of England. Sometimes known as ITV1 Westcountry. TRILT coverage: June 2001 to date.

ITV1 Granada

Quay Street, Manchester M60 9EA
☎ 0161 832 7211 **Fax:** 0161 827 2141
Web: http://www.itvregions.com/granada
Available on digital, cable and satellite as well as terrestrially, Granada is the ITV1 franchise for the North West region. TRILT coverage: June 2001 to date.

ITV1 London See **Television channels recorded by the BUFVC**

ITV1 Meridian

Solent Business Park, Whiteley, Hampshire PO15 7PA
☎ 01489 442000 **Fax:** 01489 442277
Web: http://www.meridiantv.co.uk
Available on digital, cable and satellite as well as terrestrially, Meridian is the ITV1 franchise for the South and South East of England. TRILT coverage: June 2001 to date.

ITV1 Tyne Tees Television

Television House, The Watermark, Gateshead, Tyne & Wear NE11 9SZ
☎ 0191 261 0181 **Fax:** 0191 261 2302
Web: http://www.tynetees.tv
Available on digital, cable and satellite as well as terrestrially, this channel holds the ITV1 franchise for the North East of England. Sometimes called ITV1 Tyne Tees. TRILT coverage: June 2001 to date.

ITV1 Wales

The Television Centre, Culverhouse Cross, Cardiff CF5 6XJ
☎ 029 2059 0590 **Fax:** 029 2059 9108
Web: http://www.itvregions.com/Wales
Available on digital, cable and satellite as well as terrestrially, this channel is the ITV1 franchise for Wales and was formerly known as HTV Wales. TRILT coverage: June 2001 to date.

ITV1 West of England

Television Centre, Bath Road, Bristol BS4 3HG
☎ 0117 972 2722 **Fax:** 0117 972 2400
Web: http://www.itvregions.com/west
Available on digital, cable and satellite as well as terrestrially, this channel is the ITV1 franchise for the West of England and was formerly known as HTV West. Sometimes called ITV1 West. TRILT coverage: June 2001 to date.

ITV1 Yorkshire

The Television Centre, Leeds LS3 1JS
☎ 0113 243 8283. **Fax:** 0113 244 5107
Web: http://www.itvregions.com/yorkshire
Available on digital, cable and satellite as well as terrestrially, this channel is the ITV1 franchise for Yorkshire and Lincolnshire. Sometimes called YTV. TRILT coverage: June 2001 to date.

ITV2

Channels Department, 4th Floor, 200 Grays Inn Road, London WC1X 8HF
☎ 020 7843 8140 **Fax:** 020 7843 8432
Web: http://www.itv.com/itv2
ITV2 is a general entertainment channel. Its programming consists of ITV1 repeats, imported American shows and extended coverage of Reality TV shows. TRILT coverage: June 2001 to date.

ITV3

Channels Department, 4th Floor, 200 Grays Inn Road, London WC1X 8HF
☎ 020 7843 8140 **Fax:** 020 7843 8432
Web: http://www.itv.com/itv3
ITV3 is a general entertainment channel. The programming consists largely of classic drama and comedy. TRILT coverage: March 2006 to date.

ITV4

Channels Department, 4th Floor, 200 Grays Inn Road, London WC1X 8HF
☎ 020 7843 8140 **Fax:** 020 7843 8432
Web: http://www.itv.com/itv2
ITV4 is a general entertainment channel aimed at male viewers. It mainly shows sports, US dramas and comedy. TRILT coverage: August 2006 to date.

Liberty TV

General entertainment channel showing a high proportion of religious programmes. No longer active on TRILT.

Living

Virgin Media Television, 160 Great Portland Street, London W1W 5QA
☎ 0870 043 4028
E-mail: enquiries@livingtv.co.uk Web: http://www.livingtv.co.uk
Channel available on digital, cable and satellite television, aimed at women viewers. Living shows many drama series, talk shows, soap operas and comedy programmes. Available in analogue and digital versions. TRILT coverage: June 2001 to date.

Living Analogue See Living

LWT See ITV1 London (weekend)

Men and Motors

ITV Digital Channels Ltd, Channels Department, 4th Floor, 200 Grays Inn Road, London WC1X 8HF
☎ 020 7843 8140 **Fax:** 020 7843 8432
Web: http://www.menandmotors.co.uk
Channel available on digital, cable and satellite television. Men and Motors, formerly known as Granada Men and Motors, is a men's lifestyle channel. Both analogue and digital versions are available. TRILT continues to carry listings for the channel under the old name, Granada Men and Motors. TRILT coverage: June 2001 to date.

Meridian See ITV1 Meridian

The Money Channel

The Money Channel ceased broadcasting in August 2001. The channel concentrated on financial programmes. No longer active on TRILT.

More4

124 Horseferry Road, London SW1P 2TX
E-mail: viewerenquiries@channel4.co.uk
Web: http://www.channel4.com/more4
Launched in October 2005, More4 is an entertainment channel from Channel 4. TRILT coverage: October 2005 to date.

More4 + 1

124 Horseferry Road, London SW1P 2TX
E-mail: viewerenquiries@channel4.co.uk
Web: http://www.channel4.com/more4
More4 + 1 is a time-shift channel, showing the same programmes as More4 one hour later.

MTV
180 Oxford Street, London WIN 0DS
☎ 020 7284 7777 **Fax:** 020 7284 7788
Web: http://www.mtv.co.uk
Music channel available on cable, satellite and digital television. MTV shows music videos, documentaries and entertainment series. TRILT coverage: June 2001 to date.

MTV 2
180 Oxford Street, London WIN 0DS
☎ 020 7478 6000 **Fax:** 020 7478 6007
Web: http://www.mtv.co.uk/channel/mtv2
MTV 2 specialises in alternative music. The channel is available on cable, satellite and digital television. TRILT coverage: June 2001 to date.

MTV Base
180 Oxford Street, London WIN 0DS
☎ 020 7478 6000 **Fax:** 020 7478 6007
Web: http://www.mtv.co.uk/channel/mtvbase
Music channel available on cable, satellite and digital television. It is dedicated to urban black music from around the world. TRILT coverage: June 2001 to date.

MTV Extra See **MTV Hits**

MTV Hits
180 Oxford Street, London WIN 0DS
☎ 020 7478 6000 **Fax:** 020 7478 6007
Web: http://www.mtv.co.uk/channel/mtvhits
MTV Hits, formerly known as MTV Extra, plays chart hits. It is available on cable, satellite and digital television. TRILT continues to carry listings for the channel under the old name, MTV Extra. TRILT coverage: June 2001 to date.

The Music Factory
180 Oxford Street, London WID IDS
☎ 020 7478 6000 **Fax:** 020 7478 6007
Web: http://www.mtv.co.uk/channel/tmf
Music channel from MTV, available on cable, satellite and digital television. Sometimes called TMF. TRILT coverage: March 2005 to date.

MUTV
274 Deansgate, Manchester M3 4JB
☎ 0161 868 8435 **Fax:** 0161 868 8848
E-mail: mutv@mutv.com Web: http://www.manutd.com/mutv
Television channel devoted to Manchester United Football Club. Available on cable, satellite and digital television, MUTV shows classic and live football matches, news about the team and magazine-type programmes. TRILT coverage: June 2001 to date.

National Geographic
3rd Floor, Shepherd's Building East, Richmond Way, London W14 0DQ
☎ 020 7751 7700 **Fax:** 020 7751 7698
E-mail: natgeoweb@bskyb.com Web: http://www.natgeochannel.co.uk
National Geographic is only available to cable, digital and satellite viewers.

The channel shows programmes that deal with diverse aspects of the natural world. It is available in analogue and digital versions. TRILT coverage: June 2001 to date.

National Geographic Analogue See National Geographic

Nick Jr.

Nickelodeon UK, 15-18 Rathbone Place, London WIT 1HU
☎ 020 7462 1000 **Fax:** 020 7462 1100
E-mail: letterbox@NickJr.co.uk Web: http://www.nickjr.co.uk
The UK's first television channel aimed at very young children, Nick Jr is available on analogue and digital platforms. TRILT coverage: June 2001 to date.

Nick Jr. Analogue See Nick Jr.

Nickelodeon

Nickelodeon UK, 15-18 Rathbone Place, London WIT 1HU
☎ 020 7462 1000 **Fax:** 020 7462 1100
E-mail: letterbox@nick.co.uk Web: http://www.nick.co.uk
Channel aimed at children with both animated and live action programmes. The channel is available on digital, cable and satellite television. TRILT coverage: June 2001 to date.

Nickelodeon Analogue See Nickelodeon

Onsport1

Sports channel. No longer active on TRILT.

Onsport2

Sports channel. No longer active on TRILT.

Pakistani Channel See ARY Digital

Paramount Comedy Channel

180 Oxford Street, London WID 1DS
☎ 020 7478 5300 **Fax:** 020 7478 5446
Web: http://www.paramountcomedy.com
Channel available to cable, digital and satellite viewers. The Paramount Comedy Channel is devoted to popular television comedy series, especially American sit-coms. Both analogue and digital versions of the channel are available. TRILT coverage: June 2001 to date.

Paramount Comedy Channel Analogue
See Paramount Comedy Channel

Performance

4 Farleigh Court, Bristol BS48 1UL
☎ 0870 850 8102 **Fax:** 01275 464 070
E-mail: info@performance-channel.com
Web: http://www.performance-channel.com
Performance is only available to cable, digital and satellite viewers. Devoted to the arts, it broadcasts recorded concerts, ballets, operas and cultural documentaries. TRILT coverage: June 2001 to date.

Phoenix CNE

7th Floor, The Chiswick Centre, 414 Chiswick High Road,
London W4 5TF
☎ 020 8987 4320 **Fax:** 020 8987 4333
E-mail: info@phoenixcnetv.com
Phoenix CNE (Chinese News and Entertainment) is available on digital, cable and satellite television platforms. It caters for Chinese communities in Europe. TRILT coverage: June 2001 to date.

Playboy TV

Aquis House, Station Road, Hayes, Middlesex UB3 4DX
☎ 020 8581 7000 **Fax:** 020 8581 7007
Web: http://www.playboy.co.uk
Broadcasts adult material that is permissible within British law. Available on cable and satellite, broadcasting for a limited period at night, seven days a week. TRILT coverage: June 2001 to date.

Play UK

Play UK was a part of the UKTV family and its programming largely consisted of comedy and music related series. No longer active on TRILT.

Quiz Call

iTouch, Avalon House, 57-63 Scrutton Street, London EC2A 4PF
Web: http://www.quizcall.co.uk
Quiz Call is a channel available in the UK on digital, satellite, cable and Freeview. Viewers call a premium rate number for the chance to win prizes by answering quiz questions. TRILT coverage: March 2006 to date.

QVC

Marco Polo House, 346 Queenstown Road, London SW8 4NQ
☎ 020 7705 5600
E-mail: ukstudio@qvc.com Web: http://www.qvcuk.com
QVC is a well-established general shopping channel available in the UK on Freeview, digital, cable and satellite platforms. TRILT coverage: June 2001 to date.

Racing Channel

Available on digital, cable and satellite, the Racing Channel covered racing news and meets. No longer active on TRILT.

Rapture TV

A UK channel dedicated to 'clubbing,' showing programmes relating to sport, music and clubbing as well as some films. No longer active on TRILT.

Red Hot

Suite 14, Burlington House, St Saviour's Road, St Helier, Jersey JE2 4LA
☎ 01534 703 700 **Fax:** 01534 703 760
E-mail: feedback@redhottv.co.uk Web: http://www.redhottv.co.uk
Adult entertainment channel available in the UK on a pay-per-view basis. TRILT coverage: October 2006 to date.

S4C

Lôn Ddewi, Caernarfon LL55 1ER
☎ 0870 600 4141
Web: http://www.s4c.co.uk

S4C is a television channel available in Wales on analogue television. It broadcasts Welsh and English language programmes, with the majority of the English language programming being rebroadcast from Channel 4. TRILT coverage: June 2001 to date.

S4C2

Parc Ty Glas, Llanisien, Cardiff CF4 5DU
☎ 029 20 747 444
Web: http://www.s4c.co.uk

S4C2 is a partnership between S4C and BBC Wales which provides a comprehensive broadcasting service from the National Assembly for Wales. The channel is available in the UK on digital satellite, cable and Freeview. TRILT coverage: April 2006 to date.

Science

Discovery House, Chiswick Park, Building 2, 566 Chiswick Park Road, London W4 5YB
☎ 020 8811 3000 **Fax:** 020 8811 3100

Formerly known as Discovery Science, this channel is part of the Discovery group and is available on digital, cable and satellite television. TRILT continues to carry listings under the old name, Discovery Science. TRILT coverage: May 2003 to date.

Sci-Fi

Oxford House, 76 Oxford Street, London W1D 1BS
☎ 020 7307 6600 **Fax:** 020 7307 6695
Web: http://www.scifiuk.com

Sci-Fi is only available to cable, digital and satellite viewers. It generally shows feature films and reruns of science-fiction series that have previously been shown on terrestrial television. TRILT coverage: June 2001 to date.

Sci-Fi Satellite See **Sci-Fi**

Scottish

Pacific Quay, Glasgow G51 1PQ
☎ 0141 300 3000 **Fax:** 0141 300 3030
Web: http://www.stv.tv

Scottish is the ITV franchise for Scotland. It incorporates two services, one for central Scotland and one for the north of Scotland (formerly known as Grampian). The channels are sometimes known as STV Central and STV North. TRILT coverage: June 2001 to date.

Screenshop

Sit-up House, 179-181 The Vale, London W3 7RW
☎ 07884 113635 **Fax:** 020 8746 7621
Web: http://www.screenshop.co.uk

Screenshop is a shopping channel available on Freeview, digital, cable and satellite television. It shows pre-recorded 'infomercials' and viewers can purchase products by phone or online. TRILT coverage: June 2001 to date.

Shop!

Shop! is no longer broadcasting. Shop! was a general shopping channel, available on various digital, cable and satellite platforms. No longer active on TRILT.

Simply Money

Simply Money ceased broadcasting on 16 April 2001. Showed financial programmes. No longer active on TRILT.

SkyArts

BSkyB, NHC 1, Grant Way, Isleworth TW7 5QD
☎ 020 7805 2384
E-mail: viewerr@bskyb.com Web: http://www.skyarts.co.uk
SkyArts, formerly known as Artsworld, is an arts channel available on digital television, launched on 2 December 2000. TRILT continues to carry listings for the channel under the old name, Artsworld. TRILT coverage: June 2001 to date.

Sky Box Office Events

Sky Box Office Events is no longer broadcasting. It was a pay-per-view channel that screened non-regular events such as wrestling matches. No longer active on TRILT.

Sky Cinema

British Sky Broadcasting Ltd, Grant Way, Isleworth, Middlesex TW7 5QD
Film channel available on cable, satellite and digital television. Sky Cinema screens classic Hollywood films. Both analogue and digital versions are available. TRILT coverage: June 2001 to date.

Sky Cinema Analogue See **Sky Cinema**

Sky MovieMax ONdigital

Movie channel. No longer active on TRILT.

Sky Movies Action/Thriller

British Sky Broadcasting Ltd, Grant Way, Isleworth, Middlesex TW7 5QD
Web: http://www.skymovies.com/skymovies
Part of the Sky Movies group of film channels from BSkyB. Sky Movies Action/Thriller, formerly known as Sky Movies Max, is available on digital, cable and satellite platforms in the UK as part of the Movie Mix subscription. TRILT coverage: June 2001 to date.

Sky Movies Cinema See **Sky Movies Premiere**

Sky Movies Cinema 2 See **Sky Movies Premiere +1**

Sky Movies Classics

British Sky Broadcasting Ltd, Grant Way, Isleworth, Middlesex TW7 5QD
Web: http://www.skymovies.com/skymovies
Part of the Sky Movies group of film channels from BSkyB. Sky Movies Classics, formerly known as Sky Movies Premier 3, is available on digital, cable and satellite platforms in the UK as part of the Movie Mix subscription. TRILT coverage: June 2001 to date.

Sky Movies Comedy

British Sky Broadcasting Ltd, Grant Way, Isleworth, Middlesex TW7 5QD
Web: http://www.skymovies.com/skymovies
Part of the Sky Movies group of film channels from BSkyB. Sky Movies Comedy, formerly known as Sky Movies Premier, is available on digital, cable and satellite platforms in the UK as part of the Movie Mix subscription. TRILT coverage: June 2001 to date.

Sky Movies Drama

British Sky Broadcasting Ltd, Grant Way, Isleworth, Middlesex TW7 5QD
Web: http://www.skymovies.com/skymovies
Part of the Sky Movies group of film channels from BSkyB. Sky Movies Drama, formerly known as Sky Movies Max 5, is available on digital, cable and satellite platforms in the UK as part of the Movie Mix subscription. TRILT coverage: June 2001 to date.

Sky Movies Family

British Sky Broadcasting Ltd, Grant Way, Isleworth, Middlesex TW7 5QD
Web: http://www.skymovies.com/skymovies
Part of the Sky Movies group of film channels from BSkyB. Sky Movies Family, formerly known as Sky Movies Premier 2, is available on digital, cable and satellite platforms in the UK as part of the Movie Mix subscription. TRILT coverage: June 2001 to date.

Sky Movies HD1/SD1

British Sky Broadcasting Ltd, Grant Way, Isleworth, Middlesex TW7 5QD
Web: http://www.skymovies.com/skymovies
Part of the Sky Movies group of film channels from BSkyB. Sky Movies HD1/SD1, formerly known as Sky Movies Max 4, is available on digital, cable and satellite platforms in the UK as part of the Movie Mix subscription. TRILT coverage: June 2001 to date.

Sky Movies Indie

British Sky Broadcasting Ltd, Grant Way, Isleworth, Middlesex TW7 5QD
Web: http://www.skymovies.com/skymovies
Part of the Sky Movies group of film channels from BSkyB. Sky Movies Indie, formerly known as Sky Movies Max 3, is available on digital, cable and satellite platforms in the UK as part of the Movie Mix subscription. TRILT coverage: June 2001 to date.

Sky Movies Max See **Sky Movies Action/Thriller**

Sky Movies Max 2 See **Sky Movies Sci-Fi/Horror**

Sky Movies Max 3 See **Sky Movies Indie**

Sky Movies Max 4 See **Sky Movies HD1/SD1**

Sky Movies Max 5 See **Sky Movies Drama**

Sky Movies Modern Greats

British Sky Broadcasting Ltd, Grant Way, Isleworth, Middlesex TW7 5QD
Web: http://www.skymovies.com/skymovies
Part of the Sky Movies group of film channels from BSkyB. Sky Movies Premier is available on digital, cable and satellite platforms in the UK as part of the Movie Mix subscription. TRILT coverage: June 2001 to date.

Sky Movies Premier See **Sky Movies Comedy**

Sky Movies Premier 2 See **Sky Movies Family**

Sky Movies Premier 3 See **Sky Movies Classics**

Sky Movies Premier 4 See **Sky Movies Modern Greats**

Sky Movies Premiere

British Sky Broadcasting Ltd, Grant Way, Isleworth, Middlesex TW7 5QD
Web: http://www.skymovies.com/skymovies
Part of the Sky Movies group of film channels from BSkyB. Sky Movies Premiere, formerly known as Sky Movies Cinema, is available on digital, cable and satellite platforms in the UK as part of the Movie Mix subscription. TRILT coverage: June 2001 to date.

Sky Movies Premiere +1

British Sky Broadcasting Ltd, Grant Way, Isleworth, Middlesex TW7 5QD
Web: http://www.skymovies.com/skymovies
Part of the Sky Movies group of film channels from BSkyB. Sky Movies Premiere +1, formerly known as Sky Movies Cinema 2, is available on digital, cable and satellite platforms in the UK as part of the Movie Mix subscription. It is a time shift channel. TRILT coverage: June 2001 to date.

Sky Movies Sci-Fi/Horror

British Sky Broadcasting Ltd, Grant Way, Isleworth, Middlesex TW7 5QD
Web: http://www.skymovies.com/skymovies
Part of the Sky Movies group of film channels from BSkyB. Sky Movies Sci-Fi/Horror, formerly known as Sky Movies Max 2, is available on digital, cable and satellite platforms in the UK as part of the Movie Mix subscription. TRILT coverage: June 2001 to date.

Sky News

British Sky Broadcasting Ltd, Grant Way, Isleworth, Middlesex TW7 5QD
☎ 0870 240 3000 **Fax:** 0870 240 3060
Web: http://news.sky.com/skynews
Sky News is a 24 hour news channel from BSkyB. It is available on Freeview, digital, cable and satellite television platforms. TRILT coverage: June 2001 to date.

Sky One

British Sky Broadcasting Ltd, Grant Way, Isleworth, Middlesex TW7 5QD
Sky One is available to cable, satellite and digital viewers. It promises to be the first in the UK to deliver the best television from the United States. Its flagship shows are BUFFY THE VAMPIRE SLAYER, THE SIMPSONS and FRIENDS.

Sky One Mix

British Sky Broadcasting Ltd, Grant Way, Isleworth, Middlesex TW7 5QD
☎ 0870 240 3000 **Fax:** 0870 240 3060
Web: http://www.sky.com
Sister channel to Sky One, Sky One Mix is another BSkyB channel available on digital, cable and satellite television in the UK. Sky One Mix shows much of the same general entertainment content as Sky One, but at different days and times, so it can be viewed as a catch-up channel (but not a time shift channel).

Sky One ONdigital
General entertainment channel. No longer active on TRILT.

Sky Premier ONdigital
Movie channel. No longer active on TRILT.

Sky Premier Widescreen
Movie channel. No longer active on TRILT.

Sky Sports
British Sky Broadcasting Ltd, Grant Way, Isleworth, Middlesex TW7 5QD
☎ 0870 240 3000 **Fax:** 0870 240 3060
Web: http://home.skysports.com
Sky Sports is a group of subscription sports channels from BSkyB, available on digital, cable and satellite platforms in the UK. TRILT carries listings for Sky Sports 1, 2 and 3 as well as Sky Sports Extra. These four channels are available for a monthly fee as a bundle called 'Sports Mix.' TRILT coverage: June 2001 to date.

Skysports.comTV See Sky Sports News

Sky Sports News
British Sky Broadcasting Ltd, Grant Way, Isleworth, Middlesex W7 5QD
☎ 0870 240 3000 **Fax:** 0870 240 3060
Web: http://www.skysports.com/skysports/shows/news
Sky Sports News (formerly known as Skysports.comTV). The channel is devoted to sports news coverage, predominantly football news, and broadcasts 24 hours a day in the UK. It is owned by BSkyB. The channel is available on Freeview and various digital, cable and satellite platforms on the UK. TRILT coverage: June 2001 to date.

Sky Three
British Sky Broadcasting Ltd, Grant Way, Isleworth, Middlesex TW7 5QD
☎ 0870 240 3000 **Fax:** 0870 240 3060
Web: http://www.sky.com
Sky Three offers a mix of programming including dramas, documentaries, lifestyle and factual entertainment. It showcases programmes from Sky One, Sky Travel and Artsworld. The channel is available in the UK on digital satellite, cable and Freeview. TRILT coverage: March 2006 to date.

Sky Travel
British Sky Broadcasting Ltd, Grant Way, Isleworth, Middlesex TW7 5QD
Web: http://www.skytravel.co.uk/sky
Sky Travel is a channel from BSkyB with general entertainment programming, including reality shows relating to travel, such as AIRLINE and CLUB REPS. There are also regular slots dedicated to selling holidays. The channel is available on various cable, satellite and digital platforms. TRILT coverage: June 2001 to date.

TCM
Turner House, 16 Great Marlborough Street, London W1V 1AF
☎ 020 7693 1000 **Fax:** 020 7693 1001
E-mail: tcmmailuk@turner.com Web: http://tcmonline.co.uk
TCM is available to cable, digital and satellite viewers and draws from the largest film libraries in the world. It shows classic movies from all genres and periods, including the silent era. TRILT coverage: June 2001 to date.

TCM/WCW

Channel showing feature films and wrestling. No longer active on TRILT.

Teachers' TV

16-18 Berners Street, London W1T 3LN

☎ 020 7182 7430

E-mail: info@teachers.tv Web: http://www.teachers.tv

Teachers' TV is a channel for everyone who works in education. TRILT coverage: February 2005 to date.

Television X

Suite 14, Burlington House, St Saviour's Road, St Helier, Jersey JE2 4LA

☎ 01534 703700 **Fax:** 01534 703760

Web: http://www.televisionx.co.uk

Subscription channel available to digital, cable and satellite viewers. Content consists of adult material that is legal within the UK. The channel was formerly known as The Fantasy Channel; TRILT continues to carry listings under this name. Both analogue and digital versions are available. TRILT coverage: June 2001 to date.

Thomas Cook TV

8 Park Place, 12 Lawn Lane, Vauxhall, London SW8 1UD

☎ 020 7840 7150 **Fax:** 020 7820 4471

Web: http://www.thomascooktv.com

Thomas Cook TV is a shopping channel that showcases Thomas Cook holiday destinations and packages. Viewers can phone in to book holidays. The channel is available in the UK on digital satellite, cable and Freeview. TRILT coverage: March 2006 to date.

Toonami

Toonami, Turner House, 16 Great Marlborough Street, London W1F 7HS

☎ 020 7693 1000 **Fax:** 020 7693 1001

Web: http://www.toonami.co.uk

CNX was re-branded as Toonami in 2003. As CNX the channel showed mostly action, adventure and anime aimed at males aged 12-34. As Toonami the channel shows more cartoons aimed at younger viewers. TRILT continues to carry listings for the channel under the old name, CNX. TRILT coverage: April 2003 to date.

Travel & Living

Discovery House, Chiswick Park Building 2, 566 Chiswick Park Road, London W4 5YB

☎ 020 8811 3000 **Fax:** 020 8811 3100

Web: http://www.travelandliving.co.uk

Formerly known as Discovery Travel & Adventure, Travel & Living is available on digital, cable and satellite television. TRILT continues to carry listings for the channel under the old name, Discovery Travel & Adventure. TRILT coverage: June 2001 to date.

Trouble

Virgin Media Television, 160 Great Portland Street, London W1W 5QA

☎ 0870 043 4027

E-mail: enquiries@trouble.co.uk Web: http://www.trouble.co.uk

Trouble TV is available to analogue and digital cable and satellite viewers. It shows programmes aimed at a teenage market, including soap operas, comedies, sit-coms and music shows. TRILT coverage: June 2001 to date.

Trouble Analogue See **Trouble**

Turbo

Discovery House, Chiswick Park Building 2, 566 Chiswick Park Road, London W4 5YB

☎ 020 8811 3000 **Fax:** 020 8811 3100

Web: http://www.discoveryturbo.co.uk

Turbo is available on cable, satellite and digital television. TRILT continues to carry listings for the channel under the old name, Discovery Wings. TRILT coverage: June 2001 to date.

.TV (aka **The Computer Channel**)

Ceased broadcasting at the end of August 2001. Concentrated on technology and IT. No longer active on TRILT.

Tyne Tees Television See **ITV1 Tyne Tees Television**

UK Bright Ideas See **UKTV Bright Ideas**

UK Drama See **UKTV Drama**

UK Food See **UKTV Food**

UK Gold See **UKTV Gold**

UK Gold 2 See **UKTV G2**

UK Horizons See **UKTV Documentary**

UK Style See **UKTV Style**

UKTV Bright Ideas

UKTV, 160 Great Portland Street, London W1W 5QA

Web: http://www.uktv.co.uk/brightideas

UKTV Bright Ideas (formerly known as UK Bright Ideas) is only available to cable, digital and satellite viewers. The channel mainly shows lifestyle programming repeated from the BBC, with many home make-over and cookery shows. TRILT coverage: April 2003 to date.

UKTV Documentary

UKTV, 160 Great Portland Street, London W1W 5QA

☎ 020 7299 6200

Web: http://www.uktv.co.uk/documentary

UKTV Documentary, formerly known as UK Horizons, is part of UKTV, a joint venture between BBC Worldwide and Virgin Media. It is only available to cable, digital and satellite viewers. The channel shows factual entertainment. TRILT continues to carry listings for the channel under the name UK Horizons. TRILT coverage: June 2001 to date.

UKTV Drama

UKTV, 160 Great Portland Street, London W1W 5QA

☎ 020 7299 6200

Web: http://www.uktv.co.uk/drama

UKTV Drama, formerly known as UK Drama, is only available to cable, digital and satellite viewers. It is one of ten channels that make up UKTV, a joint venture between the BBC and Virgin Media. TRILT coverage: June 2001 to date.

UKTV Food

UKTV, 160 Great Portland Street, London W1W 5QA
Web: http://www.uktv.co.uk/food
UKTV Food (formerly known as UK Food) is only available to cable, digital and satellite viewers. The channel mainly shows cookery shows. TRILT coverage: June 2001 to date.

UKTV G2

UKTV, 160 Great Portland Street, London W1W 5QA
UKTV G2 (formerly known as UK Gold 2) is only available to cable, digital and satellite viewers. The channel shows a lot of BBC comedy and quiz show repeats. TRILT coverage: June 2001 to date.

UKTV Gold

UKTV, 160 Great Portland Street, London W1W 5QA
UKTV Gold (formerly known as UK Gold) is only available to cable, digital and satellite viewers. The channel mainly shows repeats of BBC dramas, soap operas and comedies. TRILT coverage: June 2001 to date.

UKTV History

UKTV, 160 Great Portland Street, London W1W 5QA
Web: http://www.uktv.co.uk/history
UKTV History is only available to cable, digital and satellite viewers. The channel shows a wide variety of history documentaries, mostly repeated from the BBC. TRILT coverage: June 2004 to date.

UKTV Style

UKTV, 160 Great Portland Street, London W1W 5QA
Web: http://www.uktv.co.uk/style
UKTV Style (formerly known as UK Style) is only available to cable, digital and satellite viewers. The channel's programming largely consists of lifestyle shows, including DIY, property and makeover shows. TRILT coverage: June 2001 to date.

Ulster (UTV)

Havelock House, Ormeau Road, Belfast BT7 1EB
☎ 028 9032 8122 **Fax:** 028 9024 6695
Web: http://u.tv
Available on digital, cable and satellite as well as terrestrially, this channel is the ITV1 franchise for Northern Ireland. TRILT coverage: June 2001 to date.

VH1

180 Oxford Street, London W1D 1DS
☎ 020 7478 6000 **Fax:** 020 7478 6007
Web: http://www.vh1.com
Music channel that plays classic songs from the last four decades. Also features popular documentaries about artists and groups. TRILT coverage: June 2001 to date.

VH1 Classic

180 Oxford Street, London, W1D 1DS
☎ 020 7478 6000 **Fax:** 020 7478 6007
Web: http://www.vh1classic.com
Music channel which plays vintage hits and nostalgia from the sixties to the early nineties. TRILT coverage: June 2001 to date.

Yorkshire See **ITV1 Yorkshire**

Zee TV

Unit 7-9, Belvue Business Centre, Belvue Road, Northolt, Middlesex
UB5 5QQ
☎ 020 8839 4000 **Fax:** 020 8841 9550
E-mail: info@zeetv.co.uk Web: http://www.zeetv.co.uk
Channel catering for the South Asian television market. Europe Zee TV
broadcasts a wide variety of programmes in several languages to over a million
viewers across the UK and Europe. TRILT coverage: June 2001 to date.

RADIO STATIONS LISTED ON TRILT (BY REGION AND NATION)

a. NATIONAL

BBC Radio 1

Broadcasting House, Portland Place, London W1A 1AA
☎ 020 7765 4575
Web: http://www.bbc.co.uk/radio1
The BBC's national popular music radio station. It broadcasts a wide range of
music on disc as well as concerts, festivals and documentaries. TRILT coverage:
June 2001 to date.

BBC Radio 2

Broadcasting House, Portland Place, London W1A 1AA
☎ 020 7765 5712
Web: http://www.bbc.co.uk/radio2
BBC Radio 2 combines popular music and culture with a diverse range of
specialist music, features, documentaries, light entertainment, readings and
broadcasts from concerts and festivals. TRILT coverage: June 2001 to date.

BBC Radio 3

Broadcasting House, Portland Place, London W1A 1AA
☎ 020 7765 2722
Web: http://www.bbc.co.uk/radio3
BBC Radio 3 broadcasts a range of classical music and speech programmes.
Jazz, world music, dramas and documentaries are also featured. TRILT
coverage: June 2001 to date.

BBC Radio 4

Broadcasting House, Portland Place, London W1A 1AA
☎ 020 7765 5337
Web: http://www.bbc.co.uk/radio4
Predominantly a speech channel, Radio 4 broadcasts a mixture of news,
analysis, drama and comedy. On occasions it splits into two frequencies
broadcasting different programmes on long wave and FM. TRILT coverage:
June 2001 to date.

BBC Radio 4 LW See **BBC Radio 4**

BBC Radio 5 Live
Television Centre, Wood Lane, London W12 7RJ
☎ 020 7765 2139
Web: http://www.bbc.co.uk/radio5
The BBC's 24-hour news and sport radio channel. Sometimes called Five Live.
TRILT coverage: June 2001 to date.

BBC Radio 5 Live Sports Extra
Room 2605, Television Centre, Wood Lane, London W12 7RJ
☎ 08700 100 500
Web: http://www.bbc.co.uk/fivelive/sportsextra
BBC Radio 5 Live Sports Extra is a digital radio station that complements
BBC Radio 5 Live. TRILT coverage: March 2006 to date.

BBC World Service Radio
BBC World Service, Bush House, Strand, London WC2B 4PH
☎ 020 7240 3456 **Fax:** 020 7557 1258
E-mail: worldservice@bbc.co.uk Web: http://www.bbc.co.uk/worldservice
BBC World Service broadcasts news and programmes to many countries
throughout the world. It broadcasts in thirty-three different languages and its
English language programming broadcasts twenty-four hours a day. TRILT
coverage: June 2001 to date.

BBC 6 Music
Broadcasting House, Portland Place, London W1A 1AA
☎ 08700 100600
Web: http://www.bbc.co.uk/6music
BBC 6 Music is a digital radio station from the BBC, which launched on 11th
March 2002. It plays 'alternative' music. Unlike the more mainstream Radio 1
and Radio 2, 6 Music's playlist is less chart and singles focused. TRILT coverage:
March 2006 to date.

BBC 7
Room 4015, BBC Broadcasting House, London W1A 1AA
Web: http://www.bbc.co.uk/bbc7
BBC 7 is a digital radio station, drawing on the BBC Sound Archive's huge collection of spoken word programmes from across the decades. TRILT coverage: March 2006 to date.

BBC Asian Network
9 St Nicholas Place, Leicester, Leicestershire LE1 5LB
☎ 0116 201 6787 **Fax:** 0116 253 2004
Web: http://www.bbc.co.uk/asiannetwork
The BBC Asian Network is a national digital BBC radio station playing the best in new British Asian music and covering British Asian issues. TRILT coverage: March 2006 to date.

Heat
Endeavour House, 189 Shaftesbury Avenue, London WC2H 8JG
☎ 020 7437 9011
Web: http://www.heatradio.co.uk
Heat is a digital radio station from Emap, with the branding of the company's celebrity weekly magazine, *Heat*. TRILT coverage: March 2006 to date.

ITN News Channel Radio
200 Gray's Inn Road, London WC1X 8XZ
☎ 020 7833 3000 **Fax:** 020 7430 4848
Digital radio news service, with news, sport, money and weather. TRILT coverage: June 2001 to date.

Kerrang! Radio
20 Lionel Street, Birmingham B3 1A
☎ 0845 053 1052 **Fax:** 0844 583 7990
E-mail: kerrang@kerrangradio.co.uk Web: http://www.kerrangradio.co.uk
Kerrang! Radio is a digital radio station from Emap, with the branding of the company's weekly rock music magazine, *Kerrang!* TRILT coverage: March 2006 to date.

Oneword
Landseer House, 19 Charing Cross Road, London WC2H 0ES
☎ 020 79763030 **Fax:** 020 7930 9460
E-mail: general@oneword.co.uk Web: http://www.oneword.co.uk
Oneword is a digital spoken word radio station available in the UK. Programming concentrates on serialisations of books, drama, comedy, interviews with authors and book and film reviews. TRILT coverage: March 2006 to date.

Q Radio
Mappin House, 4 Winsley Street, London W1W 8HF
☎ 020 7182 8000
Web: http://www.q4music.com
Q Radio is a digital radio station from Emap, with the branding of the company's monthly music and entertainment magazine, *Q*. TRILT coverage: March 2006 to date.

Radio Atlantic 252

Radio Atlantic 252 is no longer broadcasting. The commercial station transmitted from Ireland, but was available throughout the UK. No longer active on TRILT.

Smash Hits Radio

Mappin House, 4 Winsley Street, London W1W 8HF
☎ 020 7182 8767
E-mail: smashhits@emap.com Web: http://www.smashhits.net
Smash Hits is a digital radio station from Emap. The station took its name from the company's weekly pop magazine, which is no longer published. TRILT coverage: March 2006 to date.

Virgin Radio

1 Golden Square, London W1F 9DJ
☎ 020 7434 1215 **Fax:** 020 7434 1197
E-mail: reception@virginradio.co.uk Web: http://www.virginradio.co.uk
Virgin Radio is a commercial music radio station in the UK, playing rock and pop and available nationally. TRILT coverage: June 2001 to date.

b. LONDON

102.2 Smooth FM

Smooth Radio, 26-27 Castlereagh Street, London W1H 5DL
☎ 020 7706 4100
E-mail: enquiries@gmgradio.co.uk Web: http://www.smoothfm.com
102.2 Smooth FM, formerly known as Jazz FM 102.2, is a commercial station broadcasting in the UK, covering the Greater London area. TRILT carries listings for the channel under the name Jazz FM 102.2. TRILT coverage: June 2001 to date.

BBC London 94.9

BBC London, PO Box 94.9, Marylebone High Street, London W1A 6FL
☎ 020 7224 2424
E-mail: yourlondon@bbc.co.uk Web: http://www.bbc.co.uk/london
BBC London 94.9, formerly known as London Live 94.9, is the BBC's local radio station for the Greater London area. TRILT coverage: June 2001 to date.

Capital FM

30 Leicester Square, London WC2H 7LA
☎ 020 7766 6000 **Fax:** 020 7766 6100
E-mail: info@capitalradio.com Web: http://www.capitalfm.co.uk
Independent local radio station serving the London area. Broadcasts popular contemporary music, classic hits, and local and national news. TRILT coverage: June 2001 to date.

Capital Gold

30 Leicester Square, London WC2H 7LA
☎ 020 7766 6000 Fax : 020 7766 6393
E-mail: info@capitalgold.co.uk Web: http://www.capitalgold.com
Independent local radio station serving Greater London. Broadcasts hits from the 1960s, 70s and 80s, sport and local and national news. TRILT coverage: June 2001 to date.

Choice FM
GCap Media plc, 30 Leicester Square, London WC2H 7LA
☎ 020 7766 6000 **Fax:** 020 7766 6840
E-mail: info@choicefm.com Web: http://www.choicefm.com
Independent local radio station serving south London. Based in Brixton, it broadcasts R&B, reggae, rap, gospel and local news. TRILT coverage: June 2001 to date.

Heart 106.2
The Chrysalis Building, Bramley Road, London W10 6SP
☎ 020 7468 1062 **Fax:** 020 7470 1095
Web: http://www.heart1062.co.uk
Heart 106.2 is a commercial radio station broadcasting in the UK, covering the Greater London area. TRILT coverage: June 2001 to date.

Kiss 100 FM
Mappin House, 4 Winsley Street, London W1W 8HF
☎ 020 7975 8100 **Fax:** 020 7975 8150
Web: http://www.totalkiss.com
Independent local radio station serving the Greater London area. It is also available nationally on Sky digital. Broadcasts dance music, dance-related news, national and local news. TRILT coverage: June 2001 to date.

Magic 105.4
Mappin House, 4 Winsley Street, London W1W 8HF
☎ 020 7182 8000 **Fax:** 020 7182 8165
E-mail: studio@magic.fm Web: http://www.magic1054.co.uk
Independent local radio station, serving Greater London. Broadcasts music, news and information. TRILT coverage: June 2001 to date.

Paradise FM
2A South Mall, Edmonton Green Shopping Centre, Edmonton, London N9 0TN
☎ 020 8373 1075 **Fax:** 020 8373 1074
Web: http://www.paradisefm.co.uk
Local cable radio station, encrypted and carried on the Telewest (London) cable network. Broadcasts music, local news, information and community features. TRILT coverage: June 2001 to date.

Premier Christian Radio
22 Chapter Street, London SW1P 4NP
☎ 020 7316 1300
E-mail: response@premier.org.uk Web: http://www.premier.org.uk
Premier broadcasts speech and music for the greater London area, reflecting and proclaiming the worship, thought and action of the Christian faith. It broadcasts a mixture of live and pre-recorded shows twenty-four hours a day. TRILT coverage: March 2006 to date.

Spectrum 558 AM
4 Ingate Place, Battersea, London SW8 3NS
☎ 020 7627 4433 **Fax:** 020 7627 3409
Web: http://www.spectrumradio.net
Spectrum 558 AM claims to be the only ethnic commercial radio station aimed at London audiences. The station is available at 558AM, but is also available on DAB digital radio, various digital, cable and satellite television platforms and online. No longer active on TRILT.

Sunrise Radio

Sunrise House, Merrick Road, Southall, Middlesex UB2 4AU
☎ 020 8574 6666 **Fax:** 020 8813 9700
E-mail: reception@sunriseradio.com Web: http://www.sunriseradio.com
Sunrise Radio is an independent commercial radio station in the UK, covering the West London area. It is aimed at the Asian community. TRILT coverage: June 2001 to date.

UCB Christian Radio

PO Box 255, Stoke-on-Trent ST4 8YY
☎ 0845 6040401
E-mail: ucb@ucb.co.uk Web: http://www.ucb.co.uk
UCB stands for United Christian Broadcasters. UCB Christian Radio is available on DAB radio in Staffordshire and London. TRILT coverage: June 2001 to date.

Virgin Radio 105.8FM

1 Golden Square, London W1F 9DJ
☎ 020 7434 1215 **Fax:** 020 7434 1197
E-mail: reception@virginradio.co.uk Web: http://www.virginradio.co.uk
Virgin Radio is a commercial music radio station in the UK, playing rock and pop. It is available on the FM frequency 105.8 in the Greater London region, but can be heard nationally on a variety of AM frequencies as well as on digital radio and online. No longer active on TRILT.

XFM 104.9

30 Leicester Square, London WC2H 7LA
☎ 020 7766 6600 **Fax:** 020 7766 6601
Web: http://www.xfm.co.uk
XFM is a group of UK commercial radio stations owned by GCap Media. The channels specialise in alternative music, especially indie music. TRILT coverage: June 2001 to date.

c. SOUTH EAST

BBC Radio Berkshire

P.O Box 104.4, Reading RG4 8FH
☎ 0118 946 4200 **Fax:** 0118 946 4555
E-mail: radio.berkshire@bbc.co.uk
Web: http://www.bbc.co.uk/berkshire/local_radio
BBC Radio Berkshire is the BBC's local radio station for the Berkshire area. TRILT coverage: June 2001 to date.

BBC Radio Oxford

269 Banbury Road, Oxford OX2 7DW
☎ 08459 311 444
E-mail: oxford@bbc.co.uk Web: http://www.bbc.co.uk/oxford/local_radio
BBC Radio Oxford is the BBC's local radio station for Oxfordshire. TRILT coverage: June 2001 to date.

BBC Radio Solent

Broadcasting House, Havelock Road, Southampton SO14 7PU
☎ 023 8063 1311
E-mail: hampshire@bbc.co.uk
Web: http://www.bbc.co.uk/hampshire/local_radio

BBC Radio Solent is the BBC's local radio station for the Hampshire region. TRILT coverage: June 2001 to date.

BBC Southern Counties Radio

Broadcasting House, Queens Road, Brighton, East Sussex BN1 3XB
☎ 08459 570057
E-mail: southerncounties@bbc.co.uk
Web: http://www.bbc.co.uk/southerncounties/local_radio
BBC Southern Counties Radio is the BBC's local radio station for Surrey, Sussex and North East Hampshire. TRILT coverage: June 2001 to date.

County Sound Radio

Dolphin House, North Street, Guildford GU1 4AA
☎ 01483 300964 **Fax:** 01483 531612
E-mail: onair@countysound.co.uk Web: http://www.ukrd.com
Independent local radio station serving the Surrey and North East Hampshire area. Aimed at the 35+ plus age group, it broadcasts a wide range of programmes including music, speech, news and sport. TRILT coverage: June 2001 to date.

Kestrel FM

Suite 2, Paddington House, Festival Place, Basingstoke RG21 7LJ
☎ 01256 694000 **Fax:** 01256 694111
E-mail: kestrelfm@kestrelfm.com Web: http://www.kestrelfm.com
Kestrel FM is a commercial radio station broadcasting in the UK, covering the Basingstoke area. Listeners in this area can tune into the station at 107.6FM, but it can also be heard online. TRILT coverage: June 2001 to date.

Kick FM

42 Bone Lane, Newbury, Berkshire RG14 5SD
☎ 01635 841600 **Fax:** 01635 841010
E-mail: studio@kickfm.com Web: http://www.kickfm.com
Independent local radio station serving the Newbury and west Berkshire area. Broadcasts soft adult contemporary music, local news and information. No longer active on TRILT.

Ocean FM

Ocean FM, Radio House, Whittle Avenue, Segensworth West,
Fareham PO15 5SH
☎ 01489 589911 **Fax:** 01489 589453
E-mail: info@oceanfm.co.uk Web: http://www.oceanfm.com
Ocean FM, formerly known as Radio Victory, broadcasts in the Hampshire region. No longer active on TRILT.

Radio 2CRFM

5 Southcote Road, Bournemouth, Dorset BH1 3LR
☎ 01202 234900 **Fax:** 01202 234909
Web: http://www2.crfm.co.uk
2CR FM is a commercial station broadcasting in the UK, covering the Bournemouth area in Dorset. The station is owned by GCap Media. TRILT coverage: June 2001 to date.

Radio Victory See Ocean FM

d. SOUTH WEST

BBC Radio Cornwall
BBC Cornwall, Phoenix Wharf, Truro TR1 1UA
☎ 01872 275421
E-mail: cornwall@bbc.co.uk
Web: http://www.bbc.co.uk/cornwall/local_radio/index.shtml
BBC Radio Cornwall is the BBC's local radio station for the Cornwall area.
TRILT coverage: June 2001 to date.

BBC Radio Devon
Broadcasting House, Seymour Road, Plymouth PL3 5BD
☎ 01752 229201
E-mail: radio.devon@bbc.co.uk Web: http://www.bbc.co.uk/devon/local_radio
BBC Radio Devon is the BBC's local radio station for the Devon region. TRILT
coverage: June 2001 to date.

BBC Radio Guernsey
Bulwer Avenue, St Sampsons, Guernsey GY2 4LA
☎ 01481 200600
E-mail: guernsey@bbc.co.uk Web: http://www.bbc.co.uk/guernsey/local_radio
BBC Radio Guernsey is the BBC's local radio station for the island of
Guernsey. TRILT coverage: June 2001 to date.

BBC Radio Somerset Sound
Broadcasting House, Park Street, Taunton, Somerset TA1 4DA
☎ 01823 323956
E-mail: somerset@bbc.co.uk
Web: http://www.bbc.co.uk/somerset/local_radio
BBC Radio Somerset Sound is the BBC's local radio station for the Somerset
region. TRILT coverage: June 2001 to date.

BBC Radio Swindon
Broadcasting House, 56-58 Prospect Place, Swindon, Wiltshire SN1 3RW
☎ 01793 513626
E-mail: wiltshire@bbc.co.uk
Web: http://www.bbc.co.uk/wiltshire/local_radio/radio_swindon
BBC Radio Swindon is the BBC's local radio station for the Wiltshire region.
TRILT coverage: June 2001 to date.

Classic Gold 666/954
Web: http://www.classicgolddigital.com
Independent local radio station covering the Exeter, mid and east Devon and
Torbay areas. Broadcasts music and speech. The AM sister station of Gemini
FM. TRILT coverage: June 2001 to date.

Classic Gold Plymouth 1152
Earl's Acre, Plymouth, Devon PL3 4HX
☎ 01752 275600 **Fax:** 01752 275605
Web: http://www.classicgolddigital.com
Independent local radio station covering the Plymouth area. Broadcasts classic
hits and easy listening favourites. TRILT coverage: June 2001 to date.

Galaxy 101 See **Kiss 101**

Gemini FM 97.0

Hawthorn House, Exeter Business Park, Exeter EX1 3QS
☎ 01392 444444 **Fax:** 01392 354202
Web: http://www.koko.com
Independent local radio station serving the Exeter, mid and east Devon and Torbay areas on FM frequencies. Broadcasts current hits and news. Its AM sister station is Classic Gold 666/954AM. TRILT coverage: June 2001 to date.

GWR

PO Box 2000, One Passage Street, Bristol BS99 7SN
☎ 0117 984 3200 **Fax:** 0117 984 3202
Web: http://www.gwrfmbristol.co.uk
GWR is a commercial radio station broadcasting in the UK in the Bristol and Bath area. It is owned by GCap Media. TRILT coverage: June 2001 to date.

Island FM

12 Westerbrook, St. Sampsons, Guernsey GY2 4QQ
☎ 01481 242000 **Fax:** 01481 249676
Web: http://www.islandfm.com
Island FM is a commercial radio station broadcasting in the UK, covering the Guernsey area. No longer active on TRILT.

Kiss 101

Kiss 101, 26 Baldwin Street, Bristol BS1 1SE
☎ 0117 901 0101 **Fax:** 0117 984 3204
Web: http://www.totalkiss.com
Independent local radio station covering the Severn estuary area, formerly known as Galaxy 101 and Vibe 101 FM. Broadcasts dance and r'n'b. TRILT continues to carry listings for the channel under the name Vibe 101 FM. TRILT coverage: June 2001 to date.

Lantern 96.2 FM

2b Lauder Lane, Roundswell Business Park, Barnstaple EX31 3TA
☎ 01271 340340 **Fax:** 01271 340345
Web: http://www.koko.com
Independent local radio station serving the Barnstaple area. The koko web site is shared with Gemini FM but carries little information on Lantern. TRILT coverage: June 2001 to date.

Orchard FM

Haygrove House, Taunton, Somerset TA3 7BT
☎ 01823 338448 **Fax:** 01823 368318
E-mail: orchardfm@koko.com
Web: http://www.koko.com
Independent local radio station serving the Yeovil and Tauton area. Broadcasts contemporary music. TRILT coverage: June 2001 to date.

Pirate FM

Carn Brea Studios, Wilson Way, Redruth, Cornwall TR15 3XX
☎ 01209 314400 **Fax:** 01209 314345
E-mail: reception@piratefm.co.uk Web: http://www.piratefm102.co.uk
Pirate FM is a commercial radio station broadcasting in the UK, covering the Cornwall area. Listeners in this area can tune into the station at 102FM, but it can also be heard online. TRILT no longer carries listings for this station.

South Hams Radio

Unit 1G, South Hams Business Park, Churchstow, Kingsbridge,
Devon TQ7 3QH
☎ 01548 854595 **Fax:** 01548 854595
E-mail: southhams@musicradio.com Web: http://www.southhamsradio.com
South Hams Radio is a commercial station broadcasting in the UK, covering
the South Hams region in Devon. The station is owned by GCap Media. TRILT
coverage: June 2001 to date.

Vibe 101 FM See Kiss 101

e. EAST OF ENGLAND

TRILT does not carry any listings for radio stations in the East of England.

f. NORTH EAST

3C

3C Digital Radio, 3 South Avenue, Clydebank Business Park,
Glasgow G81 2RX
☎ 0845 345 0333 or 0141 565 2307
Web: http://www3cdigital.com
3C was a radio station featuring country and western music, broadcasting in
Scotland, Newcastle and Northern Ireland. No longer active on TRILT.

BBC Radio Newcastle

BBC Tyne, Broadcasting Centre, Barrack Rd, Newcastle upon Tyne NE99 1RN
☎ 0191 232 4141
E-mail: tyne@bbc.co.uk Web: http://www.bbc.co.uk/tyne/local_radio
BBC Radio Newcastle is the BBC's local radio station in the Newcastle area.
TRILT coverage: June 2001 to date.

Magic 1152

55 Degrees North, Pilgrim Street, Newcastle upon Tyne NE1 6BF
☎ 0191 230 6100
Web: http://www.magic1152.co.uk
Independent local radio station covering the Tyne and Wear area. Broadcasts
popular music, news and sport. TRILT coverage: June 2001 to date.

Radio Borders

Tweedside Park, Tweedside, Melrose TD1 3RS
☎ 01896 759444 **Fax:** 0845 3457080
E-mail: programming@radioborders.com Web: http://www.radioborders.com
Radio Borders is a commercial radio station, based in the Borders region of
Scotland and North Northumberland. TRILT coverage: June 2001 to date

g. NORTH WEST

100.4 SmoothFM

8 Exchange Quay, Manchester M5 3EJ
☎ 0161 877 1004 **Fax:** 0161 877 1005
Web: http://www.smoothradionorthwest.com
100.4 SmoothFM, formerly known as Jazz FM 100.4, is a commercial radio
station in the UK, covering the Northwest of England. TRILT coverage: June
2001 to date.

The Bay

P.O. Box 969, St George's Quay, Lancaster LA1 3LD
☎ 01524 848747 **Fax:** 01524 848787
Web: http://www.thebay.co.uk
Independent local radio station serving the Morecambe Bay and south Lakeland areas. Broadcasts classic hits, news and community information. TRILT coverage: June 2001 to date.

The Buzz 97.1 See **Wirral's Buzz 97.1**

BBC Radio Lancashire

Darwen Street, Blackburn, Lancashire BB2 2EA
☎ 01254 262411
E-mail: lancashire@bbc.co.uk
Web: http://www.bbc.co.uk/lancashire/local_radio
BBC Radio Lancashire is the BBC's local radio station for the Lancashire region. TRILT coverage: June 2001 to date.

BBC Radio Merseyside

BBC Liverpool, P.O. Box 95.8, Liverpool L69 1ZJ
☎ 0151 708 5500
E-mail: liverpool@bbc.co.uk
Web: http://www.bbc.co.uk/liverpool/local_radio/index.shtml
BBC Radio Merseyside is the BBC's local radio station for the Liverpool region. TRILT coverage: June 2001 to date.

Jazz FM 100.4 See **100.4 SmoothFM**

Key 103FM

Castle Quay, Castlefield, Manchester M15 4PR
☎ 0161 288 5000
Web: http://www.key103.co.uk
Independent local radio station for the Manchester area. No longer active on TRILT.

Magic 1548

St Johns Beacon, 1 Houghton Street, Liverpool L1 1RL
☎ 0151 472 6800 **Fax:** 0151 472 6821
Web: http://www.magic1548.co.uk
Independent local radio station serving the Merseyside area. Aimed at the over-30s it broadcasts music, news and sport. No longer active on TRILT.

Manx Radio

Broadcasting House, Douglas Head, Douglas, Isle of Man IM99 1SW
☎ 01624 682600 **Fax:** 01624 682605
E-mail: postbox@manxradio.com Web: http://www.manxradio.com
Independent local radio station serving the Isle of Man. It broadcasts music and news. No longer active on TRILT.

Radio City 96.7

St Johns Beacon, 1 Houghton Street, Liverpool L1 1RL
☎ 0151 472 6800 **Fax:** 0151 472 6821
Web: http://www.radiocity.co.uk
Independent local radio station for Liverpool, the Northwest and Wales. Broadcasts popular music from the 1990s to today. No longer active on TRILT.

Rock FM
St Paul's Square, Preston PR1 1YE
☎ 01772 477700
Web: http://www.rockfm.co.uk
Rock FM is a commercial radio station broadcasting in the UK, based in the Preston area. TRILT coverage: June 2001 to date.

Wirral's Buzz 97.1
Media House, Claughton Road, Birkenhead CH41 6EY
☎ 0151 650 1700 **Fax:** 0151 647 5427
Web: http://www.wirralsbuzz.co.uk
Wirral's Buzz 97.1, formerly known as The Buzz 97.1, is an independent local radio station playing classic and current hits, and providing local and national news. No longer active on TRILT.

h. YORKSHIRE AND THE HUMBER

BBC Radio Leeds
Broadcasting Centre, 2 Saint Peter's Square, Leeds LS9 8AH
☎ 0113 244 2131
E-mail: leeds@bbc.co.uk Web: http://www.bbc.co.uk/leeds/local_radio
BBC Radio Leeds is the BBC's local radio station for the Leeds and West Yorkshire region. TRILT coverage: June 2001 to date.

BBC Radio Sheffield
BBC South Yorkshire, 54 Shoreham Street, Sheffield S1 4RS
☎ 0114 273 1177
E-mail: south.yorkshire@bbc.co.uk
Web: http://www.bbc.co.uk/southyorkshire/community/
radio_sheffield/index.shtml
BBC Radio Sheffield is the BBC's local radio station for the South Yorkshire region. TRILT coverage: June 2001 to date.

BBC Radio York
20 Bootham Row, York YO30 7BR
☎ 01904 641351
E-mail: radio.york@bbc.co.uk
Web: http://www.bbc.co.uk/northyorkshire/local_radio
BBC Radio York is the BBC's local radio station for North Yorkshire. TRILT coverage: June 2001 to date.

HWD Radio
The Studios, Dewsbury District Hospital, Dewsbury, West Yorkshire
WF13 4HS
☎ 08707 469507 **Fax:** 08707 468508
E-mail: onair@hwdhospitalradio.com
HWD Radio is a hospital radio station. No longer active on TRILT.

Magic 828
51 Burley Road, Leeds LS3 1LR
☎ 0113 283 5500 **Fax:** 0113 283 5501
Web: http://www.magic828.co.uk
Independent local radio station serving the Leeds area. Broadcasts popular music, and local and national news and sport. No longer active on TRILT.

Minster FM

PO Box 123, Dunnington, York YO19 5ZX
☎ 01904 488888 **Fax:** 01904 481088
E-mail: general@minsterfm.co.uk Web: http://www.minsterfm.com
Independent local radio station covering York and the north Yorkshire area.
Broadcasts music and local and national news. TRILT coverage: June 2001 to
date.

The Pulse

Foster Square, Bradford, West Yorkshire BD1 5NE
☎ 01274 203040 **Fax:** 01274 203040
Web: http://www.pulse.co.uk
The Pulse is a commercial radio station broadcasting in the UK, covering the
Bradford and West Yorkshire region. TRILT coverage: June 2001 to date

Radio Airedale

Radio Airedale is a hospital radio station. No longer active on TRILT.

i. EAST MIDLANDS

BBC Radio Derby

56 St Helen's Street, Derby DE1 3HY
☎ 01332 361111
E-mail: derby@bbc.co.uk Web: http://www.bbc.co.uk/derby/local_radio
BBC Radio Derby is the BBC's local radio station for the Derbyshire region.
TRILT coverage: June 2001 to date.

Peak 107FM

Radio House, Foxwood Road, Chesterfield S41 9RF
☎ 01246 269107 **Fax:** 01246 269933
E-mail: info@peak107.com Web: http://www.peakfm.net
Independent local radio station covering the north Derbyshire area. It
broadcasts a mix of music, and local and national news. TRILT coverage: June
2001 to date.

j. WEST MIDLANDS

Heart 100.7

1 The Square, 111 Broad Street, Birmingham B15 1AS
☎ 0121 695 0000 **Fax:** 0121 696 1007
E-mail: heartfm@heartfm.co.uk Web: http://www.heartfm.co.uk/heart1007
Heart 100.7 is a commercial radio station broadcasting in the UK, covering
the West Midlands area. TRILT coverage: June 2001 to date.

Kix 96 See **Touch FM**

Touch FM

Watch Close, Spon Street, Coventry CV1 3LN
☎ 024 7652 5656 **Fax:** 024 7655 1744
Web: http://www.intouchfm.com
Independent local radio station, formerly known as Kix 96, serving the
Coventry area. Broadcasts music news and information. No longer active on
TRILT.

UCB Christian Radio

PO Box 255, Stoke-on-Trent ST4 8YY
☎ 0845 6040401
E-mail: ucb@ucb.co.uk Web: http://www.ucb.co.uk
UCB stands for United Christian Broadcasters. Available on DAB radio in
Staffordshire and London. TRILT coverage: June 2001 to date.

k. SCOTLAND

3C

3C Digital Radio, 3 South Avenue, Clydebank Business Park,
Glasgow G81 2RX
☎ 0845 345 0333 or 0141 565 2307
Web: http://www3cdigital.com
3C was a radio station featuring country and western music, broadcasting in
Scotland, Newcastle and Northern Ireland. No longer active on TRILT.

96.3 Rock Radio

Rock Radio, PO BOX 101, Unit 1130, Parkway Court,
Glasgow Business Park, G69 6GA
☎ 0141 781 1011
E-mail: enquiries@gmgradio.co.uk Web: http://www.rockradiofm.co.uk
96.3 Rock Radio, formerly known as Q96 FM, is a commercial station
broadcasting in the UK, covering the Glasgow and Renfrewshire area. TRILT
continues to carry listings for the station under the old name, Q96 FM. TRILT
coverage: June 2001 to date.

BBC Radio Nan Gaidheal

Rosebank Church Street, Stornoway, Isle of Lewis HS1 2LS
☎ 01851 705000
E-mail: alba@bbc.co.uk Web: http://www.bbc.co.uk/scotland/alba/radio
BBC Radio Nan Gaidheal is the BBC's Gaelic language radio station, broadcasting in Scotland. TRILT coverage: June 2001 to date.

BBC Radio Orkney

Castle Street, Kirkwall, Orkney KW15 1DF
☎ 01856 873939
E-mail: radio.orkney@bbc.co.uk
Web: http://www.bbc.co.uk/scotland/radioscotland/programmes/orkney
BBC Radio Orkney is the BBC's local radio station in the Orkney Isles. It is a
local opt-out from BBC Radio Scotland. TRILT coverage: June 2001 to date.

BBC Radio Scotland

Broadcasting House, Glasgow G12 8DG
☎ 0870 010 0222
E-mail: enquiries.scot@bbc.co.uk
Web: http://www.bbc.co.uk/scotland/radioscotland
BBC Radio Scotland is the national radio station for Scotland from the BBC.
TRILT coverage: June 2001 to date.

BBC Radio Shetland

Pitt Lane, Lerwick, Shetland ZE1 0DW
☎ 01595 694 747
E-mail: radio.shetland@bbc.co.uk
Web: http://www.bbc.co.uk/scotland/radioscotland/programmes/shetland&

BBC Radio Shetland is the BBC's local radio station for the Shetland Isles. It is a local opt-out from BBC Radio Scotland. TRILT coverage: June 2001 to date.

Beat 106 See **XFM Scotland**

Central FM
201 High Street, Falkirk FK1 1DU
☎ 01324 611164 **Fax:** 01324 611168
E-mail: mail@centralfm.co.uk Web: http://www.centralfm.co.uk
A local independent radio station covering the Stirling and Falkirk areas. It broadcasts current and past hits, local news, sport and information. TRILT coverage: June 2001 to date.

Clyde 1 FM
Clydebank Business Park, Glasgow G81 2RX
☎ 0141 565 2200 **Fax:** 0141 565 2265
E-mail: info@clyde1.com Web: http://www.clyde1.com
Independent local radio station serving the Glasgow area. Broadcasts popular contemporary music, sport, and local and national news. The FM sister station of the AM station Clyde 2. TRILT coverage: June 2001 to date.

Clyde 2 AM
Clydebank Business Park, Glasgow G81 2RX
☎ 0141 565 2200 **Fax:** 0141 565 2265
E-mail: info@clyde2.com Web: http://www.clyde2.com
Independent local radio station serving the Glasgow area. Broadcasts easy listening music, local and national news and sport. The AM sister station to Clyde1. TRILT coverage: June 2001 to date.

Forth 1 See **Forth One**

Forth 2 See **Forth Two**

Forth AM See **Forth Two**

Forth FM See **Forth One**

Forth One
Forth House, Forth Street, Edinburgh EH1 3LE
☎ 0131 556 9255 **Fax:** 0131 558 3277
E-mail: info@forthone.com Web: http://www.forthone.com
Independent local radio station, formerly known as Forth FM and Forth 1, serving the Edinburgh area. Broadcasts chart and contemporary hits, news and information. TRILT coverage: June 2001 to date.

Forth Two
Forth House, Forth Street, Edinburgh EH1 3LE
☎ 0131 556 9255 **Fax:** 0131 558 3277
E-mail: info@forth2.com Web: http://www.forth2.com
Independent local radio station, formerly known as Forth AM and Forth 2, serving the Edinburgh area. Broadcasts classic hits, contemporary music, news and sport. TRILT coverage: June 2001 to date.

Kingdom FM
Web: http://www.kingdomfm.co.uk
Independent local radio station serving the Fife area. Broadcasts current and past hits, local news and community information. TRILT coverage: June 2001 to date.

Moray Firth Radio
Scorguie Place, Inverness, Scotland IV3 8UJ
☎ 01463 224433 **Fax:** 01463 243224
E-mail: mfr@mfr.co.uk Web: http://www.mfr.co.uk
Independent local radio station covering the Inverness and Moray Firth area. Broadcasts a wide range of programmes including contemporary music, sport, news, entertainment and local information. TRILT coverage: June 2001 to date.

Northsound One
Northsound Radio Ltd, Abbotswell Road, West Tullos, Aberdeen AB12 3AJ
☎ 01224 337000 **Fax:** 01224 400003
E-mail: northsound@srh.co.uk Web: http://www.northsound1.co.uk
Independent local radio station covering the Aberdeen area. Broadcasts contemporary hits, news, sport and information. No longer active on TRILT.

Northsound Two
Northsound Radio Ltd, Abbotswell Road, West Tullos, Aberdeen AB12 3AJ
☎ 01224 337000 **Fax:** 01224 400003
E-mail: northsound@srh.co.uk Web: http://www.northsound2.co.uk
Independent local radio station, covering the Aberdeen area. Broadcasts adult pop, news, sport and information. No longer active on TRILT.

Q96 FM See **96.3 Rock Radio**

Radio Borders
Tweedside Park, Tweedside, Melrose TD1 3RS
☎ 01896 759444 **Fax:** 0845 3457080
E-mail: programming@radioborders.com
Web: http://www.radioborders.com
Radio Borders is a commercial radio station, based in the Borders region of Scotland and North Northumberland. TRILT coverage: June 2001 to date

Radio Royal
Radio Royal is a hospital radio station. No longer active on TRILT.

Radio Tay AM
6 North Isla Street, Dundee DD3 7JQ
☎ 01382 200 800
E-mail: ayam@radiotay.co.uk Web: http://www.tayam.co.uk
Tay AM is a commercial radio station broadcasting in the UK, based in the Dundee and Perth area of Scotland. TRILT coverage: June 2001 to date.

Radio Tay FM
6 North Isla Street, Dundee DD3 7JQ
☎ 01382 200 800
E-mail: ayam@radiotay.co.uk Web: http://www.tayfm.co.uk
Tay FM is a commercial radio station broadcasting in the UK, based in the Dundee and Perth area of Scotland. TRILT coverage: June 2001 to date.

Real Radio

P.O. Box 101, Parkway Court, Glasgow Business Park, Glasgow G69 6GA
☎ 0141 7811011 **Fax:** 0141 7811112
Web: http://www.realradiofm.com
Real FM, formerly known as Scot FM, is an independent local radio covering the central Scotland area. Broadcasts adult contemporary music and speech. TRILT coverage: June 2001 to date.

Scot FM See **Real Radio**

Westsound

Radio House, 54a Holmston Road, Ayr KA7 3BE
☎ 01292 283662 **Fax:** 01292 283665
E-mail: info@westsound.co.uk Web: http://www.w.est-sound.co.uk
Independent local radio station based in Ayr. It plays easy listening music with local and national news plus live football. TRILT coverage: June 2001 to date.

XFM Scotland

Four Winds Pavilion, Pacific Quay, Glasgow G51 1EB
☎ 0141 566 6106 **Fax:** 0141 566 6110
E-mail: info@beat106.com Web: http://www.beatfm.com
An independent local radio station, formerly known as Beat 106, broadcasting a mixture of chart and indie music to Central Scotland. The station was re-branded as XFM Scotland in 2006. No longer active on TRILT.

I. WALES

BBC Radio Cymru

Broadcasting House, Llantrisant Road, Llandaff, Cardiff CF5 2YQ
☎ 029 2057 2888
Web: http://www.bbc.co.uk/cymru/radiocymru
BBC Radio Cymru is the BBC's local radio station for the Wales area, broadcasting in the Welsh language. TRILT coverage: June 2001 to date.

BBC Radio Wales

Broadcasting House, Llandaff, Cardiff CF5 2YQ
☎ 08700 100 110
E-mail: radio.wales@bbc.co.uk Web: http://www.bbc.co.uk/wales/radiowales
BBC Radio Wales is the national English language radio station for Wales from the BBC. TRILT coverage: June 2001 to date.

Classic Gold Marcher 1260AM

The Studios, Mold Road, Wrexham, Clwyd LL1 4AF
☎ 01978 751818 **Fax:** 01978 722209
E-mail: admin@classicgolddigital.com
Web: http://www.classicgolddigital.com
Local independent radio station serving the Wrexham, Chester and North Wales area. Formerly known as Marcher Gold. No longer active on TRILT.

Galaxy 101 See **Kiss 101**

Kiss 101

Kiss 101, 26 Baldwin Street, Bristol BS1 1SE
☎ 0117 901 0101 **Fax:** 0117 984 3204
Web: http://www.totalkiss.com/

Independent local radio station covering the Severn estuary area, formerly known as Galaxy 101 and Vibe 101 FM. Broadcasts dance and r'n'b. TRILT continues to carry listings for the channel under the name Vibe 101 FM. TRILT coverage: June 2001 to date.

Marcher Gold See Classic Gold Marcher 1260AM

MFM 103.4
Web: http://www.mfmradio.com
Independent local radio station covering the Wrexham and Chester areas. Broadcasts a mix of music, and local and national news. TRILT coverage: June 2001 to date.

Red Dragon FM
Atlantic Wharf, Cardiff Bay CF10 4DJ
☎ 029 2066 2066 **Fax:** 029 2066 2060
E-mail: mail@reddragonfm.co.uk Web: http://www.reddragonfm.co.uk
Red Dragon FM is a commercial radio station broadcasting in the UK, covering the Cardiff and Newport area. TRILT coverage: June 2001 to date.

Valleys Radio
Festival Park, Victoria, Ebbw Vale NP23 8XW
☎ 01495 301116 **Fax:** 01495 300710
E-mail: info@valleysradio.co.uk Web: http://www.valleysradio.co.uk
Valleys Radio is a commercial radio station broadcasting in the UK in the South Wales Valleys region. TRILT coverage: June 2001 to date.

Vibe 101 FM See Kiss 101

m. NORTHERN IRELAND

3C
3C Digital Radio, 3 South Avenue, Clydebank Business Park,
Glasgow G81 2RX
☎ 0845 345 0333 or 0141 565 2307
Web: http://www3cdigital.com
3C was a radio station featuring country and western music, broadcasting in Scotland, Newcastle and Northern Ireland. No longer active on TRILT.

BBC Radio Foyle
8 Northland Road, Derry BT48 7JD
☎ 028 7126 6522
Web: http://www.bbc.co.uk/northernireland/radiofoyle
BBC Radio Foyle is the BBC's local radio station for Derry and the North West of Northern Ireland. It runs an opt-out service from Radio Ulster. TRILT coverage: June 2001 to date.

BBC Radio Ulster
Broadcasting House, Ormeau Avenue, Belfast BT2 8HQ
☎ 028 9033 8000 **Fax:** 028 9032 6453
Web: http://www.bbc.co.uk/northernireland/radioulster
BBC Radio Ulster is the BBC's main local radio station for Northern Ireland. TRILT coverage: June 2001 to date.

Cool FM

PO Box 974, Belfast BT1 1RT
☎ 028 9181 7181 **Fax:** 028 9181 4974
E-mail: music@coolfm.co.uk Web: http://www.coolfm.co.uk
Independent local radio station serving Northern Ireland. Broadcasts a mix of contemporary music and news. TRILT coverage: June 2001 to date.

Downtown Radio

Newtownards, Co. Down, Northern Ireland BT23 4ES
☎ 028 9181 5555 **Fax:** 028 9181 8913
E-mail: programmes@downtown.co.uk Web: http://www.downtown.co.uk
Independent local radio station serving Northern Ireland. Broadcasts a mix of music, news and information, and specialist music. TRILT coverage: June 2001 to date.

Q102.9FM

The Riverview Suite, 87 Rossdowney Road, Waterside, Londonderry BT47 5SU
☎ 02871 344449 **Fax:** 02871 311177
E-mail: manager@q102.fm Web: http://www.q102.fm
Q102.9FM is a commercial station broadcasting in the UK, covering the Derry area. TRILT coverage: June 2001 to date.

n. EIRE

Raidio Na Gaeltachta

RTÉ, Raidió na Gaeltachta, Casla, Co. na Gaillimhe, Eire
☎ 091 506677 **Fax:** 091 506666
E-mail: nag@rte.ie Web: http://www.rte.ie/rnag
Raidio Na Gaeltachta is the Irish language radio channel from RTÉ. TRILT coverage: June 2001 to date.

COURSES AND TRAINING

The major source for information on courses and training in film, video and multimedia in the UK is the BFI/Skillset Media Courses and Multimedia Courses Directory, available at http://www.bfi.org.uk/education/talkscourses/mediacourses or http://www.skillset.org/training/coursedatabase. The Directory lists details of over 6,000 courses across England, Northern Ireland, Scotland and Wales. Film courses, television courses, video courses, radio courses and web authoring courses are included. The database provides comprehensive information both for those needing professional upgrading and anyone contemplating a career shift.

In addition to courses run by institutions of higher and further education, the following organisations offer relevant specialist training courses.

01zero-one, the Creative Learning Lab
Westminster Kingsway College, Soho Centre, Peter Street, London W1F 0HS
☎ 020 7025 1985
E-mail: info@01zero-one.co.uk Web: http://www.01zero-one.co.uk
01zero-one, the Creative Learning Lab is part of Westminster Kingsway College and runs a range of courses to train London's television, film, post production, interactive and new media and digital design industries.

4Talent
Web: http://www.channel4.com/4talent
Through an ever-growing range of cutting-edge talent schemes, 4talent offers the support and space needed to make that crucial next step for a career in the industry. The various schemes include: *Television Documentary*: FourDocs, 3 Minute Wonder, New Documentary Strand, Documentary Film Foundation, Sheffield Pitch, New Shoots; *Film*: Cinema Extreme, Dance 4 Film; *Comedy*: 4Laughs, Comedy Lab; Television Drama: Coming Up; *New Digital*: Melt; *Animation*: E Stings.

Ahead Training
1 Springvale Terrace, London W14 0AE
☎ 0800 043 0025
E-mail: learn@aheadtraining.co.uk Web: http://aheadtraining.co.uk
Ahead Training delivers expert diverse training, tuition, and skills development for the creative media and post production industries and home studio enthusiasts.

BBC Training
☎ 0870 122 0216 **Fax:** 0870 122 0145
E-mail: training@bbc.co.uk Web: http://www.bbctraining.com
The BBC is constantly innovating to meet the new demands created by audience expectations and new technology. BBC Training & Development is at the heart of that change, ensuring staff and workers in the industry have the skills to meet these ever changing challenges. The BBC works with Skillset to offer subsidised training to the UK freelance community; it offers a complete portfolio of courses and development solutions to individuals and organisations world wide; and it acts as development consultants to work with individuals and organisations, offering an end to end service from training needs analysis to evaluation.

Bill Curtis Associates
Colpetty, Westbury Terrace, Westerham, Kent TN16 1RP
☎ 01959 563326
E-mail: info@bcassociates.org Web: http://www.bcassociates.org
Training and production in broadcast and creative media affordable to broadcasters, companies and freelancers delivered by an experienced team of practitioners in London or on site. Includes Skillset-funded courses.

BKSTS – the Moving Image Society
Pinewood Studios, Iver Heath, Bucks SL0 0NH
☎ 01753 656656
Web: http://www.bksts.com/index-training.htm
BKSTS offers a range of short, part-time courses, some of them supported by the Skillset freelance fund. Topics include introduction to film technologies, television technology, audio technology for television and film, projectionist training, management in the creative industries, being an effective manager, broadcast technology, from camera to screen – the technology of television, what is HD, and HD technology.

British Interactive Media Association (BIMA)
Briarlea House, Southend Road, Billericay CM11 2PR
☎ 01277 658107 **Fax:** 0870 051 7842
E-mail: info@bima.co.uk
Web: http://www.bima.co.uk/industry-insight/training-and-accreditation.asp
BIMA is the industry association representing the interactive media and digital content sector. It takes a proactive role with academia in helping students understand what the future interactive industry might demand from them and encourages student placements with its members.

British Universities Film & Video Council (BUFVC)
77 Wells Street, London W1T 3QJ
☎ 020 7393 1512
E-mail: courses@bufvc.ac.uk Web: http://www.bufvc.ac.uk/courses
The BUFVC offers a range of one-day courses, each offered several times a year. Titles include: Authoring streaming media for the world wide web; Data projectors for education; Encoding digital video for streaming and network delivery (at introductory or advanced level); Finding and using audio-visual media in further and higher education; Copyright clearance for print, broadcast and multimedia; Shooting with HDV; Streaming and handheld technologies to support students with disabilities; Video in Flash.
From 2008, the BUFVC and the Technical Advisory Service for Images (TASI) plan jointly to provide a JISC-funded Technical Advisory Service for moving images and sound. This will include a co-ordinated programme of training courses.

Cyfle
33-35 West Bute Street, Cardiff CF10 5LH
☎ 029 2046 5533 **Fax:** 029 2046 3344
E-mail: Cyfle@cyfle.co.uk Web: http://www.cyfle.co.uk
Cyfle is the training company for the Welsh television, film and interactive media industry. In 2000 the company became a Skillset-accredited Training Partner and a national provider for the industry across Wales. Cyfle provides a variety of training schemes covering a wide spectrum of activity from the Summer Schools for the young people to Newcomer Schemes and courses for the professional seeking to update and acquire new skills.

Documentary Filmmakers Group (DFG)

4th Floor Shacklewell Studios, 28 Shacklewell Lane, London E8 2EZ
☎ 020 7249 6600
E-mail: info@dfgdocs.com Web: http://www.dfgdocs.com/Training
DFG offers an extensive programme of short courses from 1-5 days in length. These courses offer an opportunity to acquire a range of skills specifically for documentary filmmaking. In addition, DFG also runs Doclab, an intensive training course and documentary production factory in partnership with Goldsmiths University of London.

DV Talent

Studio 451, Highgate Studios, 53-79 Highgate Road, London NW5 1TL
☎ 020 7267 2300 **Fax:** 020 7428 0527
E-mail: rob@dvtalent.co.uk Web: http://www.dvtalent.co.uk
DV Talent are agents to top-end DV people, and are training providers and DV consultants. Training courses include some subsidised by Skillset.

Film Design International

Pinewood Studios, Pinewood Road, Iver Heath, Buckinghamshire SL0 0NH
☎ 01753 656 678
E-mail: Terry@filmdi.com Web: http://www.filmdi.com
Draughtsmanship training for the film and television industry, offering an Art Direction and an Advanced Art Direction course, based at Pinewood Film Studios. Skillset film skills funding is available for the Art Direction Courses depending on experience.

FOCAL

Pentax House, South Hill Avenue, Northolt Road, South Harrow, Middlesex HA2 0DU
☎ 020 8423 5853 **Fax:** 020 8933 4826
E-mail: info@focalint.org Web: http://www.focalint.org/training.htm
FOCAL International organises regular training events for those working in the footage industry. Several of its consultant members are professional trainers who can provide bespoke training to individuals or groups. FOCAL has also established the Jane Mercer Training Award in memory of Jane Mercer, footage researcher and Chair of FOCAL International 2000-2005. The Award is intended to provide assistance to those wishing to further their professional development in the footage industry and its associated areas.

FT2

3rd Floor, 18-20 Southwark Street, London SE1 1TJ
☎ 020 7407 0344 **Fax:** 020 7407 0366
E-mail: ft2@ft2.org.uk Web: http://www.ft2.org.uk
FT2 is the Film and Television Freelance Training's web site. FT2 is committed to assisting the film and television industry achieve a diverse workforce, which more closely represents the makeup of society as a whole.

Pact

Procter House, 1 Procter Street, Holborn, London WC1V 6DW
☎ 020 7067 4367
E-mail: enquiries@pact.co.uk Web: http://www.pact.co.uk/training
Pact's Skills Team aims to maintain and improve the competitiveness of Pact member companies. To meet this aim, it provides over 100 courses a year through the short course programme; provides in-house and bespoke

versions of Pact short courses for members; offers in-company skills development support and funding through in.indie; collects and distributes training funds for the sector through the Independent Production Training Fund; and actively lobby skills policy makers on members' behalf.

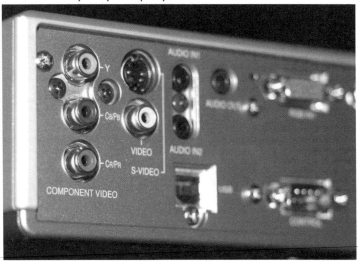

Praxis Films
Suite 3N, Leroy House, 436 Essex Road, London N1 3QP
☎ 020 7682 1865 **Fax:** 0779 111 4691
E-mail: info@praxisfilms.co.uk Web: http://www.praxisfilms.co.uk
Praxis Films offer a variety of short training courses for freelancers tailored to meet skills shortages identified by the television and film industry. Substantial discounts are available for courses funded by Skillset.

Raindance
81 Berwick Street, London W1F 8TW
☎ 020 7287 3833
E-mail: courses@raindance.co.uk Web: http://www.raindance.co.uk/courses
Raindance offers courses aimed at directors, producers, writers, actors, agents, film and media students. All tutors are working industry professionals. Around thirty-three different one- and two-day courses are offered for those wishing to focus on particular aspects of writing, producing or directing. Other short courses run one day or evening a week. Diplomas are also offered for those taking a number of short courses to study an area in depth.

Scottish Screen New Entrants Training Scheme (NETS) and New Entrants Animation Scheme (NEATS)
249 West George Street, Glasgow G2 4QE
☎ 0845 300 7300
E-mail: info@scottishscreen.com Web: http://www.scottishscreen.com
NETS provides the opportunity for eight trainees to undertake extensive work experience, providing the support and guidance to progress to assistant level in a diverse range of areas across the technical, craft, design and production grades. Most of a trainee's time is spent on productions, working in the areas they have chosen to specialise in across television production,

feature film and commercials. NEATS is a pilot initiative funded by Skillset, Scottish Enterprise and Scottish Screen. It is an industry-approved ten-month training course, with up to six places available for trainees in animation studios across Scotland.

Skillset

Prospect House, 80-110 New Oxford Street, London WC1A 1HB
☎ 020 7520 5757 **Fax:** 0)20 7520 5758
E-mail: info@skillset.org Web: http://www.skillset.org/training
Skillset is the national training organisation for broadcast, film, video and multimedia. Whether you are an employee or a freelancer, you need to know that any training you do is up to date and relevant to the industry. And companies want to be sure that business development training will help them gain and maintain a competitive edge. It is Skillset's role to ensure that individuals and organisations can access high quality vocational training. It works with industry, training and education providers and public agencies to make sure training provision meets industry needs. It accredit courses and approves providers on the basis of quality and relevance to industry.

Technical Advisory Service for Images (TASI)

Institute for Learning and Research Technology, University of Bristol, 8-10 Berkeley Square, Bristol BS8 1HH
☎ 0117 928 7091
E-mail: info@tasi.ac.uk Web: http://www.tasi.ac.uk/training/training.html
TASI runs a programme of full and half-day training workshops at venues around the country aimed at those involved in image digitisation projects or who wish to use digital images in learning and teaching. The small-group workshops consist of presentations and expert advice as well as practical exercises. The current programme of workshops covers four main areas: Image capture skills; Digital imaging skills; Using images to enhance learning and teaching; Building image collections. Several of the practical courses are offered at beginner, intermediate or advanced level.

From 2008, TASI and the BUFVC plan jointly to provide a JISC-funded Technical Advisory Service for moving images and sound. This will include a co-ordinated programme of training courses.

Training and Performance Showcase (TAPS)

Shepperton Studios, Shepperton, Middlesex TW17 0QD
☎ 01932 592151 **Fax:** 01932 592233
Web: http://www.tapsnet.org
TAPS is an organisation committed to seeking out, training and showcasing emerging talented writers by putting their original voices in front of leading drama and comedy producers and script executives. It runs courses designed to help UK writers crack into television.

VET

Lux Building, 2-4 Hoxton Square, London N1 6US
☎ 020 7505 4700 **Fax:** 020 7505 4800
E-mail: info@vet.co.uk Web: http://www.vet.co.uk
VET's reputation as a leading media industry training provider is built on fifteen years of successful training delivery. It offers regular short courses and AVID certified courses. Freelance rates are available on some courses with financial support from Skillset.

DISCUSSION LISTS

The following e-mail discussion lists cover areas of audio-visual media of interest to UK higher education and research. All can be freely subscribed to and will send regular e-mails under discussion threads on topics relevant to the list. Some discussion lists are open; others have a moderator who will vet submissions before publication and may guide discussion topics or advise on 'netiquette.' Most are provided through JISCmail, the National Academic Mailing List funded by the Joint Information Systems Committee. 'Announce' lists are used to disseminate news, not for discussion of topics. All the lists below are open to all, unless indicated otherwise.

The BUFVC currently manages four JISCmail discussion lists: BUFVC-Movies, Newsreels, ShakespeareAV and TRILT-Talk.

AHDS-ALL
Web: http://www.jiscmail.ac.uk/lists/AHDS-ALL.html
Discussion list for disseminating news about the Arts and Humanities Data Service.

AMIA-L
Web: http://lsv.uky.edu/archives/amia-l.html
Discussion list for members of the Association of Moving Image Archivists and anyone interested in issues surrounding the archiving of motion pictures.

ARLIS-Link
Web: http://www.jiscmail.ac.uk/lists/ARLIS-LINK.html
Discussion list for ARLIS/UK & Ireland, the Art Libraries Society, covering issues relating to librarianship of the visual arts.

BBC History
http://www.jiscmail.ac.uk/lists/BBC-HISTORY.html
Discussion list for researchers investigating the history of the BBC.

BISA
Web: http://www.jiscmail.ac.uk/lists/BISA.html
Discussion list for the British and Irish Sound Archives Forum.

BUFVC-Movies
Web: http://www.jiscmail.ac.uk/lists/BUFVC-MOVIES.html
BUFVC discussion list on the online delivery of moving images, also used for general BUFVC news.

Cinephoto
Web: http://www.jiscmail.ac.uk/lists/CINEPHOTO.html
An interdisciplinary mailing list for cinema and photography.

Clickandgovideo
Web: http://www.jiscmail.ac.uk/lists/CLICKANDGOVIDEO.html
Discussion on the educational value and implementation issues behind using streaming video lectures as a teaching method.

Creativity-in-Education
Web: http://www.jiscmail.ac.uk/lists/CREATIVITY-IN-EDUCATION.html
Designed to stimulate discussion and disseminate information on the subject of creativity in education.

Elearning
Web: http://www.jiscmail.ac.uk/lists/ELEARNING.html
Discussion list for sharing ideas and best practice in e-learning projects in museums, libraries, archives, galleries and HE/FE organisations.

Film-Philosophy
Web: http://www.jiscmail.ac.uk/lists/FILM-PHILOSOPHY.html
Discussion 'salon' devoted to serious debate about film.

Film-Screening
Web: http://www.jiscmail.ac.uk/lists/FILM-SCREENING.html
Discussion list for screening films in a higher education context.

H-Film
Web: http://www.h-net.org/~film
H-Film encourages scholarly discussion of cinema history and uses of the media.

History-Digitisation
Web: http://www.jiscmail.ac.uk/lists/HISTORY-DIGITISATION.html
The application of optical character recognition (OCR) and imaging technology to historical material.

IAMS
Web: http://www.jiscmail.ac.uk/lists/IAMS.html
Discussion list for the International Association for Media in Science.

IASA
Web: http://www.nb.no/cgi-bin/wa?A0=IASALIST
Discussion list for the International Association of Sound and Audiovisual Archives.

Intute-Announce
Web: http://www.jiscmail.ac.uk/lists/INTUTE-ANNOUNCE.html
Latest news from Intute, a national JISC service which provides the academic community with access to the best web resources for education and research.

JISC-Announce
Web: http://www.jiscmail.ac.uk/lists/JISC-ANNOUNCE.html
An announcement list for news from the Joint Information Systems Committee.

JISC-Development
Web: http://www.jiscmail.ac.uk/lists/JISC-DEVELOPMENT.html
JISC development discussion forum.

JISC-E-Collections
Web: http://www.jiscmail.ac.uk/lists/JISC-E-COLLECTIONS.html
Discussion list for electronic collection managers.

LIS-Link
Web: http://www.jiscmail.ac.uk/lists/LIS-LINK.html
A general library and information science list for news and discussion.

LIS-MMIT
Web: http://www.jiscmail.ac.uk/lists/LIS-MMIT.html
Discussion for the CILIP Multimedia Information & Technology Group, covering issues of multimedia information and technology developments in library and information science.

LondonScreenArchives
Web: http://www.mailtalk.ac.uk/lists/londonsscreenarchives.html
Discussion list for the network of London's screen archives.

MECCSA
Web: http://www.jiscmail.ac.uk/lists/MECCSA.html
Discussion list for MECCSA, the Media, Communication and Cultural Studies Association, covering aspects of academic research and teaching within media.

Medialib
Web: http://www.jiscmail.ac.uk/lists/MEDIALIB.html
Forum for media librarians and information professionals.

Media-Support-Services
Web: http://www.jiscmail.ac.uk/lists/MEDIA-SUPPORT-SERVICES.html
Discussion list for media departments in the UK.

MLAnews
Web: http://www.jiscmail.ac.uk/lists/MLANEWS.html
News from the Museums, Libraries and Archives Council.

Newsreels
Web: http://www.jiscmail.ac.uk/lists/NEWSREELS.html
BUFVC list for the study of cinema newsreels and their use in historical research.

Podcasting
Web: http://www.jiscmail.ac.uk/lists/PODCASTING.html
Academic podcasting and related issues.

Radio-Studies
Web: http://www.jiscmail.ac.uk/lists/RADIO-STUDIES.html
Debate on all issues related to radio.

SCUDD
Web: http://www.jiscmail.ac.uk/lists/SCUDD.html
Discussion list for the Standing Conference of University Drama Departments (SCUDD).

ShakespeareAV
Web: http://www.jiscmail.ac.uk/lists/SHAKESPEAREAV.html
BUFVC discussion list for its audio-visual Shakespeare database project, and general issues relating to Shakespeare on film, television and radio.

Shaksper
Web: http://www.shaksper.net
Moderated list for Shakespearean researchers, instructors, students, and those who share their academic interests and concerns. Requires an application to be made before one can join the list.

Streaming
Web: http://www.jiscmail.ac.uk/lists/STREAMING.html
Discussion list for issues around streaming technology for delivering presentations.

TRILT-Talk
Web: http://www.jiscmail.ac.uk/lists/TRILT-TALK.html
Broadcasting and education mailing list, managed by the BUFVC. Particularly relates to the BUFVC's Television and Radio Index for Learning and Teaching.

UK-Colleges
Web: http://www.jiscmail.ac.uk/lists/UK-COLLEGES.html
Use of the Internet to support curriculum activity in further education colleges.

Video
Web: http://www.jiscmail.ac.uk/lists/VIDEO.html
Issues on the use of video in education.

Visualisation Tools
Web: http://www.jiscmail.ac.uk/lists/VISUALISATION-TOOLS.html
The use of visualisation tools.

VLE
Web: http://www.jiscmail.ac.uk/lists/VLE.html
Discussion list on all issues relating to Virtual Learning Environments.

DISTRIBUTORS

The BUFVC selects and describes audio-visual programmes available in the UK which will be of interest to UK higher education users, and publishes the details through its HERMES database (http://www.bufvc.ac.uk/hermes). Below is a listing of some of the main distributors currently referred to by the BUFVC, providing specialist content suitable for higher education and research.

2 entertain
33 Foley Street, London W1W 7TL
☎ 020 7612 3000 **Fax:** 020 7612 3003
E-mail: emma.burch@2entertain.co.uk Web: http://www.2entertain.co.uk
Specialises in distributing archival film and television titles, predominantly licensed from Granada.

4 Learning
PO Box 400, Wetherby LS23 7LG
☎ 08701 246 444 **Fax:** 08701 246 446
E-mail: sales@channel4learning.com Web: http://www.channel4.com/learning
The educational broadcasting arm of Channel 4.

Acorn Media UK
10 Smith's Yard, Summerley Street, London SW18 4HR
☎ 020 8879 7000 **Fax:** 020 8879 1616
E-mail: info@acornmedia.com Web: http://www.acornmedia.com
Founded in 1997, it distributes mainly archival television programmes predominantly licensed from the BBC and ITV.

Artificial Eye Film Company
14 Kings Street, London WC2E 8HN
☎ 020 7240 5353 **Fax:** 020 7240 5242
E-mail: info@artificial-eye.com Web: http://www.artificial-eye.com
Independent film and video distributor with an emphasis on foreign language titles.

AVP
School Hill Centre, Chepstow, Monmouthshire NP16 5PH
☎ 01291 625439 **Fax:** 01291 629671
E-mail: info@avp.co.uk Web: http://avp.100megs28.com
Since 1969 a major supplier of audio-visual materials to schools in the UK.

BBC Active
Mezzanine, 80 The Strand, London WC2R 0RL
☎ 020 7010 6965 **Fax:** 020 8433 2916
E-mail: bbcactive.bbcstudies@pearson.com Web: http://www.bbcactive.com
Previously known as BBC Videos for Education and Training and BBC Learning, this distributor of specialist BBC programmes is now run by Pearson Education and will provide some content 'on demand' to educational institutions.

BBC Radio Collection

BBC Audiobooks, St James House, The Square, Lower Bristol Road, Bath BA2 3BH
☎ 0800 136919 **Fax:** 01225 448005
E-mail: radio.collection@bbc.co.uk
Web: http://www.bbcworldwide.com/spokenword
BBC audio materials available commercially.

BFI Distribution

21 Stephen Street, London W1P 2LN
☎ 020 7957 8938
Web: http://www.bfi.org.uk
Specialist distributor of international fiction and documentary films on 16mm and 35mm film as well as VHS and DVD video.

BFI Video

21 Stephen Street, London W1P 2LN
☎ 020 7957 8957
Web: http://www.bfi.org.uk/booksvideo/video/catalogue
The British Film institute releases its own productions as well as a variety of film and television materials made by European, American and Japanese companies.

British Library Sound Archive

96 Euston Road, London NW1 2DB
☎ 020 7412 7676 **Fax:** 020 7412 7441
E-mail: sound-archive@bl.uk Web: http://www.bl.uk/nsa
National UK repository for sound, which produces a range of audio publications related to its collections.

British Universities Film & Video Council

77 Wells Street, London W1T 3QJ
☎ 020 7393 1503 **Fax:** 020 7393 1555
E-mail: services@bufvc.ac.uk
Web: http://www.bufvc.ac.uk/services/distribution
The BUFVC's distribution library includes Stanley Milgram's OBEDIENCE, Virgilio Tosi's THE ORIGINS OF SCIENTIFIC CINEMATOGRAPHY and InterUniversity History Film Consortium films.

Cinenova

113 Roman Road, London E2 0QN
E-mail: info@cinenova.org.uk Web: http://www.cinenova.org.uk
Films made by, and predominantly for, women.

Classroom Video

St Thomas Court, Thomas Lane, Redcliffe, Bristol BS1 6JG
☎ 0870 850 8256 **Fax:** 0870 850 8424
E-mail: customerservice@classroomvideo.co.uk
Web: http://www.classroomvideo.com.au
Educational films specialists, based in Australia.

Coachwise
Chelsea Close, Off Amberley Road, Armley, Leeds LS12 4HP
☎ 0113 201 5555 **Fax:** 0113 231 9606
E-mail: enquiries@1st4sport.com Web: http://www.1st4sport.com
Specialists in sports coaching, training and education.

Concord Media
22 Hines Rd, Ipswich IP3 9BG
☎ 01473 726012, **Fax:** 01473 274 531
E-mail: sales@concordmedia.org.uk Web: http://www.concordvideo.co.uk
Long-established distributor of educational documentaries on a wide variety
of subjects, with a special interest in subjects of social concern; also handles
titles made by the Arts Council. Formerly Concord Video and Film Council.

Construction Industry Training Board
CITB-ConstructionSkills, Bircham Newton, Kings Lynn, Norfolk PE31 6RH
☎ 01485 577577
E-mail: information.centre@citb.co.uk Web: http://www.citb.org.uk
Films made for training within the construction industry.

Contemporary Arts Media
PO BOX 245, South Fremantle 6162, Western Australia
☎ +61 0 8 9336 1587 **Fax:** +61 0 8 9335 3198
E-mail: info@hushvideos.com Web: http://www.hushvideos.com
Supplier of films and books for Art education.

Contender Entertainment
120 New Cavendish Street, London W1W 6XX
☎ 020 7907 3773 **Fax:** 020 7907 3777
E-mail: gchurch@contendergroup.com Web: http://www.contendergroup.com
Distributes contemporary film and television titles, many licensed from the
BBC.

Dance Books
The Old Bakery, 4 Lenten Street, Alton, Hampshire GU34 1HG
☎ 01420 86138 **Fax:** 01420 86142
E-mail: http://www.dancebooks.co.uk/contact.asp
Web: http://www.dancebooks.co.uk
Handles international video titles relating to all types of dance.

DD Home Entertainment
PO Box 738, High Street, Jersey JE4 0QW
☎ 0870 060 0286 **Fax:** 0845 126 1111
E-mail: http://www.ddhe.co.uk/contactus.aspx Web: http://www.ddhe.co.uk
Large-scale mail-order and online distributor with a special interest in
historical subjects.

Documentary Educational Resources
101 Morse Street, Watertown, MA 02472 USA
☎ +800-569-6621 or 617-926-0491 **Fax:** +617-926-9519
E-mail: docued@der.org Web: http://www.der.org
American company with an extensive catalogue of ethnographic films.

Earthstation1.com

J.C. Kaelin, PO Box 1432, Bayonne, NJ 07002-6432, USA
E-mail: jckaelin@prosperohouse.com Web: http://www.earthstation1.com
Specialises in audio and video CDs, mainly from archival sources.

Educational Broadcasting Services Trust

12 Printing House Yard, Hackney Road, London E2 7PR
☎ 020 7613 5082 **Fax:** 020 7613 5220
E-mail: mail@ebstrust.u-net.com Web: http://www.shotlist.co.uk
Produces and distributes educational films which can be re-edited and customised for specific institutional use.

Einstein Network

67-74 Saffron Hill, London EC1N 8QX
☎ 020 7693 7777 **Fax:** 020 7693 7788
E-mail: info@einstein-network.com Web: http://www.einstein-network.com
Focuses on content to aid professional development. Formerly Television Education Network.

Fenman Training

28 St Thomas Place, Cambridgeshire Business Park, Ely CB7 4EX
☎ 01353 665533 **Fax:** 01353 663644
E-mail: service@fenman.co.uk Web: http://www.fenman.co.uk
Training materials dealing with issues in the workplace.

Film Education

27-31 Charing Cross Road, London WC2H 0AU
☎ 020 7976 2291 **Fax:** 020 7839 5052
E-mail: postbox@filmeducation.org Web: http://www.filmeducation.org
Producer of DVD and CD-ROM materials for students studying Media Studies within the National Curriculum.

Filmbank Distributors

Warner House, 98 Theobalds Road, London WC1X 8WB
☎ 020 7984 5957/5958 **Fax:** 020 7984 5951
E-mail: E-mail: info@filmbank.co.uk Web: http://www.filmbank.co.uk
The main source in the UK for non-theatrical presentations of feature films, available on 16mm as well as VHS and DVD video.

Films for the Humanities & Sciences

PO Box 2053, Princeton NJ 08543-2053, USA
☎ +1 609671-1000 **Fax:** +1 609-671.0266
E-mail: custserv@films.com Web: http://www.films.com
American company specialising in video materials aimed at the HE and FE education market.

Gower Publishing

Direct Sales, Bookpoint Ltd, 130 Milton Park, Oxon OX14 4SB
☎ 01235 827730 **Fax:** 01235 400454
E-mail: gower@bookpoint.co.uk Web: http://www.gowerpub.com
Publishes several training DVDs as well as books on various media-related topics.

Grant and Cutler
55-57 Great Marlborough Street, London W1F 7AY
☎ 020 7734 2012 **Fax:** 020 7734 9272
E-mail: contactus@grantandcutler.com Web: http://www.grantandcutler.com
An important source of foreign language VHS and DVD releases.

Health and Safety Executive Videos
Publications Section, Room 313, Daniel House, Trinity Road,
Bootle L20 3TW
☎ 0151-951 4446
E-mail: hsebooks@hse.gsi.gov.uk Web: http://www.hsebooks.com
Training films made by the government.

Human Kinetics Europe
107 Bradford Road, Stanningley, Leeds LS28 6AT
☎ 0113 255 5665 **Fax:** 0113 255 5885
E-mail: custserv@hkeurope.com Web: http://www.humankinetics.com
A US company with a UK affiliate specialising in productions dealing with physical activity including Health and Sport.

I.A. Recordings
PO Box 476, Telford, Shropshire TF7 4RB
☎ 01907 224509
E-mail: info@iarecordings.org Web: http://www.iarecordings.org
Productions depicting industrial archaeology.

Illuminations
19-20 Rheidol Mews, Rheidol Terrace, Islington, London N1 8NU
☎ 020 7288 8400 **Fax:** 020 7288 8488
Email: louise@illuminationsmedia.co.uk Web:
http://www.illuminationsmedia.co.uk
Documentaries on the arts, artists and architecture.

Imperial War Museum
Lambeth Road, London SE1 6HZ
☎ 020 7416 5293 **Fax:** 020 7416 8299
E-mail: film@iwm.org.uk Web: http://www.iwm.org.uk
The IWM produces a range of CD and DVD titles covering the two World Wars.

Institution of Civil Engineers
Library, 1 Great George Street, London SW1P 3AA
☎ 020 7665 2251 **Fax:** 020 7976 7610
E-mail: library@ice.org.uk Web: http://www.ice.org.uk
Maker of several training productions in the field.

International Broadcasting Trust
143-145 Farringdon Road, London EC1R 3AB
☎ 020 7239 1441 **Fax:** 020 7833 8347
E-mail: mail@ibt.org.uk Web: http://www.ibt.org.uk
Specialises in content dealing with Third World development.

Leeds Animation Workshop
45 Bayswater Row, Leeds LS8 5LF
☎ 0113 248 4997 **Fax:** 0113 248 4997
E-mail: info@leedsanimation.org.uk Web: http://www.leedsanimation.org.uk
Maker and distributor of its own animated films since 1976.

London Mathematical Society
De Morgan House, 57-58 Russell Square, London WC1B 4HS
☎ 020 7637 3686 **Fax:** 020 7323 3655
E-mail : lms@lms.ac.uk Web: http://www.lms.ac.uk
Videocassettes and DVDs of popular Mathematics lectures, for purchase and hire.

Lux
18 Shacklewell Lane, London E8 2EZ
☎ 020 7503 3980 **Fax:** 020 7503 1606
E-mail: info@lux.org.uk Web: http://www.lux.org.uk
The premiere UK source for non-theatrical video and film materials made by artists and experimental filmmakers, including the London Film-maker's Co-op.

Media Education Foundation
60 Masonic Street, Northampton, Massachusetts 01060, USA
☎ +1 0800 897 0089 **Fax:** +1 0800 659 6882
E-mail: info@mediaed.org Web: http://www.mediaed.org
Produces and distributes documentary films and other educational resources to inspire critical reflection on the social, political and cultural impact of American mass media.

Mental Health Media
356 Holloway Road, London N7 6PA
☎ 020 7700 8171 **Fax:** 020 7686 0959
E-mail: info@mhmedia.com Web: http://www.mhmedia.com
Producer and distributor of video materials relating to various aspects of Mental Health.

Old Pond Publishing
Dencora Business Centre, 36 White House Road, Ipswich IP1 5LT
☎ 01473 238200 **Fax:** 01473 23821
E-mail: enquiries@oldpond.com Web: http://www.oldpond.com
Specialises in titles relating to Agriculture and Farming.

Open University Worldwide – Learning Resources
Walton Hall, Milton Keynes MK7 6AA
☎ 01908 858793 **Fax:** 01908 858787
E-mail: ouw-customer-services@open.ac.uk Web: http://www.ouw.co.uk
Materials created as part of Open University courses.

Oxfam Publishing
c/o BEBC Distribution, PO Box 1496, Parkstone, Dorset BH12 3YD
☎ 01202 712933 **Fax:** 01202 712930
E-mail: oxfam@bebc.co.uk Web: http://www.oxfam.org.uk
Materials made to support the work of the charity to aid the poor, especially in developing countries.

Oxford Educational Resources

PO Box 106, Kidlington, Oxon OX5 1HY
☎ 01865 84255 **Fax:** 01865 842551
E-mail: enquiries@oer.co.uk   Web: http://www.oer.co.uk
Maker of training materials on film and video since 1972, most notably in the area of Medicine and Health.

Pavilion Publishing

Richmond House, Richmond Road, Brighton, East Sussex BN2 3RL
☎ 01273 623222 **Fax:** 01273 625526
E-mail: info@pavpub.com Web: http://www.pavpub.com
Training materials for people working in social services.

Pidgeon Digital

World Microfilms, Microworld House, PO Box 35488, London NW8 6WD
☎ 020 7586 4499 **Fax:** 020 7722 1068
E-mail: microworld@ndirect.co.uk Web: http://www.pidgeondigital.com
Films on architects and their work.

Quantum Leap

1A Great Northern Street, Huntingdon, Cambridgeshire PE29 7HJ
☎ 01480 450006 **Fax:** 01480 456686
E-mail: customerservices@qleap.co.uk Web: http://www.qleap.co.uk
Distributor of many non-fiction titles on a wide variety of subjects.

Roland Collection

Peasmarsh, East Sussex TN31 6XJ
☎ 01797 230421 **Fax:** 01797 230677
E-mail: info@rolandcollection.com Web: http://www.rolandcollection.com
Broad range of documentaries on Fine Art and Humanities, now available online via subscription.

Royal Anthropological Institute

50 Fitzroy Street, London W1T 5BT
☎ 020 7387 0455 **Fax:** 020 7388 8817
E-mail: film@therai.org.uk
Web: http://www.therai.org.uk/film/video_sales.html
Distributor of anthropological films and video productions.

Safety Media

5a Kinmel Park, Abergele Road, Bodelwyddan, Rhyl LL18 5TX
☎ 0845 3451703 **Fax:** 01745 536195
E-mail: sales@safetymedia.co.uk Web: http://www.safetymedia.co.uk
Producer of DVD and video materials covering aspects of Health and Safety at work and in the workplace.

Teachers' TV

6-18 Berners Street, London W1T 3LN
☎ 020 7182 7430
E-mail: info@teachers.tv Web: http://www.teachers.tv
A large new resource providing material for educators across the curriculum to use in the classroom as well as advice on best practice, available to view on digital television or for download.

Trumedia
PO Box 316, Kidlington, Oxon OX5 2ZY
☎ 01865 847837 **Fax:** 01865 847837
E-mail: sales@trumedia.co.uk Web: http://www.trumedia.co.uk
Distributor specialising in titles for the English Literature National Curriculum along with other subjects such as Business Studies, Natural History, Art, History and materials for primary schools.

Trust for the Study of Adolescence
23 New Road, Brighton BN1 1WZ
☎ 01273 693311 **Fax:** 01273 679907
E-mail: info@tsa.uk.com Web: http://www.tsa.uk.com
Creates resources for professionals working with young people.

TV Choice
PO Box 597, Bromley, Kent BR2 0YB
☎ 020 8464 7402 **Fax:** 020 8464 7845
E-mail: tvchoiceuk@aol.com Web: http://www.tvchoice.uk.com
A producer and distributor of educational materials since 1982 covering a variety of subject areas including Drama, History, Geography, Business Studies and Science.

Undercurrents
Old Exchange, Pier Street, Swansea SA1 1RY
☎ 01792 45590
E-mail: info@undercurrents.org Web: http://www.undercurrents.org
A not-for-profit producer and distributor of counter-culture content outside of the mainstream as well as video material on animal welfare, radical music and various types of activism.

United Nations Centre for Human Settlements (Habitat)
PO Box 30030, GPO, Nairobi, 00100 Kenya
☎ +254 2 7621 234 **Fax:** +254 2 7624 266
E-mail: videos@unchs.org
Web: http://www.unchs.org/pmss/getPage.asp?page=latestVideos
Makes and distributes video materials pertaining to the Centre's city and town settlement programmes.

University of Sheffield: Learning Development and Media Unit
5 Favell Road Sheffield S3 7QX
☎ 0114 222 0400
E-mail: ldmu@shef.ac.uk Web: http://www.shef.ac.uk/ldmu
LDMU offers a wide range of educational video titles across a wide range of subject disciplines, including Biology, Chemistry, Earth Sciences, Health & Safety, Law, Medicine and Sociology.

Uniview Worldwide
PO Box 20, Hoylake, Wirral, Cheshire CH48 7HY
☎ 0151 625 3453 **Fax:** 0151 625 3707
E-mail: sales@uniview.co.uk Web: http://www.uniview.co.uk
Distributor for a wide range of educational materials with particular strengths in Psychology as well as Biology and Sports Science.

Vega Science Trust
Sussex Innovation Centre, Science Park Square, Brighton BN1 9SB
☎ 01273 678726 **Fax:** 01273 234645
E-mail: vega@vega.org.uk Web: http://www.vega.org.uk
Well-established maker and distributor of Science, Engineering and Technology-related films and video productions for the education sector.

Video Arts
6-7 St Cross Street, London EC1N 8UA
☎ 0845 601 2531 **Fax:** 0207 400 4900
E-mail: info@videoarts.co.uk Web: http://www.videoarts.com
Maker of highly regarded business training films, well-known for featuring such celebrities as John Cleese, its co-founder in 1972. Now owned by Tinopolis.

Videos for Patients
The Production Tree, Unit G16, Shepherd's Building, Rockley Road, London W14 0DA
☎ 020 7610 5599 **Fax:** 020 7610 5333
E-mail: sales@productiontree.co.uk Web: http://www.videosforpatients.co.uk
Sister company to Video Arts, which makes programmes dealing with improving patient care.

Videotel International
84 Newman Street, London W1P 3LD
☎ 020 7299 1800 **Fax:** 020 7299 1818
E-mail: mail@videotelmail.com Web: http://www.videotel.co.uk
Maker and distributor of training products originally made for maritime crews and focusing on shipping and legislation.

Viewtech Educational Media
7-8 Falcons Gate, Northavon Business Centre, Dean Road, Yate,
Bristol BS37 5HN
☎ 01454 858055
E-mail: mail@viewtech.co.uk Web: http://www.viewtech.co.uk
A leading producer and distributor of educational films, incorporating the Gateway, Rank Aldis (including Gaumont-British Instructional), Hugh Baddeley Productions and Educational Media Film & Video collections.

Wellcome Trust, Moving Image and Sound Collections
183 Euston Road, London NW1 2BE
☎ 020 7611 8766
E-mail: mfac@wellcome.ac.uk Web: http://library.wellcome.ac.uk/misc.html
World leader in producing content relating to medical matters.

Women Make Movies
462 Broadway, 500WS (at Grand Street), New York NY 10013, USA
☎ +1 212 925 0606 **Fax:** +1 212 925 2052
E-mail: info@wmm.com Web: http://www.wmm.com
US company distributing films made by, and predominantly for, women.

Woodhead Publishing
Abington Hall, Abington, Cambridge CB1 6AH
☎ 01223 891358 **Fax:** 01223 893694
E-mail: wp@woodheadpublishing.com
Web: http://www.woodheadpublishing.com

Established in 1989, the company has videos in the fields of Engineering, Metallurgy, and Material Science.

World Microfilms
PO Box 35488, St John's Wood, London NW8 6WD
☎ 020 7586 4499 **Fax:** 020 722 1068
E-mail: microworld@ndirect.co.uk Web: http://www.microworld.uk.com
Includes Pidgeon Digital (qv), Sussex Publications collection of audio and video material on English, History and Music; Audio-Forum audiotapes for Language Learning.

York Films of England
23 Bradstone Avenue, Folkestone, Kent CT19 5AQ
☎ 01303 226 2345 **Fax:** 01303 858 196
E-mail: office@yorkfilms.com Web: http://www.yorkfilms.com
Established in 1982, the company specialises in content relating to science, especially astronomy and space, and makes programmes for home video and television broadcast.

This is a select listing of film festivals in the UK and overseas. The major source of information on film festivals worldwide is the British Council's Directory of International Film and Video Festivals, listing over 600 international events, including television and video festivals. It is available at http://www.britfilms.com/festivals.

10secfilmfest
Web: http://www.tensec.com
An Internet-based rolling competition taking submissions throughout the year. Any kind of film that lasts only ten seconds is eligible. The best films submitted are screened on the web site.

Africa in Motion
Web: http://www.africa-in-motion.org.uk
An annual festival, first held in 2006, that showcases classic and contemporary films from Africa as well as holding complementary events. Held in Edinburgh.

Angel Film Festival
Web: http://www.angelfilmfestival.org
Founded in 2006, the Angel Film Festival exists to give unknown, but talented film-makers an opportunity to showcase their short films in an informal atmosphere alongside the work of more experienced short film directors. A selection of the best films are screen in venues across Islington, London.

Aurora Festival
Web: http://www.aurora.org.uk
Aurora is the new name for the Norwich International Animation Festival, which challenges the boundaries of animation. An art-focused, progressive event, it fuses artist retrospectives and thematic film programmes with debate, live performance and installations, alongside a selection of new work from across the world in wide-ranging competition programmes.

AV Festival
Web: http://www.avfest.co.uk
A biennial international festival of electronic arts first held across venues in Newcastle, Gateshead, Sunderland and Middlesbrough in 2003. It showcases film, digital arts, music, games and new media, including many specially commissioned works. The programme features concerts, performances, film screenings, exhibitions and installations, and outdoor projections. The next festival is planned for Spring 2008.

Belfast Film Festival
Web: http://www.belfastfilmfestival.org
Belfast Film Festival has a defined 'socio-political' focus on films, comple-mented by a commitment to bring the best of new international documentaries to Ireland in the Maysles Documentary Competition. Each year a range of films, speakers and seminars focussing on a selected theme provides a platform for debate and engagement between diverse sections of the audience.

Beyond TV

Web: http://www.undercurrents.org/beyondtv
BeyondTV is a week-long festival presented by Undercurrents, consisting of short movies, documentaries, music videos & animation. All films have a theme of social or environmental activism. Hosted in Swansea Marina, all proceeds from the festival go support the charity work of Undercurrents.

Birds Eye View Film Festival

Web: http://www.birds-eye-view.co.uk
Begun in 2005, the Birds Eye View film festival showcases the best features, shorts and documentaries from women filmmakers around the world. The festival is held in London across three venues: the ICA, the National Film Theatre and the Barbican.

Bradford Animation Festival

Web: http://www.nationalmediamuseum.org.uk/baf
The animation festival, which has been running since 1994, also hosts screentalks, workshops and special events led by some of the industry's top names. The festival culminates in the annual BAF Awards, which celebrate the very best in new animation from around the world.

Bradford International Film Festival

Web: http://www.nationalmediamuseum.org.uk/bff
Based at the National Media Museum, the Bradford International Film Festival has been held every March since its launch in 1995 and shows a range of new and classic film. The festival includes a number of diverse strands, such as Cinefile, which features documentaries about films and film-makers, and Uncharted States of America, showcasing emerging talent in the US independent film sector.

BritDoc

Web: https://www.britdoc.org/festival/index.php
Held in Oxford in July, Britdoc is a three-day annual festival showcasing short and feature-length documentaries from the UK. It provides a venue for leading international film producers, distributors, and financiers to meet British film-makers face to face.

British Silent Cinema Festival

Web: http://www.britishsilentcinema.com
The British Silent Film Festival, based in Nottingham, is a celebration of British cinema before 1930 and is organized in collaboration with the British Film Institute. The festival showcases both fiction and non-fiction silent film; many of the films have not been exhibited for decades. The screenings are accompanied by academic papers and special events.

Cambridge Film Festival

Web: http://www.cambridgefilmfestival.org.uk
Running from 1977 to 1997 and then re-launched in 2001, the Cambridge Film Festival is held annually in early July. Its programme includes new features, shorts, revivals and documentaries from around the world. In addition, the Festival offers visits from actors and directors, fora, conferences, workshops and education events.

CPH:DOX Copenhagen International Documentary Film Festival

Web: http://www.cphdox.dk

An annual international documentary festival founded in 2003 and held in July in Denmark. Films can be selected for the CPH:DOX Award, Amnesty Award, New Vision Award (short and long category), Sound & Vision Award and non-competitive thematic categories.

Document 5 International Human Rights Documentary Film Festival

Web: http://www.variant.randomstate.org/Doc5/doc5.html

Held annually in Glasgow, Document 5 presents a platform for both established and emerging documentary filmmakers to screen their work at the only UK festival dedicated to raising awareness of international human rights issues.

DOCUSUR

Web: http://www.docusur.es

DOCUSUR is an International Southern Documentary Film Festival and Market, for international documentary productions, with a unique focus on documentaries produced or shot in Africa, Asia, and Latin America, or thematically related to southern countries.

DOK.FEST

Web: http://www.dokfest-muenchen.de

The Munich International Documentary Film Festival showcases documentaries from around the world.

Eat Our Shorts

Web: http://www.nahemi.org/eatourshorts

Annual two-day festival bringing together student filmmakers from all over the UK and Ireland to see each other's work and share experiences. This non-competitive festival is organised by the National Association for Higher Education in the Moving Image (NAHEMI) and twenty member schools from the UK and Ireland including all the Skillset Screen Academies are represented at the event.

Edinburgh International Film Festival

Web: http://www.edfilmfest.org.uk

An international film festival forming part of the annual Edinburgh Arts Festival. Categories include features, shorts, documentary, animation, music promos, experimental and young person's films. Established in 1947 as a documentary-based event, it is the longest continually running film festival in the world.

Edinburgh International Television Festival

Web: http://www.mgeitf.co.uk

The wide ranging programme of this major television event deals with key issues of the day and involves keynote lectures, preview screenings, master-classes, interviews and networking parties. Founded in 1976 the Festival is held annually over the August bank holiday weekend and is attended by UK and international delegates representing the full spectrum of the industry including controllers, commissioners, producers, directors, marketers, new media companies, distributors and press.

Encounters Short Film Festival

Web: http://www.encounters-festival.org.uk

The Brief Encounters International Short Film Festival merged with the Animated Encounters International Animation Festival to form the Encounters Short Film Festival. It celebrates and provides a competitive showcase for short films from around the world. A forum for emerging talent and established industry alike, designed to nurture creativity and innovation. Held annually in Bristol.

Exposures UK Student Film Festival

Web: http://www.exposuresfilmfestival.co.uk

A four-day festival of student films held annually in Manchester. As well as featuring the best new filmmaking in categories – drama, documentary, animation, experimental and music video – Exposures also hosts a range of masterclasses, premieres, workshops and discussions with key figures from film and television. There are four competitive categories – animation, drama, documentary or experimental.

German Film Festival

Web: http://www.germanfilmfestival.co.uk

Since 1997 this annual festival has been organised by the German Film Service to promote German films worldwide. Screenings are held at the Curzon in London, but for the last few years a selection of the films has been shown at the Irish Film Institute in Dublin.

Glasgow Film Festival

Web: http://www.glasgowfilmfestival.org.uk

The international Glasgow Film Festival, first held in 2005, includes a section featuring some of the best of classic and contemporary documentaries as well as feature films.

Hotdocs

Web: http://www.hotdocs.ca

Hot Docs Canadian International Documentary Festival is North America's largest documentary festival. Each year, the festival presents a selection of more than 100 cutting-edge documentaries from Canada and around the globe. Through its industry programmes, the Festival also provides a full range of professional development, market and networking opportunities for documentary professionals.

Human Rights Watch International Film Festival

Web: http://www.hrw.org/iff/2007/about.html

Documentary and animated films and videos with a distinctive human rights theme. Each year, the festival's programming committee screens more than 500 films and videos to create a program that represents a range of countries and issues.

Image et Science

Web: http://www.image-science.cnrs.fr

Established in 1988 and organised by CNRS (Centre National de la Recherche Scientifique) the international festival is held each year in Paris. The festival includes awards for international television science programmes.

Images of Black Women Film Festival

Web: http://www.imagesofblackwomen.com

An international festival, held annually in London, which aims to celebrate women of African descent in their roles both on and behind the screen. It includes a competition for the best short film (under fifteen minutes).

Imperial War Museum Student Film Festival

Web: http://london.iwm.org.uk/server/show/ConWebDoc.2310

Since 2000 the IWM has held an annual Student Film Festival. The Festival offers the opportunity to students who have made films and videos incorporating archive film from the Museum's collection or about its subject matter, to have their work screened publicly in the cinema. Each title screened in the Festival is also eligible to be entered into a competition.

International Festival of Ethnographic Film

Web: http://www.raifilmfest.org.uk

Sponsored by the Royal Anthropological Institute since 1985, this biennial festival is an itinerant event, moving from one university host to another. The principal aims of the Festival are: to promote cultural diversity and inter-cultural dialogue through ethnographic film; to screen outstanding recent work in ethnographic film and related documentary genres; to showcase the work of young film-makers in these genres; to explore new trends in these genres and their influence upon one another and on visual anthropology; to provide a marketing platform for both international and British productions.

International Science Film Festival

Web: http://www.caid.gr/isffa/about.html

Established in 2006, the Festival is held in Athens and organised by CAID (the Centre of Applied Industrial Design). The festival is for scientific films aimed at the general public and provides an informal forum in which topical and thought-provoking scientific issues can be discussed with scientists. Seven awards are presented during the festival.

Leeds International Film Festival

Web: http://www.leedsfilm.com

Films are shown in three strands: Official Selection highlights some of the best new films of the year; Cinema Versa – dedicated to inspirational documentary filmmaking and the exploration of unconventional cinema; Fanomenon – screening the best horror, sci-fi, fantasy, anime and action films from around the world. The Festival also includes UK Film Week, retrospectives and archive film. The Leeds Young People's Festival (see below) is incorporated within the Leeds International Film Festival.

Leeds Young People's Film Festival

Web: http://www.leedsfilm.com

Organised and run by Leeds City Council as part of the Leeds International Film Festival, the Leeds Young People's Film Festival features films from around the world that are aimed at young people, as well as a series of workshops and masterclasses to encourage talented young people to get involved in the film industry. Awards are also made in two age categories.

London Film Festival See The Times BFI London Film Festival

London International Animation Festival (LIAF)
Web: http://www.liaf.org.uk
The London International Animation Festival showcases the best of the world's most recent short and feature-length animated films. It includes a strand for student animated films as well as digital animation, abstract animation and animated documentaries.

London International Documentary Festival:
A Conversation in Film
Web: http://www.lidf.co.uk
The LIDF is a new collaboration with the American Museum of Natural History's Margaret Mead Film & Video Festival, covering innovative documentaries (10-120 minutes long) from the UK, Europe and USA, with foyer events, Q & A sessions with the directors and panel discussions with guest speakers and industry professionals.

Munich International Short Film Festival
Web: http://www.muc-intl.de
Founded in 2006, the Munich Short Film Festival film festival is held in June, immediately prior to the main Munich film festival. It showcases the world's best contemporary short films.

Onedotzero
Web: http://www.onedotzero.com/home.php
A global network of film festivals which, since 1996, has been showcasing the best of new digital film and animation. Held each year at the ICA in London, Onedotzero explores new ideas and innovation through curated compilation screenings, features, exhibitions, live audio-visual performances, club nights, presentations and panel discussions from internationally acclaimed artists and creatives.

One World International Human Rights Film Festival
Web: http://www.jedensvet.cz/ow/2007/index_en.php?id=199
An annual international festival, based in Prague, of films on human rights issues, including investigative and activist films. The festival gives awards and includes a discussion forum, as well as having an educational brief to involve Czech schoolchildren and provide teaching materials to accompany the use of the films in schools.

Raindance
Web: http://www.raindance.co.uk/festival
This annual festival held at venues in central London celebrates the best of independent filmmaking worldwide, including feature films, shorts, documentaries and special events. Films have not been previously released in the UK and must be independently produced. Raindance also hosts the British Independent Film Awards.

Real to Réel
Web: http://www.institut-francais.org.uk/realtoreel
As part of France's annual worldwide Documentary Film Month (Le Mois du film documentaire), Ciné Lumière and the Médiathèque of the Institut Français in London have joined forces to present Real to Réel, a week of films and encounters with key documentarists and producers, complemented by a documentary film workshop for students from the NFTS and la FEMIS. The season's aim is to provide an insight into documentary filmmaking on both sides of the Channel and beyond.

Scinema Festival of Science Film

Web: http://www.csiro.au/scinema
An annual international festival celebrating the science and the art of scientific filmmaking. Established in 2000 and originally based in Canberra, the festival is intended to serve as a tool for communication between scientists and the public and forge links between the sciences and the arts.

Screen07

Web: http://www.screenfilmfestival.com
An international student film festival organised each year by the University of Winchester. Categories are Documentary, Drama and Experimental. There is also a Best Film and a Best Director category. The festival is open to schools and colleges across Hampshire as well as national universities and colleges and student filmmakers in Asia, Africa and America.

SEE: The Brighton Documentary Film Festival

Web: http://www.seefestival.org
SEE was founded in 2005 to showcase documentary talent in the south-east of England. It brings together a selection of the UK's most well-respected documentary film-makers to encourage and inspire new work. SEE aims to provide an opportunity for knowledge-transfer from professional film-makers and industry pundits to professional and up-and-coming film-makers.

Sheffield Doc/Fest

Web: https://sheffdocfest.com
The first Sheffield International Documentary Festival was held in 1994. It is the UK's premiere documentary festival. It was launched as a two pronged event – an international film festival and a conference for professionals working in documentary film and television production. It has retained this approach; as well as showcasing around 100 documentaries, the programme offers many opportunities for people working in the documentary field to network, obtain advice and pitch their ideas.

Televisual Intelligent Factual Festival

Web: http://www.televisual.com/festival
Founded in 2006, Televisual's Intelligent Factual Festival is devoted to the best of factual television and looks at the latest trends and the future for the genre. There are seminars, panel discussions, free workshops and master classes providing a hands-on overview of the latest production theories, techniques and technology.

The Times BFI London Film Festival

Web: http://www.lff.org.uk
The Festival, which celebrated its 50th anniversary in 2006, showcases the best new films from around the world. Non-competitive, the LFF was originally conceived as a 'festival of festivals,' screening a selection of films from other European festivals. The Festival's aim is to bring film to the public and offer opportunities for people to see films that have never been screened before in the UK and may not go into distribution.

United Nations Association Film Festival

Web: http://www.unaff.org
An annual festival organised by Stanford University originally conceived to celebrate the fiftieth anniversary of the signing of the Universal Declaration of Human Rights.

Videomed – International Contest of Medical, Health and Telemedicine Cinema

Web: http://videomed.dip-badajoz.es

The festival aims to boost the production of cinema and video relating to medicine and healthcare, with a particular emphasis on new communication techniques, medical imaging and telemedicine. Although based in Badajoz in Spain, Videomed has been held in many different cities over the years.

Wildscreen Festival

Web: http://www.wildscreenfestival.org

The Wildscreen Festival was founded 1982 in association with WWF-UK and is now a biennial fixture held in Bristol. Its aim is to encourage and applaud excellence in the production of moving images about the natural world, and so increase the global viewing public's awareness and understanding of nature and the need to conserve it. The centrepiece of every Wildscreen is the bestowing of its Panda Awards – the wildlife film industry's equivalent of the Hollywood Oscars.

HE ACADEMY SUBJECT CENTRES

The HE Academy was established in 2002, from a merger of the Institute for Learning and Teaching in Higher Education (ILTHE), the Learning and Teaching Support Network (LTSN), and the TQEF National Co-ordination Team (NCT). Its mission is to help institutions, discipline groups and all staff to provide the best possible learning experience for their students. The HE Academy provides discipline-based support through its Subject Network of twenty-four Subject Centres. These are a mix of single-site and consortium-based centres located within relevant subject departments and hosted by higher education institutions. Each centre engages in a wide variety of activities to support practitioners, subject departments and discipline communities.

Art, Design and Media
Art Design Media Subject Centre, University of Brighton, Faculty of Arts & Architecture, 68 Grand Parade, Brighton, East Sussex BN2 9JY
☎ 01273 643119 **Fax:** 01273 643429
E-mail: adm@heacademy.ac.uk Web: http://www.adm.heacademy.ac.uk
Supporting and developing learning and teaching in Art, Design, Media, History of Art and the History of Design in higher education.

Bioscience
The Centre for Bioscience, the Higher Education Academy, Room 9.15, Worsley Building, University of Leeds, Leeds LS2 9JT
☎ 0113 343 3001 **Fax:** 0113 343 5894
E-mail: heabioscience@leeds.ac.uk
Web: http://www.bioscience.heacademy.ac.uk
The Centre for Bioscience is the Subject Centre for the Life, Food, Agricultural and Biomedical Sciences. The Centre provides support for discussion, dissemination and innovation in all aspects of learning, teaching and assessment.

Built Environment
Architecture, Landscape, Planning, Housing & Transport,
Centre for Education in the Built Environment (CEBE), Cardiff University, Bute Building, King Edward VII Avenue, Cardiff CF10 3NB
☎ 029 2087 4600 **Fax:** 029 2087 4601
Construction, Surveying & Real Estate,
University of Salford, Room 436, The School of The Built Environment, Maxwell Building, The Crescent, Salford M5 4WT
☎ 0161 295 5944 **Fax:** 0161 295 5011
Web: http://www.cebe.heacademy.ac.uk
The Centre provides discipline based support to enhance the quality of learning and teaching in the UK Higher Education Built Environment community.

Business, Management, Accountancy and Finance
BMAF, Oxford Brookes University, Business School, Wheatley Campus, Wheatley, Oxford OX33 1HX
☎ 01865 485670 **Fax:** 01865 485830
E-mail: bmaf@brookes.ac.uk Web: http://www.business.heacademy.ac.uk
The Centre aims to enhance the education experience of students by communicating and disseminating ideas and promoting good practice and

innovations in higher education teaching and learning. It acts as a hub of information and resources across academic communities in Business, Management and Accountancy.

Dance, Drama and Music

PALATINE, The Great Hall, Lancaster University, Lancaster LA1 4YW
☎ 01524 592614
E-mail: palatine@lancaster.ac.uk Web: http://www.palatine.ac.uk
PALATINE is the Higher Education Academy Subject Centre for Dance, Drama and Music, established in 2000 to support and enhance learning and teaching in Performing Arts higher education across the UK.

Economics

The Economics Network, ILRT, University of Bristol, 8-10 Berkeley Square, Bristol BS8 1HH
☎ 0117 928 7071 **Fax:** 0117 928 7112
E-mail: econ-network@bristol.ac.uk
Web: http://www.economicsnetwork.ac.uk
The Centre provides a range of services that support university teachers of Economics in the UK.

Education

ESCalate, 35 Berkeley Square, Bristol BS8 1JA
☎ 0117 331 4291 **Fax:** 0117 925 1537
E-mail: heacademy-escalate@bristol.ac.uk Web: http://escalate.ac.uk
The ESCalate partnership includes the universities of Bristol, St Martin's College and Stirling. Together these produce and disseminate resources for staff and students in higher and further education involved in Education Studies, Continuing Education and Lifelong Learning and Initial Teacher Education. The Centre supports and advises on pedagogy, curriculum enhancement across foundation, undergraduate, masters, PhD and EdD programmes.

Engineering

Engineering Subject Centre, Sir David Davies Building, Loughborough University, Leicestershire LE11 3TU
☎ 01509 227 170 **Fax:** 01509 227 172
E-mail: enquiries@engsc.ac.u Web: http://www.engsc.ac.uk
The Engineering Subject Centre's mission is to improve the student learning experience in partnership with the UK engineering community. It is based in the Faculty of Engineering at Loughborough University. It draws upon the expertise of engineering academics and educationalists from across the higher education sector, and works closely with the engineering professional bodies.

English

English Subject Centre, Royal Holloway, University of London, Egham, Surrey TW20 OEX
☎ 01784 443221 **Fax:** 01784 470684
E-mail: esc@rhul.ac.uk Web: http://www.english.heacademy.ac.uk
The English Subject Centre supports the teaching of English Literature, Language and Creative Writing in UK higher education.

Geography, Earth and Environmental Sciences

GEES Subject Centre, Buckland House, University of Plymouth, Drake Circus, Plymouth PL4 8AA

☎ 01752 233530 **Fax:** 01752 233534

E-mail: info@gees.ac.uk Web: http://www.gees.ac.uk

The aim of the Subject Centre is to support and enhance learning and teaching in these three disciplines in UK higher education.

Health Sciences and Practice

Health Sciences & Practice Subject Centre, King's College London, Room 3.12, Waterloo Bridge Wing, Franklin-Wilkins Building, 150 Stamford Street, London SE1 9NN

☎ 020 7848 3141 **Fax:** 020 7848 3130

Web: http://www.health.heacademy.ac.uk

The Centre aims to promote the development of good practices in Health Care through enhancing the quality of learning, teaching and assessment, both in higher education institutions and in practice-based education.

History, Classics and Archaeology

The Subject Centre for History, Classics and Archaeology, University Gardens, University of Glasgow, Glasgow G12 8QQ Scotland

☎ 0141 330 4942 **Fax:** 0141 330 5518

E-mail: hca@gla.ac.uk Web: http://www.hca.heacademy.ac.uk

The Centre aims to provide a comprehensive framework for the support and development of learning and teaching in History, Classics and Archaeology, produce and disseminate resources for staff and students, and advise on pedagogy and curriculum enhancement.

Hospitality, Leisure, Sport and Tourism

Hospitality, Leisure, Sport & Tourism Network (HLST), Oxford Brookes University, Wheatley Campus, Wheatley, Oxford OX33 1HX

☎ 01865 483861

E-mail: hlst@brookes.ac.uk Web: http://www.hlst.heacademy.ac.uk

The Hospitality, Leisure, Sport & Tourism Network aims to encourage and broker the sharing of good learning and teaching practice across these subject areas of UK higher education.

Information and Computer Sciences

Computer Science

Higher Education Academy, Room 16G28, Faculty of Engineering, University of Ulster at Jordanstown, Newtownabbey, Co. Antrim BT37 0QB

☎ 028 90368020 **Fax:** 028 90368206

E-mail: heacademy-ics@ulster.ac.uk

Information Science

Higher Education Academy – ICS, Research School of Informatics, Loughborough University, Hollywell Park, Loughborough, Leicestershire LE11 3TU

☎ 01509 635708

E-mail: j.l.marsh@lboro.ac.uk Web: http://www.ics.heacademy.ac.uk

The primary aim is to enhance the student learning experience in ICS environments. This is done by providing subject-based support to both ICS individuals and departments to promote quality learning and teaching by stimulating the sharing of good practice and innovation.

Languages, Linguistics and Area Studies

Subject Centre for Languages, Linguistics and Area Studies (LLAS), School of Modern Languages, University of Southampton, Highfield, Southampton SO17 1BJ

☎ 023 8059 4814 **Fax:** 023 8059 4815

E-mail: llas@soton.ac.uk Web: http://www.llas.ac.uk

The Centre's mission is to foster world-class education in these subject areas. It does this by supporting stakeholders and helping them to provide the best possible learning experience for students. LLAS is responsive to the needs of its stakeholders and also offers academic leadership in promoting good practice and identifying emerging issues.

Law

UK Centre for Legal Education – UKCLE, University of Warwick, Coventry CV4 7AL

☎ 024 7652 3117 **Fax:** 024 7652 3290

E-mail: ukcle@warwick.ac.uk Web: http://www.ukcle.ac.uk

The UK Centre for Legal Education (UKCLE) supports effective practice in learning, teaching and assessment in Law.

Materials

UK Centre for Materials Education, 2nd Floor, Civil Engineering Tower, University of Liverpool, Liverpool L69 3GQ

☎ 0151 794 5364 **Fax:** 0151 794 4466

E-mail: ukcme@liv.ac.uk Web: http://www.materials.ac.uk

The UKCME supports high quality student learning in Materials Science and related disciplines. It promotes, encourages and coordinates the development and adoption of effective practices in learning, teaching and assessment.

Mathematics, Statistics and Operational Research

Maths, Stats & OR Network (MSOR), School of Mathematics, The University of Birmingham, Edgbaston, Birmingham B15 2TT

☎ 0121 414 7095 **Fax:** 0121 414 3389

E-mail: info@mathstore.ac.uk Web: http://mathstore.ac.uk

Supporting lecturers in Mathematics, Statistics and Operational Research and promoting, disseminating and developing good practice in learning and teaching across the UK.

Medicine, Dentistry and Veterinary Medicine

Higher Education Academy Subject Centre for Medicine, Dentistry and Veterinary Medicine (MEDEV), School of Medical Education Development, Faculty of Medical Sciences, Newcastle University, Newcastle upon Tyne NE2 4HH

☎ 0191 222 5888 **Fax:** 0191 222 5016

E-mail: enquiries@medev.ac.uk Web: http://www.medev.ac.uk

Working together with educators, communities and organisations to promote and enhance student learning in the health-related disciplines.

Philosophical and Religious Studies

The Subject Centre for Philosophical and Religious Studies (PRS), School of Theology and Religious Studies, University of Leeds, Leeds LS2 9JT

☎ 0113 3434184 **Fax:** 0113 3433654

E-mail: enquiries@prs.heacademy.ac.uk Web: http://prs.heacademy.ac.uk

The Centre's mission is to support and promote Philosophical, Theological and Religious Studies higher education in the UK, and to build on its culture of dialogue and reflection.

Physical Sciences

Higher Education Academy Physical Sciences Centre, Department of Chemistry, University of Hull, Hull HU6 7RX

☎/**Fax:** 01482 465418

E-mail: psc@hull.ac.uk Web: http://www.physsci.heacademy.ac.uk

Enhancing the student experience in Chemistry, Physics and Astronomy within the university sector.

Psychology

The Higher Education Academy Psychology Network, Department of Psychology, 1st Floor, Information Centre, Market Square, University of York, York YO10 5NH

☎ 01904 433 154 **Fax:** 01904 433 655

E-mail: psychology@heacademy.ac.uk

Web: http://www.psychology.heacademy.ac.uk

The Centre exists to promote excellence in the learning, teaching and assessment of Psychology across the full range of curricula and activities relevant to UK higher education.

Sociology, Anthropology and Politics

C-SAP, Nuffield Building, The University of Birmingham, Edgbaston, Birmingham B15 2TT

☎ 0121 414 7919 **Fax:** 0121 414 7920

E-mail: enquiries@c-sap.bham.ac.uk Web: http://www.c-sap.bham.ac.uk

C-SAP aims to promote a scholarly and disciplinary-specific approach to the innovation and reform of learning and teaching in the Social Sciences.

Social Policy and Social Work

SWAP HE Academy Subject Centre, School of Social Sciences, University of Southampton, Southampton SO17 1BJ
☎ 023 8059 7782 **Fax:** 023 8059 2779
E-mail: m.locke@swap.ac.uk Web: http://www.swap.ac.uk
SWAP aims to enhance the student learning experience by promoting high quality learning, teaching and assessment and by supporting Social Work and Social Policy educators.

MEDIA LEGISLATION AND REPORTS

This annotated bibliography comprises mainly government publications, but also diverse reports published by industry bodies and independent pressure groups. The documents cited here are those published since the previous edition of the BUFVC Handbook in 2001, and are given in chronological order. Please note that some of the web pages cited will open as PDF (.pdf) documents.

The full text of all legislation enacted by the UK parliament and delegated legislation (Statutory Instruments) is made available free of charge on the web site: http://www.hmso.gov.uk/legislation/uk.htm – simultaneously or at least within twenty-four hours of its publication in printed form. The official revised edition of the primary legislation of the United Kingdom is made available through the UK Statute Law Database at http://www.statutelaw.gov.uk.

2001 *Statutory Instrument 2001 (No. 2378): The Broadcasting (Subtitling) Order 2001*
TSO. ISBN 011029643 5
Web: http://www.opsi.gov.uk/si/si2001/20012378.htm
This Order amends section 20(3)(a) of the Broadcasting Act 1996 to increase from fifty to eighty the percentage in relation to subtitling for the deaf on digital programme services.

2001 *Directive 2001/29/EC: Copyright and Related Rights in the Information Society: Harmonisation of Certain Aspects*
Web: http://europa.eu.int/scadplus/leg/en/lvb/l26053.htm
This Directive aims to adapt legislation on copyright and related rights to technological developments and particularly to the information society. The objective is to transpose at Community level the main international obligations deriving from the two Treaties concerning copyright and related rights, adopted in December 1996 in the framework of the World Intellectual Property Organisation. It covers reproduction rights, right of communication, distribution rights, exemptions and limitations, mandatory exception to the right of reproduction, rights of reproduction and communication, legal protection, protection of rights-managed information, and amendments to existing directives on rental and lending rights.

2001 *Statutory Instrument 2001 (No. 223): The Broadcasting (Limit on the Holding of Licences to Provide Television Multiplex Services) Order 2001*
TSO. ISBN 0110191803
Web: http://www.opsi.gov.uk/si/si2001/20010223.htm
This Order changes the limit, as specified in Paragraph 5 of Part III of Schedule 2 to the Broadcasting Act 1990, on the number of licences to provide television multiplex services which a person may at any time hold, from three to six, and makes consequential changes to other limits placed on the holding of those licences.

2001 *European Convention for the Protection of the Audiovisual Heritage*
Council of Europe (CETS no. 183)
Web: http://conventions.coe.int/Treaty/en/Treaties/Html/183.htm
The aim of this Convention is to ensure the protection of the European audio-visual heritage and its appreciation both as an art form and as a record of our past by means of its collection, its preservation and the availability of

moving image material for cultural, scientific and research purposes, in the public interest.

2002 *Co-production Agreements*
Creative Industries Division of DCMS
Web: http://www.culture.gov.uk/NR/rdonlyres/B8068FD1-9AB8-4943-813D-1318D76A75C2/0/coproductionagreements.pdf
Gives details of the co-production agreements under which films may qualify for benefits available to national films in more than one country.

2002 *Decision no. 676/2002/EC on a Regulatory Framework for Radio Spectrum Policy in European Community (Radio Spectrum Decision)*
Official Journal of the European Communities L108, vol. 45, 24 April 2002
Web: http://eur-lex.europa.eu/LexUriServ/
LexUriServ.do?uri=CELEX:32002D0676:EN:HTML
The aim of this Decision is to establish a policy and legal framework in the Community in order to ensure the coordination of policy approaches and, where appropriate, harmonised conditions with regard to the availability and efficient use of the radio spectrum necessary for the establishment and functioning of the internal market in Community policy areas such as electronic communications, transport and research and development.

2002 *Media Diversity in Europe*
Media Division, Council of Europe
Web: http://www.coe.int/T/E/human_rights/media/
HAPMD%282003%29001_en.pdf
Report covering freedom of expression and information, media ownership regulations, public service broadcasting, new technologies and diversity, trade liberalisation and audio-visual services.

2002 *Communications: Fourth Report of Session 2001-2002: Vol. I – Report and Proceedings of the Committee – Culture Media and Sport Committee*
ISBN 0215003179
Vol. II – Minutes of Evidence and Appendices
ISBN 0215003128
Web: http://www.publications.parliament.uk/pa/cm200102/
cmselect/cmcumeds/539/53902.htm
Report of the committee, chaired by Gerald Kaufman, which preceded the publication of the draft Communications Bill. Published on 1 May 2002.

2002 *Communications: Government Response to the Fourth Report of the Culture, Media and Sport Select Committee Session 2001-2002 (Cm 5554)*
DCMS/DTI. ISBN 0101555423
Web: http://www.culture.gov.uk/NR/rdonlyres/46252C4A-FD22-471D-85D0-7EF4504672E8/0/Communicationsgovtresp.pdf
Presented to Parliament in July 2002.

2002 *Report of the Joint Committee on the Draft Communications Bill*
ISBN 0104130024 (HL Paper 169-I, HC 876-I)
Web: http://www.publications.parliament.uk/pa/jt200102/jtselect/
jtcom/169/16901.htm
The Committee, chaired by Lord Puttnam, published its report on 31 July 2002, making recommendations in relation to the framework for the new regulator; economic regulation; media ownership; and content regulation. The report also contained, as an annex, a report by Peter Kiddle, Specialist Adviser

on Radio and Radio Spectrum Issues in relation to the draft Communications Bill, and minutes of the evidence given to the committee.

2002 *Government's Response to the Report of the Joint Committee on the Draft Communications Bill (Cm 5646)*
DTI/DCMS
Web: http://www.communicationsact.gov.uk/pdf/Joint_cttee_CBill.pdf
Published on 29 October 2002.

2002 *Office of Communications Act 2002*
TSO. ISBN 0105411027
Web: http://www.opsi.gov.uk/acts/acts2002/20020011.htm
Established the Office of Communications (Ofcom) as a body to inherit the duties of the five regulators it was to replace: the Broadcasting Standards Commission (BSC), the Independent Television Commission (ITC), Oftel, the Radio Authority and the Radiocommunications Agency. Published 20 November 2002.

2002 *Copyright, etc. and Trade Marks (Offences and Enforcement) Act 2002*
TSO. ISBN 0105625027
Web: http://www.opsi.gov.uk/acts/acts2002/20020025.htm
This Act extends the criminal provisions in intellectual property law covered by the Copyright, Designs and Patents Act 1988. It details criminal offences in relation to making available for sale or hire copies of material such as music, films and computer software that have been recorded without the authorisation of the copyright owner or person having recording rights to the performance. It also covers devices, including software, that allow access to encrypted transmissions without paying the normal fee e.g. for satellite broadcasts, cable programmes or information services.

2002 *Building a Sustainable UK Film Industry*
Film Council
Web: http://www.ukfilmcouncil.org.uk/usr/ukfcdownloads/102/BaSFI.pdf
Report by Sir Alan Parker, Chairman of the Film Council, presented to the UK film industry in November 2002. A study of the recent history of the industry and discussion of how the Film Council, government and industry should work together to fulfil the industry's creative and industrial potential. Announcement of the plan to build a sustainable and growing UK film industry through investment in the UK's film distribution sector, investment in the production sector's infrastructure and increased investment in the film industry workforce.

2002 *Directive 2002/19/EC of the European Parliament and of the Council on access to, and interconnection of, electronic communications networks and associated facilities (Access Directive)*
Web: http://europa.eu.int/scadplus/leg/en/lvb/l24108i.htm
Intended to harmonise the way in which Member States regulate access to, and interconnection of, electronic communications networks and associated facilities. To establish a regulatory framework for the relationships between suppliers of networks and services that will result in sustainable competition and interoperability of electronic communications services.

2003 *Statutory Instrument 2003 No. 2498: The Copyright and Related Rights Regulations 2003*
TSO. ISBN 011047709X
Web: http://www.opsi.gov.uk/si/si2003/20032498.htm
These Regulations implement Directive 2001/29/EC of the European Parliament and of the Council of 22nd May 2001 on the harmonisation of certain aspects of copyright and related rights in the information society, amending, where necessary, provisions in the Copyright, Designs and Patents Act 1988. It deals specifically with rights of reproduction (copying) and communication to the public (electronic transmission, including digital broadcasting and "on-demand" services). It also limits the type and scope of permitted exceptions to these rights and provides legal protection for technological measures used to safeguard rights and identify and manage copyright material.

2003 *Statutory Instrument 2003 No. 187: The Copyright (Certification of Licensing Scheme for Educational Recording of Broadcasts) (Open University) Order 2003*
TSO. ISBN 0110450027
Web: http://www.opsi.gov.uk/si/si2003/20030187.htm
Sets out terms and conditions for the recording of Open University broadcasts under section 35 of the Copyright, Designs and Patents Act 1988. Supersedes those set out in the Schedule to the Copyright (Certification of Licensing Scheme for Educational Recording of Broadcasts) (Open University Educational Enterprises Limited) Order 1993.

2003 *Statutory Instrument 2003 No. 1672: The Broadcasting (Independent Productions) (Amendment) Order 2003*
TSO. ISBN 0110467175
Web: http://www.opsi.gov.uk/si/si2003/20031672.htm
This Order amends the Broadcasting (Independent Productions) Order 1991 which, together with the provisions of the Broadcasting Act 1990 under which it is made, makes provision as to the proportion of a broadcaster's programmes which are to consist of works created by producers who are independent of broadcasters. This amendment extends the scope of television services to which the 1991 Order applies and modifies the definition of an independent producer.

2003 *Television Content in the Digital Age*
BBC
Web: http://www.bbc.co.uk/info/policies/pdf/ukcontent_digital_age.pdf
An independent report, by Mark Oliver of Oliver & Ohlbaum Associates, commissioned by the BBC. It examines the role of a publicly-funded television broadcaster in supporting high-quality, domestically produced television. It finds that the UK spends more per head on domestic television programmes than any other country in the world. This enables British television to play a prominent role in reflecting and reinforcing our culture and national identity. It concludes that in the past, publicly funded services, in the shape of the BBC, have been a critical factor in sustaining the UK's rich mix of home-grown output. This role will be just as important as competition intensifies in the digital age.

2003 *Communications Act 2003*
TSO. ISBN 0105421030
Web: http://www.opsi.gov.uk/acts/acts2003/20030021.htm
Transferred the functions of the five pre-commencement broadcasting and telecoms regulators to Ofcom, restructuring licensing and regulation across the converging areas of television, radio, telephony and allocation of the radio spectrum. Amongst other measures the Act introduced legal recognition of Community Radio services and lifted many restrictions on cross-media ownership. The web site http://www.communicationsact.gov.uk has links to debates, reports, consultations, government responses, regulatory impact assessments, etc. relating to the passage of the Act.

2003 *Statutory Instrument 2003 No. 3299: The Media Ownership (Local Radio and Appointed News Provider) Order 2003*
TSO. ISBN 0110483677
Web: http://www.opsi.gov.uk/si/si2003/20033299.htm
This Order is made under section 282 of, and Schedule 14 to, the Communications Act 2003 and contains rules and restrictions on local sound broadcasting licenses and services.

2003 *Statutory Instrument 2003 no. 1901: The Advanced Television Services Regulations 2003*
TSO. ISBN 011047189X
Web: http://www.opsi.gov.uk/si/si2003/20031901.htm
These Regulations implement Article 4(2) of Directive 2002/19/EC of the European Parliament on access to, and interconnection of, electronic communications networks and associated facilities and on universal service and users' rights relating to electronic communications networks and services. Digital television has to be transmitted in wide-screen format and all television sets have to be able to descramble the common scrambling algorithm.

2003 *The British Film Industry: HCP 667-I: Sixth Report of Session 2002-03*
TSO. ISBN 0215012798
Web: http://www.publications.parliament.uk/pa/cm200203/cmselect/cmcumeds/667/667.pdf
Culture, Media and Sport Committee report on issues facing the British film industry, including the maintenance of an attractive tax regime; resources, assistance and strategic leadership offered by the UK Film Council; and improvements in training and development. Public policy has a role to play in strengthening the industry in order to generate substantial economic rewards and important cultural benefits.

2003 *The Future of European Regulatory Audiovisual Policy: Communication from the Commission to the Council, the European Parliament, the European Economic and Social Committee and the Committee of the Regions COM(2003) 784*
Web: http://europa.eu.int/scadplus/leg/en/lvb/l24107.htm
In 2003 the European Commission launched a public consultation on the 'Television without Frontiers' (1989) Directive and its possible revision. This Communication presents the main results of the consultation and announces a number of initiatives to be adopted in the short and medium term. The Communication also draws attention to recent developments in the audio-visual field and analyses the different Community policies that affect the sector.

2003 *British Film Industry Government Response to the Select Committee Report on the British Film Industry Session 2002-2003 CM 6022*
TSO. ISBN 0101602227
Web: http://www.culture.gov.uk/NR/rdonlyres/
454EF51B-EC50-4180-911B-24E212B4FAC3/0/907134Cm6022Film.pdf
Department for Culture, Media and Sport reply to 6th report, HCP 667-I, session 2002-03, looking at the first three years of the UK Film Council's work and considering issues including film finance, industry training, intellectual property rights and the threats of piracy.

2003 *Film Council: Improving Access to, and Education about, the Moving Image through the British Film Institute*
TSO. ISBN 021501393X
Web: http://www.nao.gov.uk/publications/nao_reports/02-03/0203593.pdf
Report of the House of Commons Public Accounts Committee, chaired by Leigh Edward, containing formal minutes, oral and written evidence. Considers the relationship between the Film Council and the British Film Institute and addresses the issue of access to the BFI's holdings.

2004 *Broadcasting in Transition*
Culture, Media and Sport Committee
TSO. ISBN 0215015711
Web: http://www.publications.parliament.uk/pa/cm200304/
cmselect/cmcumeds/380/380.pdf
A short inquiry into the implications of the merger of Carlton Communications and Granada for the fulfilment of ITV's public service broadcasting responsibilities including, but not confined to, regional programming and news.

2004 *Hidden Treasures: The UK Audiovisual Archives Strategic Framework*
UK Audiovisual Archives Group/Museum, Libraries and Archives Council
Web: http://www.bufvc.ac.uk/faf/HiddenTreasures.pdf
This document provides a blueprint for the future development of audio-visual archives across the UK. It argues that the lack of a strategic focus for national and regional planning in the audio-visual archives sector has led to insufficient levels of funding and investment for core activities, and a very real concern that a significant amount of the UK's moving image and sound archive heritage could be lost. The document proposes that the national strategic and funding bodies should work with the audio-visual archives to develop a national framework of institutional provision in which national, regional and local responsibilities are respectively understood and well resourced, with the aim of ensuring comprehensive coverage for audio-visual archive activity across the UK.

2004 *Listening to the Past, Speaking to the Future: Report of the Archives Task Force*
Museums, Libraries and Archive Council
Web: http://www.mla.gov.uk/resources/assets//A/atf_report_pdf_6716.pdf
The aim of the Archives Task Force was to carry out an in-depth review and analysis of the state of the UK's archives. The Report recognises the major role that the UK's audio-visual archives play in contributing to the cultural life of the nation. The Report notes the concurrent development of the UK Audio-visual Archives Strategy, and supports the key recommendations of that strategy.

2004 *Statutory Instrument 2004 no. 1944: The Community Radio Order 2004*
TSO. ISBN 0110496051
Web: http://www.opsi.gov.uk/si/si2004/20041944.htm
This Order, made under section 262 of the Communications Act 2003, contains provision to create a special regulatory framework for a new category of radio broadcasting services, to be known as 'community radio services.' The provision includes modifications to the Broadcasting Act 1990 and the 2003 Act.

2004 *Directive 2004/48/EC of the European Parliament and of the Council on the Enforcement of Intellectual Property Rights*
Web: http://europa.eu.int/scadplus/leg/en/lvb/l26057a.htm
This Directive seeks to create equal conditions for the application of intellectual property rights in the Member States by aligning enforcement measures throughout the European Union. It also aims to harmonise Member States' legislation in order to ensure an equivalent level of intellectual property protection in the internal market.

2004 *Ofcom's Decision on the Future Regulation of Broadcast Advertising*
Ofcom
Web: http://www.ofcom.org.uk/consult/condocs/reg_broad_ad/
future_reg_broad/regofbroadadv.pdf
Ofcom's decision, following consultation, to contract out its broadcast advertising regulatory functions to a self-regulator in a co-regulatory partnership.

2004 *Independent Review of the BBC's Digital Radio Services*
Tim Gardam for DCMS
Web: http://www.culture.gov.uk/NR/rdonlyres/
3B853E57-D459-44A3-9247-934B128C1ECC/0/
FullReportIndependentReviewoftheBBCsDigitalRadioServices.pdf
Commissioned by the DCMS and delivered in October 2004 as part of a series of reviews of the BBC's new services. The report follows the Secretary of State's approval for five new digital radio stations: 1Xtra, BBC 6 Music, BBC7, BBC Asian Network and Five Live Sports Extra. The approvals were subject to a number of conditions, one of which was that the services would be reviewed periodically. This report, and its sister review on digital television services, is supported by a market impact assessment conducted by Ofcom. BBC submissions to the review and responses to it are available at: http://www.bbc.co.uk/info/policies/digital_review.shtml.

2004 *Independent Review of the BBC's Digital Television Services*
Patrick Barwise for DCMS
Web: http://www.culture.gov.uk/NR/rdonlyres/2101F101-C5AB-4AC3-82F1-
A39EA6E4F796/0/IndependentReviewoftheBBCsDigitalTelevisionServices.pdf
Commissioned by the DCMS and delivered in October 2004 as part of a series of reviews of the BBC's new services. This report follows the Secretary of State's approval of the BBC's proposals for the re-launch of their digital channels, BBC Choice and BBC Knowledge, as BBC3, BBC4, CBeebies and CBBC. All the approvals were subject to a number of conditions, one of which was that the services would be subject to a review after two years. This report, and its sister review on the BBC's digital radio services, are supported by a market impact assessment conducted by Ofcom. Two supplementary reports, one on BBC3 and BBC4 and the other on CBeebies and CBBC are

also available from: http://www.culture.gov.uk/NR/rdonlyres/6AA15DAC-C2F5-44CA-B506-B4431FB90ADB/0/DCMSreviewofBBCdigitalservices.pdf and: http://www.culture.gov.uk/NR/rdonlyres/6AA15DAC-C2F5-44CA-B506-B4431FB90ADB/0/DCMSreviewofBBCdigitalservices.pdf respectively. BBC submissions to the review and responses to it are available at: http://www.bbc.co.uk/info/policies/digital_review.shtml.

2004 *Progress Towards Achieving Digital Switchover – A BBC Report to the Government*
Web: http://www.culture.gov.uk/Reference_library/Publications/archive_2004/bbc_report_on_digital_switchover.htm
The report discusses availability and coverage of the public service channels; understanding viewers; barriers to adopting digital television; market developments which could drive digital take-up; forecast of digital television take-up; technical challenges and solutions to implementing switchover.

2004 *Assessment of the Market Impact of the BBC's New Digital TV and Radio Services*
Ofcom
Web: http://www.ofcom.org.uk/tv/psb_review/reports/bbcnews.pdf
An analysis by Ofcom, conducted as an input into the independent reviews of the BBC's new digital television and radio services.

2004 *Independent Review of BBC Online*
DCMS
Web: http://www.culture.gov.uk/NR/rdonlyres/45F9953F-CE61-4325-BEA6-400DF9722494/0/BBCOnlinereview.pdf
A review conducted for the DCMS by Philip Graf into the BBC's online services, following the BBC's own review of its online services (August 2003) and a public consultation. Examines the BBC's priorities, performance and plans for the future. BBC submissions to the review and response to it are available at: http://www.bbc.co.uk/info/policies/online_review.shtml.

2004 *Emerging Themes*
Report of the Independent Panel chaired by Lord Burns for the DCMS
Web: http://www.bbccharterreview.org.uk/pdf_documents/041130_emerging_themes.pdf
The report brings together the evidence from the public consultation, seminars and research undertaken between 11 December 2003 and 31 March 2004 for the BBC Charter Review, covering issues such as the clarity of the BBC's public purposes and remit, and how the BBC is funded. These themes were brought together to allow for a debate around their implications for three models of governance and regulation. Following the final seminar Lord Burns sent a document giving final advice from the independent panel, detailing a preferred model of governance. This is available online at: http://www.bbccharterreview.org.uk/publications/in_pubs/pub_final_advice.html.

2004 *Report of the Inquiry into the Circumstances Surrounding the Death of Dr David Kelly (HCP 247)*
Lord Hutton. TSO. ISBN 0102927154
Web: http://www.the-hutton-inquiry.org.uk/content/report
The Hutton Report looks into the death of Dr David Kelly, who was the source for the story broadcast by the BBC TODAY reporter Andrew Gilligan

about claims that the government 'sexed up' its 2002 dossier about Iraqi weapons.

2004 *Audiovisual Archiving: Philosophy and Principles*
Ray Edmondson for UNESCO
Web: http://unesdoc.unesco.org/images/0013/001364/136477e.pdf
An update of the first report on this topic, published in 1998. This revision takes into account the challenge of digitisation and the associated techno-logical changes.

2004 *Proposals for a Co-regulatory System for Training and the Development of Skills in Television and Radio*
Ofcom
Web: http://www.ofcom.org.uk/consult/condocs/train_dev/train_dev/training_tv_radio.pdf
Consultation document on proposals drawn up by Ofcom, radio and tele-vision broadcasters and Skillset. The proposals were adopted, with certain amendments, outlined at:
http://www.ofcom.org.uk/consult/condocs/train_dev/skillsstat.

2004 *A Public BBC*
Culture, Media and Sport Committee. ISBN 0215020960
Web: http://www.publications.parliament.uk/pa/cm200405/cmselect/cmcumeds/82/82i.pdf
The Committee's report on the BBC's Charter review focuses on four inter-related issues: i) the scope and remit of the BBC in the context of the growth of digital television and on-going technological developments in audio-visual communications; ii) its funding mechanism; iii) its governance and regulation; and iv) whether a Charter provides the most appropriate means of estab-lishing the Corporation in a rapidly-changing communications environment. Key aspects considered include the role, definition and scope of public service broadcasting, the growth of multi-channel television, the on-going roll-out of broadband networks, and the Government's plans to switch off the analogue television signal.

2005 *A Strong BBC, Independent of Government*
DCMS
Web: http://www.bbccharterreview.org.uk/have_your_say/green_paper/bbc_cr_greenpaper.pdf
Following the consultation exercise the Green Paper puts forward proposed changes to the BBC's Royal Charter and highlights key areas for further discussion. Further documents relating to the pre- and post-Green Paper research as well as responses to the Green Paper are available online at http://www.bbccharterreview.org.uk/publications/cr_pubs/pub_gp_summaryresponses.html#1.

2005 *Statutory Instrument 2005 No. 222: The Copyright (Certification of Licensing Scheme for Educational Recording of Broadcasts) (Educational Recording Agency Ltd) Order 200*
TSO. ISBN 0110722981
Web: http://www.opsi.gov.uk/si/si2005/20050222.htm
This Order certifies the licensing scheme to be operated by the Educational Recording Agency Limited for the granting of licences to educational establishments for the recording by them of broadcasts, other than television

programmes broadcast on behalf of the Open University, which are the subject of a separate licensing scheme. This supersedes the 1990 Order and subsequent amendments to it. Changes now allow the 'communication' of recordings to students and teachers within the premises of licensed educational establishments. This extended use helps to reflect increased use of computers for access to material stored on school servers and the use of whiteboards for presenting material in classrooms.

2005 *The Economics of Delivering Local Digital Audio-visual and Interactive Services*
Spectrum Strategy Consultants for Ofcom and DCMS
Web: http://www.culture.gov.uk/NR/rdonlyres/C8B7D87A-1AF5-48CD-A62B-E7B85051E272/0/051118PLocaldigitalserviceseconomicanalysis10866final.pdf
A report on the factors affecting the potential development of digital local services including the economics of local services, the likely demand for such services in a digital media environment, and technological and commercial issues, following Ofcom's review of public service television broadcasting.

2005 *Legislative Proposal for an Audiovisual Media Services Directive: Towards a Modern Framework for Audiovisual Content (COM(2005)646final)*
Web: http://europa.eu.int/comm/avpolicy/reg/tvwf/modernisation/proposal_2005/index_en.htm
This proposal to update the EU's 1989 'TV without Frontiers' Directive, to keep pace with rapid technological and market developments in Europe's audio-visual sector, was tabled by the European Commission on 13 December 2005. Separate documents provide an impact assessment and a statistical annex. Supplementary information on the proposal is available at http://europa.eu.int/information_society/newsroom/cf/itemlongdetail.cfm?item_id=2343 and http://europa.eu.int/comm/avpolicy/reg/tvwf/index_en.htm.

2005 *The UK and International Film Co-production Agreeements: A Policy Paper*
DCMS/UK Film Council
Web: http://www.culture.gov.uk/NR/rdonlyres/CA925348-257C-4285-BCB4-CD2A76969C9A/0/int_filmagreement_pp.pdf
A review of the existing co-production treaties that exist between the UK and partners around the world and examination of the scope for new film treaties with other countries.

2005 *The Economic Contribution of the UK Film Industry*
Oxford Educational Forecasting for the UK Film Council/Pinewood Shepperton plc
Web: http://www.ukfilmcouncil.org.uk/usr/ukfcdownloads/117/The%20Economic%20Contribution%20of%20the%20UK%20Film%20Industry.pdf
A report providing a comprehensive evaluation of the economic contribution of the UK film industry. The study's aim was to inform the government consultation on the fiscal support regime for the UK film industry, *The Reform of Film Tax Incentives: Promoting the sustainable production of culturally British films*, published in July 2005.

2005 *The Economic Impact of the UK Screen Industries*
Cambridge Econometrics and Optima for the UK Film Council
Web: http://www.ukfilmcouncil.org.uk/usr/ukfcdownloads/118/The%20Economic%20Impact%20of%20the%20UK%20Screen%20Industries.pdf

The study assessed the size and analysed the economic impact of the screen industries in the UK, separated out by nation and region, focussing on the economic multipliers of the various screen industries.

2005 *The Reform of Film Tax Incentive: Promoting the Sustainable Production of Culturally British Film*
HM Treasury
Web: http://www.hm-treasury.gov.uk./media/624/CA/filmcondocv1.pdf
A consultation document on proposals for a new tax regime to cover incentives for both small and large budget films. It clarifies the core aim of tax reliefs as that of promoting the sustainable production of culturally British films.

2005 *Television Production Sector Review: A Survey of TV Programme Production in the UK*
Ofcom
Web: http://www.ofcom.org.uk/research/tv/tpsr/tpsr_report.pdf
This presentation summarises the key findings of the statistical analysis of the UK television production sector conducted by Ofcom over the period from June to September 2005. The evidence presented was intended to inform Ofcom's development of policy proposals.

2005 *Government Response to the Creative Industries Forum on Intellectual Property*
The Patent Office/DTI, DCMS
Web: http://www.culture.gov.uk/NR/rdonlyres/12017917-F8D5-4CEB-B898-D839BFC90DA7/0/GovernmentResponse_CIF.pdf
Government response to recommendations made by the Creative Industries Forum on Intellectual Property, chaired by Lord Sainsbury and James Purnell. The areas studied by the three working groups were intellectual property crime and online infringements; business opportunities; education and communication. The Forum's recommendations are available online at: http://www.culture.gov.uk/NR/rdonlyres/50C34315-E215-4D06-9FC8-BC0832B5A1DC/0/WorkingGroup_rec_papers.pdf.

2005 *Cultural Test for British Films: Final Framework*
DCMS
Web: http://www.culture.gov.uk/NR/rdonlyres/6D9D9EA2-220E-4ED2-B46A-D39B4FC3476B/0/CulturalTestFilm.pdf
Following a period of consultation, the DCMS produced this amended framework for a test better to identify culturally British films that might be considered eligible for the new tax relief. This test was supported by guidelines that the Department developed with industry input.

2005 *i2010 Digital Libraries Communication (COM 2005) 465 final*
European Commission
Web: http://europa.eu.int/information_society/activities/digital_libraries/doc/communication/en_comm_digital_libraries.pdf
Communication adopted by the Commission addressing the issues of digitisation, on-line accessibility and digital preservation of Europe's cultural and scientific record. A supporting Staff Working Paper gives further background information and the two provide the basis for an online consultation.

2005 *Review of ITV Networking Arrangements*
Ofcom
Web: http://www.ofcom.org.uk/consult/condocs/itv1/main/itv.pdf
The ITV Networking Arrangements are a set of arrangements between the ITV Network and the fifteen regional Channel 3 licensees. They are designed to coordinate the provision of a national television service capable of competing effectively with other broadcasters in the UK. Under the Communications Act Ofcom has a statutory duty to review the working of these arrangements from time to time.

2005 *Planning Options for Digitial Switchover*
Ofcom
Web: http://www.ofcom.org.uk/consult/condocs/pods1/main/pods.pdf
This consultation seeks views on which of the digital terrestrial television (DTT) planning options set out in this document is best suited to the achievement of digital switchover in the UK. Although most households will be able to choose between digital terrestrial, satellite and cable services (and possibly other platforms) for their television viewing after switchover, the migration from analogue terrestrial television and the extension of the DTT network raise particular planning and regulatory issues.

2005 *A Guide to Digital Television and Digital Switchover*
DTI
Web: http://www.digitaltelevision.gov.uk/pdf_documents/publications/ guide_dtvswitchover_june05.pdf
A guide to the benefits of digital television, facts about it and planning for the switchover.

2005 *Radio – Preparing for the Future: Phase 2 Implementing the Framework*
Ofcom
Web: http://www.ofcom.org.uk/consult/condocs/radio_reviewp2/p2.pdf
Consultation document reviewing proposals for the regulatory framework for radio for the years ahead. Follows on from the Phase 1 consultation *Developing a New Framework* (December 2004): http://www.ofcom.org.uk/ consult/condocs/radio_review/radio_review2/radio_review.pdf.

2006 *Statutory Instrument 2006 No. 18: The Performances (Moral Rights, etc.) Regulations 2006*
ISBN 0110739310
Web: http://www.opsi.gov.uk/si/si2006/20060018.htm
These Regulations make the necessary amendments to the Copyright, Designs and Patents Act 1988 to enable the United Kingdom to ratify the WIPO Performers and Phonograms Treaty. These Regulations create two new moral rights for performers of qualifying performances - the right to be identified as the performer and the right to object to derogatory treatment.

2006 *A Public Service for All: The BBC in the Digital Age (Cm 6763)*
TSO. ISBN 0101676328
Web: http://www.bbccharterreview.org.uk/have_your_say/white_paper/ bbc_whitepaper_march06.pdf
A White Paper forming part of the on-going review of the BBC's Royal Charter, due for renewal at the end of 2006. It confirms that the BBC will be overseen by a new Trust that is separate from its management and will actively work to ensure the interests of the public are paramount at all times.

Central to this will be ensuring that the cycle of Charter reviews does not dictate the BBC's approach to its services. The White Paper also sets out in further detail how the BBC will be expected to reach a more consensual relationship with the media industry, providing transparency, certainty and clarity where its activities could have an impact on the wider market.

2006 *Review of the BBC's Royal Charter: Draft Royal Charter and Framework Agreement*
DCMS
Web: http://www.bbccharterreview.org.uk/have_your_say/white_paper/rchter_fwagreeement_mar06.pdf
Published in March 2006 alongside the White Paper, the draft Royal Charter and the Framework Agreement contain all the substantive legal provisions needed to give effect to the policy decisions set out in the White Paper. Neither document is in its final form. Some technical provisions are still to be added, and modifications made in light of debates in parliament and comments received during the consultation process.

2006 *Regulatory Impact Assessment: BBC Charter Review*
Web: http://www.bbccharterreview.org.uk/have_your_say/bbccr_ria_mar06.pdf
Published alongside the White Paper, the Regulatory Impact Assessment (RIA) on the Charter review process looks at the impact - both positive and negative – that the changes the DCMS has proposed for the BBC may have on small businesses, charities and voluntary sector organisations.

2006 *Review of the BBC Value for Money and Efficiency Programmes*
PKF for DCMS
Web: http://www.bbccharterreview.org.uk/pdf_documents/pkfreport_bbcfundin0406.pdf
An independent financial report assessing the BBC's value for money plans, its bid for the next licence fee settlement and its commercial services.

2006 *Response from the Department of Culture Media and Sport to the Communication from the Commission i2010: Digital Libraries*
Web: http://www.culture.gov.uk/NR/rdonlyres/F503F40B-FA5F-4E3E-AAF9-F29183ED396B/0/i2010dcmsresponse.pdf
A response from the DCMS and the DTI to the Commission working document on the establishment of a European Digital Library, following consultation with UK cultural organisations. It raises questions about online accessibility, public-private-funding partnerships, copyright materials, and the priorities for selecting materials for digitisation.

2006 *Review of the Television Production Sector: Consultation Document*
Ofcom
Web: http://www.ofcom.org.uk/consult/condocs/tpsr/tpsr.pdf
A document looking at key aspects of the television production sector, both in-house and external production from independent producers, with the aim of exploring developments in the sector, and how the interests of television viewers are met by the industry. The particular focus is on production quotas, the operation of the commissioning system between producers and broadcasters, and the Codes of Practice.

2006 *Television Access Services: Review of the Code and Guidance*
Ofcom
Web: http://www.ofcom.org.uk/consult/condocs/accessservs
Published online together with a literature review and research study. Ofcom consulted on whether changes should be made to the Code on Television Access Services and associated guidance, which deals with subtitling, audio description and signing on television.

2006 *Bolton Digital Television Trial*
DCMS
Web: http://www.digitaltelevision.gov.uk/pdf_documents/publications/2006/7885BoltonDigital.pdf
The aim of the Bolton Digital TV Trial was to investigate what type of support would be needed at digital switchover by people aged seventy-five and over and the likely cost this would entail. The trial was a partnership between the Government, the BBC and Bolton Metropolitan Borough Council.

2006 *European Charter for the Development and Take Up of Film Online*
European Commission
Web: http://ec.europa.eu/comm/avpolicy/docs/other_actions/film_online_en.pdf
The European Film Online Charter, which was jointly developed under the auspices of the European Commission by major representatives of the film and content industry, Internet service providers and telecom operators from the EU, was endorsed in May 2006. The Charter identifies the preconditions for enabling content and infrastructure providers to make film online services a commercial success. The Charter will serve as reference for future commercial agreements as well as for a broader Content Online policy of the European Commission.

2006 *Gowers Review of Intellectual Property: Call for Evidence*
DTI/DCMS. HM Treasury
Web: http://www.hm-treasury.gov.uk/media/978/9B/gowers_callforevidence230206.pdf
At the Enterprise Conference in December 2005 the Chancellor of the Exchequer announced he was asking Andrew Gowers to lead an independent review to examine the UK's intellectual property framework. The review reported to the Chancellor, the Secretary of State for Trade and Industry and the Secretary of State for Culture, Media and Sport in Autumn 2006.

2006 *Gowers Review of Intellectual Property: Final Report*
DTI/DCMS. HM Treasury. December 2006
Web: http://www.hm-treasury.gov.uk/media/583/91/pbr06_gowers_report_755.pdf
Following the consultation phase, the final report sets out a number of targeted, practical recommendations to deliver a robust intellectual property framework fit for the digital age. The principal recommendations are: tackling IP crime and ensuring that rights are well enforced; reducing the costs and complexity of the system; reforming copyright law to allow individuals and institutions to use content in ways consistent with the digital age.

2006 *Intellectual Property: A Balance*
British Library
Web: http://www.bl.uk/news/pdf/ipmanifesto.pdf

Launched at a fringe event at the Labour Party Conference on 25 September 2006 entitled 'IP: Fee or Free? Public Access Verses Commercial Opportunity in the Digital Age,' the manifesto sets out the British Library's position on the reform of copyright law and intellectual property in the digital age.

2006 *Report into Digital Rights Management*
All Party Parliamentary Internet Group
Web: http://www.apig.org.uk/current-activities/apig-inquiry-into-digital-rights-management/DRMreport.pdf
The inquiry into copy protection technologies received oral evidence and over ninety written submissions from industry groups, consumers and media makers (available at http://www.apig.org.uk/current-activities/apig-inquiry-into-digital-rights-management.html). The report's recommendations include the OFT bringing forward appropriate labelling regulations to make it clear to consumers what they will and will not be able to do with digital content that they purchase and that the Government consider granting a much wider-ranging exemption to the anti-circumvention measures in the 1988 Copyright, Designs and Patents Act for genuine academic research.

2006 *The Provision of Current Affairs – Report on: The Current Affairs Audit 2005, Current Affairs Qualitative Viewer Research and Ofcom's Symposium on the Future of Current Affairs*
Ofcom
Web: http://www.ofcom.org.uk/research/tv/reports/currentaffairs/report.pdf
A summary of a symposium organised by Ofcom on the future of current affairs held in March 2006 and synopses of three pieces of original research conducted by Ofcom to inform debate at the event. These were: an audit of current affairs output on the network public service broadcasters; an audit of the current affairs output in the nations and regions; qualitative research into viewers' attitudes towards current affairs programming.

2006 *Willingness to Pay for the BBC During the Next Charter Period*
The Work Foundation
Web: http://www.theworkfoundation.com/Assets/PDFs/DCMS.pdf
An independent report, commissioned by the Department of Culture, Media and Sport as part of the BBC Charter Review, to analyse the preferences of British citizens regarding the level of the BBC licence fee, and what services would be most valuable to people in the future. The majority of the 7,000 people interviewed would support a sizeable increase on the current licence fee and the report gives their preferred proportions to be spent on BBC television, radio, and online and proposed new activities. Among the corporation's proposed new activities, the four that are favoured most strongly are: new digital and online learning opportunities for 14-18 year olds; the launch of a new free-to-air satellite service; more local news; and improving quality programming.

2006 *Public Innovation: Intellectual Property in a Digital Age*
William Davies and Kay Withers/Institute for Public Policy Research
Web: http://www.ippr.org.uk/publicationsandreports
This report presents an overview of the arguments and evidence that underpin Intellectual Property Rights and the development of IPR policy in the UK and internationally. It calls for copyright laws to be updated and provide a 'private right to copy,' to take account of new ways people listen to music, watch films and read books. It argues that that the idea of all-rights reserved is no longer appropriate for the digital era and the emphasis should be on tackling illegal distribution rather than personal copying.

2006 *BBC Independent Television Commissioning*
Independent report by Deloitte and Touche LLP for BBC Governors
Web: http://www.bbcgovernorsarchive.co.uk/docs/rev_valueformoney.html
Report presented to the BBC Governors' Audit Committee, September 2006 as part of the value for money review.

2006 *Wireless Telegraphy Act 2006 (c.36)*
TSO. ISBN 0 10 543606 2
Web: http://www.opsi.gov.uk/acts/acts2006/20060036.htm
The Wireless Telegraphy Act 2006 brings together into a single statute the legislation under which Ofcom manages the radio spectrum. This replaces six separate Acts of Parliament.

2006 *Legislative Proposal for an Audiovisual Media Directive: Towards a Modern Framework for Audiovisual Content*
European Parliament
Web: http://www.europarl.europa.eu/sides/getDoc.do?pubRef=
-//EP//TEXT+TA+P6-TA-2006-0559+0+DOC+XML+V0//EN&language=EN
Text adopted by the European Parliament after the first reading in December 2006 of a legislative proposal based on a report by Ruth Hieronymi on the modernisation of the audio-visual services directive, particularly with reference to taking into account non-linear (on-demand) services, strengthening the country of origin principle, restriction of advertising, and ensuring pluralism of information in television broadcasting. Further information on the updating of the 'Television without Frontiers' Directive is available at http://ec.europa.eu/comm/avpolicy/reg/tvwf/modernisation/proposal_2005/index_en.htm and http://www.openrightsgroup.org/orgwiki/index.php/TV_Without_Frontiers_Directive.

2006 *Digital PSB – Public Service Broadcasting Post Digital Switchover*
Ofcom
Web: http://www.ofcom.org.uk/tv/psb_review/digitalpsb/digitalpsb.pdf
This document outlines some of Ofcom's developing views with regard to provision of Public Service Broadcasting in UK television in the digital age. The document's primary purpose is to outline the areas of importance for the future provision of PSB and set out where Ofcom will be undertaking further work during 2006-2007.

2006 *Final Report: Study on Co-Regulation Measures in the Media Sector*
Hans-Bredow-Institute and the Institute of European Media Law for the European Commission, Directorate Information Society and Media
Web: http://ec.europa.eu/comm/avpolicy/docs/library/studies/coregul-final-report.pdf
This EU Commission study points the way forward for better regulation of new media and the digital economy. In a rapidly evolving digital world, self- and co-regulatory models can be attractive alternatives to traditional regulations. This study on co-regulation measures in the media sector concluded that, in general, industry needs sufficient incentives to support such a regime. Having a state-run regulator in the background often gives self-regulatory bodies the power they need to work effectively. In addition, sufficient means to enforce regulations, such as adequate and proportional sanctions seem to be necessary for a co-regulatory system to be workable.

2006 *Digital Dividend Review*
Ofcom
Web: http://www.ofcom.org.uk/consult/condocs/ddr/ddrmain.pdf
A document consulting on the proposed approach to the award of the digital dividend spectrum (470-862MHz) to ensure it brings maximum value to society over time.

2007 *Mission Staff Working Document: Media Pluralism in the Member States of the European Union, Sec(2007)32*
Commission of the European Communities
Web: http://ec.europa.eu/information_society/media_taskforce/doc/media_pluralism_swp_en.pdf
This document is the first stage of a three-step approach to be implemented by the European Commission's Task Force for Co-ordination of Media Affairs in advancing debate in response to political concerns about media concentration, and its possible effects on pluralism and freedom of information and expression. The paper includes a concise first survey of Member States' audio-visual and print media markets. The baseline analysis also includes information on national media ownership regulations and the diverse regulatory models of the twenty-seven Member States. This discussion will be followed by an independent study on media pluralism in EU Member States later in 2007, and a Commission Communication on the indicators for media pluralism in the EU member states (in 2008), on which broad public consultation will take place.

2007 *New Approach to Public Service Content in the Digital Media Age: The Potential Role of the Public Service Publisher*
Ofcom
Web: http://ofcom.org.uk/consult/condocs/pspnewapproach/newapproach.pdf

A discussion document further developing Ofcom's initial views on public service broadcasting, following the Creative Forum workshops (see http://www.openmedianetwork.org.uk) and the publication of *Digital PSB* in July 2006. The current document addresses how the delivery of public service purposes and characteristics might need to evolve given the continuing rapid development of digital media. It also describes the role that a new Public Service Publisher might play in the new system.

2007 *Consultation on Revised Ofcom Guidance for Broadcasters on Codes of Practice*
Ofcom
Web: http://www.ofcom.org.uk/consult/condocs/cop/cop.pdf
A consultation published by Ofcom on revised guidance for Public Service Broadcasters (PSBs) in drafting Codes of Practice for commissioning programmes from independent producers.

2007 *Audiovisual Media Services Without Frontiers*
European Parliament and the Council of the European Union
Web: http://ec.europa.eu/information_society/newsroom/cf/
itemdetail.cfm?item_id=3430
After a legislative process of eighteen months, a political agreement was reached on the new 'Audiovisual Media Services without Frontiers' Directive. Both the European Parliament and Council agreed on the main aims of the Commission's original proposal (http://ec.europa.eu/comm/ avpolicy/docs/ reg/modernisation/proposal_2005/avmsd_cons_amend_0307_en.pdf)   to modernise the rules governing the audio-visual services industry. It offers a comprehensive legal framework that covers all audio-visual media services, less detailed and more flexible regulation, and modernised rules on television advertising to better finance audio-visual content. The Directive will allow the audio-visual sector to confront the profound changes it faces to accommodate technological and market developments, and changing viewing habits resulting from convergence. The Directive rules cover all audio-visual media services, regardless of the transmission technology used – from traditional television broadcasts to emerging on-demand television-like services.

2007 *Consultation on the Future of Radio*
Ofcom
Web: http://www.ofcom.org.uk/consult/condocs/futureradio/future.pdf
A consultation on the future of radio that sets out a possible framework for future regulation and licensing of the radio sector. The framework takes into account the ongoing transition of analogue radio listening to digital platforms, including Digital Audio Broadcasting, digital television and the Internet. The consultation focuses on three main areas: the regulation of content and ownership in commercial radio; the regulation of community radio; and the migration of listening from analogue to digital platforms, opening up the possible use of analogue radio spectrum for other services when the time is right.

2007 *BBC High Definition Television Channel Public Value Test*
BBC Trust/Ofcom
Web: http://www.bbc.co.uk/bbctrust/assets/files/pdf/consult/hdtv/
hdtv_service_description.pdf
The BBC Trust decided to apply a Public Value Test (PVT) to the BBC Executive's proposals for a high definition television channel. The PVT

comprises a Public Value Assessment, carried out by the BBC Trust, and a Market Impact Assessment, carried out by Ofcom. The four-week consultation began in May and provisional conclusions are expected in September, with a final decision in November. Further information is available at: http://www.bbc.co.uk/bbctrust/framework/public_value_test/current_proposals.html and from Ofcom at: http://www.ofcom.org.uk/research/tv/bbcmias/hdtv.

2007 *Caring for Our Collections: Culture, Media and Sport Committee, Sixth Report of Session 2006-07*
TSO. ISBN 9780215034649
Web: http://www.publications.parliament.uk/pa/cm200607/cmselect/cmcumeds/176/176i.pdf
Caring for Our Collections (HC 176-I) examines issues of concern in the museums and galleries sector, the archives sector and the audio-visual sector, including funding, with particular reference to the adequacy of budgets and the impact of the London 2012 Olympics on Lottery funding, and acquisition and disposal policies, including due diligence obligations. The report finds that archives of moving images are a significant and valuable part of our cultural heritage, but that they have severe problems relating to funding, the nature of the materials with which they are concerned, and problems specific to the structure (or lack of it) of the UK's audio-visual archive sub-sector.

2007 *Digital Switchover (Disclosure of Information) Act 2007 (c.8)*
TSO. ISBN 978 0 10 540807 X
Web: http://www.opsi.gov.uk/acts/acts2007/20070008.htm
Legislation to allow social security information to be shared with the BBC in order to assist the delivery of the Digital Switchover Help Scheme.

2007 *Strategy for UK Screen Heritage*
UK Film Heritage Group, June 2007
Web: http://www.bfi.org.uk/screenheritage
The British Film Institute is leading a consultation on a strategy for promoting UK Screen Heritage. The strategy has been drafted by the UK Film Heritage Group, which collectively believes the public is entitled to access, learn about and enjoy the UK's rich moving image heritage, wherever they live and wherever the materials are held. This is an important strategy which could have a far-reaching effect on film and television archives in the UK. The strategy document was published in June 2007, with a consultation period to September 2007.

This section offers a selection of organisations within the United Kingdom which are likely to be useful to those interested in audio-visual media in higher education and the work of the BUFVC. Further, comprehensive listings can be found in the Directory of British Associations, or sector-specific publications such as the Guardian Media Guide and the ASLIB Directory. Organisations outside the UK are listed separately.

3WE
143-145 Farringdon Road, London EC1R 3AB
☎ 020 7239 1441 **Fax:** 020 7833 8347
E-mail: mail@ibt.org.uk Web: http://www.ibt.org.uk
3WE is a coalition of international development and environment charities, lobbying for sustained, high quality and imaginative coverage of international subjects on UK television. IBT (International Broadcasting Trust) represents these interests through the programming side, encouraging producers and broadcasters to make the best possible programmes about and in the developing world.

Advertising Association
7th Floor North, Artillery House, 121019 Artillery Row, London SW1P 1RT
☎ 020 7340 1100
E-mail: aa@adassoc.org.uk Web: http://www.adassoc.org.uk
A federation of thirty-one trade bodies and organisations representing the advertising and promotional marketing industries including advertisers, agencies, media and support services.

Advertising Standards Authority (ASA)
2 Torrington Place, London WC1E 7HW
☎ 020 7580 5555 **Fax:** 020 7631 3051
Web: http://www.asa.org.uk
The ASA was set up in 1962 to make sure that non-broadcast advertisements appearing in the UK are legal, decent, honest and truthful. The Authority protects the public by ensuring that the rules in the British Codes of Advertising and Sales Promotion are followed by everyone who prepares and publishes advertisements.

All Party Parliamentary Group on Telecommunications
John Robertson MP, Room 315 Portcullis House, Bridge Street,
London SW1A 2LW
☎ 020 7219 6964
The aim of the Group is to provide a forum for discussion of issues relevant to the UK telecommunications industry and to raise matters with the government, the industry regulators and the industry itself.

All Party Parliamentary Internet Group (APIG)
APIG Secretariat, 23 Palace Street, London SW1E 5HW
Web: http://www.apig.org.uk
APIG exists to provide a discussion forum between new media industries and Parliamentarians for the mutual benefit of both parties. Accordingly, the group considers Internet issues as they affect society informing current parliamentary debate through meetings, informal receptions and reports. The group

is open to all parliamentarians in both the House of Commons and the House of Lords.

Alliance Against IP Theft

167 Wardour Street, London W1F 8WL
☎ 020 7534 0595 **Fax:** 020 7534 0581
E-mail: info@allianceagainstiptheft.co.uk
Web: http://www.allianceagainstiptheft.co.uk
The Alliance provides a single voice for those who share an interest in preventing intellectual property theft in the UK. The Alliance seeks to strengthen and bring consistency to existing laws in the area of intellectual property.

Animation Research Centre (ARC)

Faculty of Arts & Media, Surrey Institute of Art & Design, University College, Falkner Road, Farnham, Surrey GU9 7DS
☎ 01252 892 806 **Fax:** 01252 892 787
E-mail: arcinfo@ucreative.ac.uk Web: http://www.surrart.ac.uk/arc
The ARC aims to promote, contribute to and support the under-researched discipline of animation theory. The aims of the archive are to maintain and expand holdings of UK animation and to develop and produce teaching and other support materials for animation curricula and other disciplines affiliated with international archival institutions.

Art Libraries Society (ARLIS)

18 College Road, Bromsgrove, Worcestershire B60 2NE
☎/**Fax:** 01527 579298
Web: http://www.arlis.org.uk
ARLIS/UK & Ireland is an independent body, founded in 1969, which became an educational charity in 1995. It aims to promote all aspects of the librarianship of the visual arts, including architecture and design.

Arts & Humanities Data Service (AHDS)

King's College London, Library, Strand, London, WC2R 2LS
☎ 020 7848 2935 **Fax:** 020 7848 2939
E-mail: info@ahds.ac.uk Web: http://www.ahds.ac.uk
The AHDS is a national service aiding the discovery, creation and preservation of digital resources in and for research, teaching and learning in the arts and humanities.

Arts & Humanities Research Council (AHRC)

Whitefriars, Lewins Mead, Bristol, BS1 2AE
☎ 0117 987 6500 **Fax:** 0117 987 6544
E-mail: enquiries@ahrc.ac.uk Web: http://www.ahrb.ac.uk
The AHRC funds research and postgraduate study within the UK's higher education institutions. In addition, on behalf of the Higher Education Funding Council for England, it provides funding for museums, galleries and collections that are based in, or attached to, higher education institutions in England.

Arts Council of England

14 Great Peter Street, London SW1P 3NQ
☎ 0845 300 6200 **Fax:** 020 7973 6590
E-mail: enquiries@artscouncil.org.uk Web: http://www.artscouncil.org.uk
The Arts Council of England is the national funding body for the arts in England. It is responsible for developing, sustaining and promoting the arts

through the distribution of public money from central government and revenue generated by the National Lottery.

Arts Council of Northern Ireland

77 Malone Road, Belfast BT9 6AQ
☎ 028 9038 5200 **Fax:** 028 9066 1715
E-mail: info@artscouncil-ni.org Web: http://www.artscouncil-ni.org
The Council distributes government and National Lottery funds for the arts throughout Northern Ireland.

Arts Council of Wales

9 Museum Place, Cardiff CF1 3NX
☎ 029 2037 6500 **Fax:** 029 2022 1447
Web: http://www.artswales.org.uk
The Council distributes government and National Lottery funds for the arts throughout Wales.

Aslib – the Association for Information Management

Staple Hall, Stone House Court, London EC3A 7PB
☎ 020 7903 0000 **Fax:** 020 7903 0011
E-mail: aslib@aslib.co.uk Web: http://www.aslib.co.uk
Aslib actively promotes best practice in the management of information resources, represents its members, and lobbies on all aspects of the management of and legislation concerning information at local, national and international levels.

Associate Parliamentary Media Literacy Group (APMLG)

E-mail: APMLG@ofcom.org.uk
Web: http://www.apmlg.org.uk/index.htm
The Associate Parliamentary Media Literacy Group has been set up to promote a greater understanding of the importance of media literacy within Parliament and more widely.

Association for Database Services in Education & Training (ADSET)

Britannia House, 29 Station Road, Kettering, Northamptonshire NN15 7HJ
Telephone: 01536 410500 or 0779 627 3792
E-mail: info@adset.org.uk Web: http://www.adset.org.uk
ADSET is a membership organisation which seeks to improve the quality, management, use and usefulness of information about learning opportunities, occupations and careers, student and client records, job vacancies, the labour market, and qualifications.

Association for Learning Technology (ALT)

ALT Administration, Gipsy Lane, Headington, Oxford OX3 0BP
☎ 01865 484125 **Fax:** 01865 484165
E-mail: alt@brookes.ac.uk Web: http://www.alt.ac.uk
ALT is the leading UK body bringing together practitioners, researchers, and policy makers in learning technology.

Association for Measurement and Evaluation of Communication (AMEC)

55 Ramsden Road, London SW12 8RA
☎ 0208 675 4442
E-mail: jacquelinemilton@amecorg.com Web: http://www.amecorg.com

AMEC is the global trade body and professional institute for companies and individuals involved in research, measurement and evaluation in editorial media coverage and related communications issues.

Association for the Study of Medical Education (ASME)

12 Queen Street - Edinburgh EH2 1JE
☎ 0131 225 9111 **Fax:** 0131 225 9444
E-mail: info@asme.org.uk Web: http://www.asme.org.uk
The Association seeks to improve the quality of medical education by bringing together individuals and organisations with interests and responsibilities in medical and healthcare education.

Association of Commonwealth Universities (ACU)

Woborn House, 20-24 Tavistock Square, London WC1H 9HF
☎ 020 7380 6700 **Fax:** 020 7387 2655
E-mail: info@acu.ac.uk Web: http://www.acu.ac.uk
The ACU is a voluntary association of over 460 universities throughout the Commonwealth. Its aim is to promote contact and co-operation between member universities; to support the movement of academic staff and students between member universities; to provide information about Commonwealth universities; to host the consultancy, the Commonwealth Higher Education Management Service (CHEMS).

Association of UK Media Librarians (AUKML)

PO Box 14254, London SE1 9WL
E-mail: Chair@aukml.org.uk Web: http://www.aukml.org.uk
AUKML was formed in 1986 to create links between librarians and information workers in all areas of the media industry. AUKML aims to improve the professional standing of information workers through exchanging knowledge and experience and by organising meetings, events and conferences to keep members up-to-date with emerging techniques in information management.

Audiobook Publishing Association (APA)

☎ 07971 280788
E-mail charlotte.mccandlish@ntlworld.com
Web: http://www.theapa.net
The APA is the UK trade association for the audiobook industry with membership open to anyone involved in the publishing of spoken word audio, including those working in BBC radio, cassette and CD duplication, actors' agencies, retail, producers and abridgers.

Audio-Visual Association

Herkomer House, 156 High Street, Bushey, Watford WD2 3DD
☎ 020 8959 5959 **Fax:** 020 8950 7560
The Association is the professional body established to protect and enhance the interests of people – creative, technical, administrative and supply – involved in the non-broadcast sector of the UK audio-visual conference and multimedia industry.

Authors' Licensing and Collecting Society (ALCS)

The Writers' House, 13 Haydon Street, London, EC3N 1DB
☎ 020 7264 5700 **Fax:** 020 7264 5755
E-mail: aclc@acls.co.uk Web: http://www.alcs.co.uk

The ALCS represents the interests of all UK writers and aims to ensure writers are fairly compensated for any works that are copied, broadcast or recorded.

The British Academy
10 Carlton House Terrace, London SW1Y 5AH
☎ 020 7969 5200 **Fax:** 020 7969 5300
E-mail: secretary@britac.ac.uk Web: http://www.britac.ac.uk
The British Academy was established by Royal Charter in 1902, under the full title of The British Academy for the Promotion of Historical, Philosophical and Philological Studies. It is an independent and self-governing fellowship of scholars. It is the national academy for the humanities and the social sciences, the counterpart to the Royal Society which exists to serve the natural sciences.

British Academy of Film & Television Arts (BAFTA)
195 Piccadilly, London W1V 5DE
☎ 020 7734 0022 **Fax:** 020 7734 1792
Web: http://www.bafta.org
BAFTA is the UK's leading organisation promoting and rewarding the best in film, television and interactive media. A membership-led organisation, it runs a wide range of events covering topical issues on all areas, which are open to Academy members and non-members as well. Based in central London, the Academy provides a meeting place for members, as well as being a unique venue which hosts many prestigious events organised through its conference facilities department.

British Advertising Clearance Centre (BACC)
2nd Floor, 4 Roger Street, WC1N 2JX
☎ 0207 339 4700
Web: http://www.bacc.org.uk
The BACC is a specialist body responsible for the pre-transmission examination and clearance of television advertisements. All advertisements being transmitted as a national television campaign on UK terrestrial and satellite channels should be submitted to the BACC for approval. The BACC is funded by commercial broadcasters who pay a quarterly copy clearance fee.

British and Irish Sound Archives Forum
Web: http://www.jiscmail.ac.uk/lists/BISA.html
A British and Irish Sound Archives Forum was established in 2007, following the model of the BUFVC-supported Film Archive Forum. Initial members include the British Library Sound Archive, EMI, and the Wessex Film and Sound Archive. A JISCmail list has been created for the sharing of information among the Forum and those interested in sound archives in the UK.

British Association of Picture Libraries and Agencies (BAPLA)
18 Vine Hill, London EC1R 5DZ
☎ 020 7713 1780, **Fax:** 020 7713 1211
E-mail enquiries@bapla.org.uk Web: http://www.bapla.org.uk
BAPLA is the UK trade association for over 400 picture libraries and agencies in the UK. It is dedicated to fostering the picture library industry through promoting established best practice and standard contracts, providing

information services and representing the industry through marketing and lobbying.

British Board of Film Classification (BBFC)

3 Soho Square, London W1V 6HD
☎ 020 7440 1570 **Fax:** 020 7287 0141
E-mail: contact_the_bbfc@bbfc.co.uk Web: http://www.bbfc.co.uk
The British Board of Film Classification is an independent, non-governmental body, which has classified cinema films since it was set up in 1912, and videos since the passing of the Video Recordings Act in 1984.

British Computer Society (BCS)

First Floor, Block D, North Star House, North Star Avenue,
Swindon, SN2 1FA
☎ 01793 417417 **Fax:** 01793 41744
E-mail: bcshq@hq.bcs.org.uk Web: http://www.bcs.org.uk
Established in 1957, the British Computer Society is the leading body for those working in IT. Its objects are to promote the study and practice of computing and to advance knowledge of and education in IT for the benefit of the public.

British Copyright Council

29-33 Berners Street, London W1T 3AB
☎ 01986 788 122 **Fax:** 01986 788 847
E-mail secretary@britishcopyright.org Web: http://www.britishcopyright.org
The British Copyright Council is an umbrella organisation bringing together organisations which represent those who create or hold rights in literary, dramatic, musical and artistic works and those who perform such works. It functions principally as a liaison committee for its member associations, providing them with a forum for the discussion of matters of copyright interest. It also acts as a pressure group for changes in copyright law at UK, European and International level.

The British Council

10 Spring Gardens, London SW1A 2BN
☎ 0161 957 7755 **Fax:** 0161 957 7762
E-mail: general.enquiries@britishcouncil.org
Web: http://www.britishcouncil.org
Film Department:
☎ 020 7389 3051 **Fax:** 020 7389 3175
E-mail: film.department@britishcouncil.org
Web: http://www.britishcouncil.org/arts-film.htm
The British Council is the United Kingdom's international organisation for educational and cultural relations. The Council's Film Department promotes contemporary and innovative work from the UK to audiences around the world through the British Council's global network.

British Educational Communications & Technology Agency (BECTa)

Milburn Hill Road, Science Park, University of Warwick,
Coventry CV4 7JJ
☎ 024 7641 6994 **Fax:** 024 7641 1418
Web: http://www.becta.org.uk

BECTa leads the national drive to improve learning through technology. It does this by working with industry to ensure the right technology for education is in place. It also supports the education sector to make the best use of technology so that all learners in the UK are able to benefit from its advantages and achieve the best they can.

British Educational Supplies Association (BESA)

20 Beaufort Court, Admirals Way, London E14 9XL

☎ 020 7537 4997 **Fax:** 020 7537 4846

E-mail: besa@besa.org.uk Web: http://www.besanet.org.uk

BESA is a trade association promoting and providing information about its member companies which include manufacturers and distributors of equipment, materials, books, consumables, furniture, technology, ICT hardware and digital content to the education market.

British Federation of Film Societies (BFFS)

Unit 315, The Workstation, 15 Paternoster Row, Sheffield S1 2BX

☎ 0845 6037278

E-mail: info@bffs.org.uk Web: http://www.bffs.org.uk

The BFFS is a national body which promotes voluntary film exhibition and represents the interests of film societies in the United Kingdom. It receives some financial support from the British Film Institute and works with other bodies such as local Arts Boards and the National Lottery Commission to support film societies.

British Film Institute (BFI)

21 Stephen Street, London W1P 2LN

☎ 020 7255 1444

Web: http://www.bfi.org.uk

The BFI promotes understanding and appreciation of Britain's rich film and television heritage and culture. Established in 1933, the BFI runs a range of activities and services: BFI Southbank (previously the National Film Theatre), the BFI IMAX Cinema, BFI Publishing, *The Times* BFI London Film Festival, the London Lesbian and Gay Film Festival, the BFI National Archive, video and DVD releases, film releases, the BFI National Library, BFI Education, and *Sight and Sound* magazine.

British Interactive Multimedia Association (BIMA)

Briarlea House, Southend Road, Billericay CM11 2PR

☎ 01277 658107 **Fax:** 0870 051 7842

E-mail: info@bima.co.uk Web: http://www.bima.co.uk

BIMA is the trade association for the UK's interactive media sector. It provides its members with a forum for the exchange of information and views on the market and promotes the sector to government, industry and education.

British Internet Publishers Alliance (BIPA)

Web: http://www.bipa.co.uk

The core purpose of the Alliance is to promote the growth and development of new Internet services in a way which permits a wide diversity of entrants to the market, on a free and fair competitive basis in order to deliver a wide range of choice for the public and maximise the potential for British enterprise in e-commerce and other areas.

British Kinematograph, Sound & Television Society (BKSTS)
aka **The Moving Image Society**
Pinewood Studios, Iver Heath, Bucks SL0 0NH
☎ 01753 656656 **Fax:** 01753 657016
E-mail: wendy@bksts.com Web: http://www.bksts.com
The BKSTS exists to encourage, sustain, educate, train and represent all those who, creatively or technologically, are involved in the business of providing moving images and associated sound in any form and through any media; to encourage and promote excellence in all aspects of moving image and associated sound technology; to promote these aims throughout the world, while remaining independent of all governments and commercial organisations, to promote these aims throughout the world.

British Library
96 Euston Road, London NW1 2DB
☎ 0870 444 1500
Web: http://www.bl.uk
The British Library is the national library of the United Kingdom.

British Library Sound Archive
96 Euston Road, London NW1 2DB
☎ 020 7412 7676 **Fax:** 020 7412 7441
E-mail: sound-archive@bl.uk Web: http://www.bl.uk/soundarchive
The Sound Archive holds over a million discs, 185,000 tapes, and many other sound and video recordings. The collections come from all over the world and cover the entire range of recorded sound from music, drama and literature, to oral history and wildlife sounds. They range from cylinders made in the late 19th century to the latest CD, DVD and minidisc recordings.

British Literary and Artistic Copyright Association (BLACA)
Web: http://www.blaca.org.uk
BLACA is the UK national group of the International Literary and Artistic Association (ALAI). Since its foundation in 1981 BLACA has provided a forum for discussion of matters affecting the rights of authors and other copyright owners. Its members are mostly practising or academic lawyers and others interested in upholding the principles of copyright.

British Music Rights
British Music House, 26 Berners Street, London W1T 3LR
☎ 020 7306 4446 **Fax:** 020 7306 4449
E-mail: britishmusic@bmr.org Web: http://www.bmr.org
British Music Rights is an umbrella organisation which represents the interests of composers, songwriters and music publishers. Formed in 1996 by the British Academy of Composers & Songwriters, the Music Publishers Association (MPA), the Mechanical-Copyright Protection Society (MCPS) and the Performing Right Society (PRS), it provides a consensus voice promoting the interests of creators and publishers of music at all levels.

British Phonographic Industry (BPI)
Riverside Building, County Hall, Westminster Bridge Road, London SE1 7JA
☎ 020 7803 1300 **Fax:** 020 7803 1310
E-mail: general@bpi.co.uk Web: http://www.bpi.co.uk
The BPI is the British record industry's trade association. Its membership comprises hundreds of music companies including all four 'major' record

companies, associate members such as manufacturers and distributors, and hundreds of independent music companies representing literally thousands of labels.

British Screen Advisory Council (BSAC)
13 Manette Street, London W1D 4AW
☎ 020 7287 1111 **Fax:** 020 7287 1123
E-mail: bsac@bsacouncil.co.uk Web: http://www.bsac.uk.com
The BSAC is an independent, advisory body to government and policy makers at national and European level. It is a source of information and research for the screen media industries. The BSAC provides a unique forum for the audio-visual industry to discuss major issues which affect the industry.

British Universities Film & Video Council (BUFVC)
77 Wells Street, London W1T 3QJ
☎ 020 7393 1500 **Fax:** 020 7393 1555
E-mail: ask@bufvc.ac.uk Web: http://www.bufvc.ac.uk
The British Universities Film & Video Council is a representative body which promotes the production, study and use of moving image, sound and related media in higher education and research. The Council is a related body of the Higher Education Funding Council for England and receives part funding as grant via the Joint Information Systems Committee.

British Video Association (BVA)
167 Great Portland Street, London W1N 5FD
☎ 020 7436 0041 **Fax:** 020 7436 0043
Web: http://www.bva.org.uk
The BVA is the trade body that represents the interests of publishers and rights owners of video home entertainment. It liaises with government, the media, other industry bodies and carries out extensive market research.

Broadband Stakeholder Group (BDG)
Russell Square House, 10-12 Russell Square, London WC1B 5EE
☎ 020 7331 2028 **Fax:** 020 7331 2040
E-mail: camilla.young@intellectuk.org Web: http://www.broadbanduk.org
The Broadband Stakeholder Group is the industry-government forum tackling strategic issues across the converging broadband value chain.

Broadcasters' Audience Research Board (BARB)
E-mail: enquiries@barb.co.uk Web: http://www.barb.co.uk
BARB is responsible for providing estimates of the number of people watching television. This includes which channels and programmes are being watched, at what time, and the type of people who are watching at any one time within the UK. The data is available for reporting nationally and at ITV and BBC regional level and covers all analogue and digital platforms.

Broadcast Journalism Training Council (BJTC)
c/o 18 Miller's Close, Rippingale nr. Bourne, Lincolnshire, PE10 0TH
☎ 01778 440025
E-mail: sec@bjtc.org.uk Web: http://www.bjtc.org.uk
BJTC is a partnership of all the main employers in the UK broadcast industry. It develops training programmes to improve the skills and knowledge across the broadcast journalism industry. It sets the criteria for course accreditation

and then sends teams of professional journalists and tutors to inspect courses and provide advice.

Broadcasting, Entertainment & Cinematograph Technicians Union (BECTU)

373-377 Clapham Road, London SW9 9BT
☎ 020 7346 0900 **Fax:** 020 7346 0901
E-mail: info@bectu.org.uk Web: http://www.bectu.org.uk
BECTU is the independent union for those working in broadcasting, film, theatre, entertainment, leisure, interactive media and allied areas. The union represents permanently employed, contract and freelance workers who are primarily based in the United Kingdom.

Broadcasting Standards Commission See Ofcom

The Broadcasting Trust

Web: http://freespace.virgin.net/local.tv/TV%20Trust%20for%20Scotland.html
Formed in 2004 from the merger of The Television Trust for Scotland and the Association of Scottish Small-scale Broadcasters. The Broadcasting Trust's brief is to focus on all electronic community media developments – radio, television and Internet – and to continue to support training and other initiatives which increase awareness of community broadcasting opportunities.

BUFVC/CBA Committee for Audiovisual Education (CAVE)

c/o BUFVC, 77 Wells Street, London W1T 3QJ
☎ 020 7393 1507 **Fax:** 020 7393 1555
E-mail: cathy@buvc.ac.uk
CAVE exists to promote the use of audio-visual materials in the teaching of archaeology at all levels. Members are drawn from the educational, media and archaeology sectors. CAVE administers the Channel 4 Awards, part of the biennial British Archaeological Awards

Campaign for Digital Rights

Web: http://www.ukcdr.org
The Campaign for Digital Rights campaigns for fair and balanced laws for the information society.

Campaign for Press and Broadcasting Freedom (CPBF)

2nd Floor, Vi & Garner Smith House, 23 Orford Road, Walthamstow, London E17 9NL
☎ 020 8521 5932
E-mail: freepress@cpbf.org.uk Web: http://www.cpbf.org.uk
The Campaign for Press and Broadcasting Freedom is an independent voice for media reform. Since 1979 it has been working for a more accountable, freer and diverse media.

Chartered Institute of Library and Information Professionals (CILIP)

7 Ridgmount Street, London WC1E 7AE
☎ 020 7255 0500 **Fax:** 020 7255 0501
E-mail: info@cilip.org.uk Web: http://www.cilip.org.uk
Provides access to knowledge, information and resources to support members in their continuing professional development. Membership is open to anyone working with knowledge, information or in library services.

CILT – The National Centre for Languages
20 Bedfordbury, London WC2N 4LB
☎ 020 7379 5101 **Fax:** 020 7379 5082
E-mail: info@cilt.org.uk Web: http://www.cilt.org.uk
CILT, the National Centre for Languages, is the Government's recognised centre of expertise on languages. The organisation's mission is to promote a greater capability in languages amongst all sectors of the UK population.

Cimtech
Cimtech Limited, Innovation Centre, University of Hertfordshire, College Lane, Hatfield AL10 9AB
☎ 01707 281060 **Fax:** 01707 281061
E-mail: c.cimtech@herts.ac.uk Web: http://www.cimtech.co.uk
Cimtech is the UK's centre of expertise on all aspects of information management and technology. It was established in 1967 and numbers amongst its members and clients over 1,000 of the UK and Europe's leading organisations in both the public and private sectors.

Cinema Exhibitors Association See **Independent Cinema Office**

Commercial Radio Companies Association See **The Radiocentre**

Commonwealth Broadcasting Association (CBA)
17 Fleet Street, London EC4Y 1AA
☎ 020 7583 5550 **Fax:** 020 7583 5549
E-mail: cba@cba.org.uk Web: http://www.cba.org.uk
The CBA is an association of more than 100 broadcasting organisations in Europe, Asia, Africa, the Caribbean, Australasia, the Pacific, North and South America.

Commonwealth Institute
New Zealand House, 80 Haymarket, London SW1Y 4TQ
☎ 020 7024 9822 **Fax:** 020 7024 9833
E-mail: information@commonwealth-institute.org
Web: http://www.commonwealth-institute.org
The Institute's mission is promoting awareness and knowledge of the Commonwealth. It is an independent statutory body funded by the UK Government, other Commonwealth governments, business partners and through its own activities.

Community Media Association (CMA)
The Workstation, 15 Paternoster Row, Sheffield S1 2BX
☎ 0114 279 5219 **Fax:** 0114 279 8976
E-mail: cma@commedia.org.uk
CMA Scotland:
E-mail: scotland@commedia.org.uk Web: http://www.commedia.org.uk
The Community Media Association is the UK representative body for the Community Media sector and is committed to promoting access to the media for people and communities. It aims to enable people to establish and develop community-based communications media for empowerment, cultural expression, information and entertainment.

Community TV Trust (CTVT)
10 Denman Road, London SE15 5NP
☎ 020 7701 0878
E-mail: chris@communitytrust.org Web: http://www.communitytvtrust.org
CTVT promotes the use of media and new media in local organisations and schools in the belief that self esteem and general personal empowerment come from participating in local media making, and that it also aids cross-cultural understanding in communities. The CTVT provides a forum for debate, as well as supplying information and promoting local initiatives, talent and needs.

Copyright Licensing Agency (CLA)
Saffron House, 6-1- Kirby Street, London EC1N 8TS
☎ 020 7400 3100 **Fax:** 020 7400 3101
E-mail: cla@cla.co.uk Web: http://www.cla.co.uk
The CLA is the UK's Reproduction Rights Organisation and a member of the International Federation of Reproduction Rights Organisations. Formed in 1982, it is a non-profit making company owned by its members, the Authors' Licensing and Collecting Society and the Publishers Licensing Society, to encourage and promote respect for copyright.

Council for British Archaeology (CBA)
St Mary's House, 66 Bootham, York YO30 7BZ
☎ 01904 671417 **Fax:** 01904 671384
E-mail: info@britarch.ac.uk Web: http://www.britarch.ac.uk
The CBA works to improve and promote public interest in and understanding of Britain's past and concerns itself with conservation, information, research, publishing, education and training in archaeology. The CBA Education Department works with the BUFVC on a joint Working Party to review and co-ordinate the listing of films, videos and new media on archaeology suitable for use in education. The CBA also runs, again in conjunction with the BUFVC, the biennial Channel 4 Awards for the best video and television programme on an archaeological subject.

Cyfle
33-35 West Bute Street, Cardiff CF10 5LH
☎ 029 2046 5533 **Fax:** 029 2046 3344
E-mail: Cyfle@cyfle.co.uk Web: http://www.cyfle.co.uk
Cyfle is the training company for the Welsh television, film and interactive media industry. The organisation was originally formed in order to train Welsh-speaking technicians for the television industry which formed as a result of the creation of S4C. In 2000 the Company became a Skillset (Sector Skills Council) accredited Training Partner and a national provider for the industry across Wales.

Department for Children, Schools and Families (DCSF)
Sanctuary Buildings, Great Smith Street, London SW1P 3BT
☎ 0870 000 2288 **Fax:** 01928 794248
E-mail: info@dfes.gsi.gov.uk Web: http://www.dfes.gov.uk
The Department for Children, Schools and Families (DCSF) is respon-sible for improving the focus on all aspects of policy affecting children and young people, as part of the Government's aim to deliver educational excellence.

Department for Innovation, Universities and Skills (DIUS)
☎ 020 7215 5555 or 01928 794666

Web: http://www.dius.gov.uk

This new Department brings together functions from the former Department of Trade and Industry, including responsibilities for science and innovation, with further and higher education and skills, previously part of the Department for Education and Skills. The Department will bring together the nation's strengths in science, research, universities and colleges to build a dynamic, knowledge-based economy.

Department of Culture, Media and Sport (DCMS)
2-4 Cockspur Street, London SW1Y 5D

☎ 020 7211 6200

E-mail: enquiries@culture.gov.uk Web: http://www.culture.gov.uk

The DCMS is responsible for Government policy on the arts, sport, the National Lottery, tourism, libraries, museums and galleries, broadcasting, creative industries including film and the music industry, press freedom and regulation, licensing, gambling and the historic environment.

Design and Artists Copyright Society (DACS)
33 Great Sutton Street, London EC1V 0DX

☎ 020 7336 8811 **Fax:** 020 7336 8822

Web: http://www.dacs.org.uk

DACS is the UK's copyright and collecting society for artists and visual creators. It exists to promote and protect the copyright and related rights of artists and visual creators.

Digital Content Forum (DCF)
c/o ELSPA, 167 Wardour Street, London W1F 8WL

☎ 020 7534 0589

E-mail: info@dcf.org.uk Web: http://www.dcf.org.uk

The DCF works in an advisory and collaborative capacity with government departments in delivering policy and strategy for the digital content sector. The DCF collaborates with groups such as the Broadband Stakeholders Group, the Information Age Partnership and HMSO's Crown Copyright Advisory Panel, and actively engages with government consultations, UK and EU legislation and its implementation.

Digital Curation Centre
University of Edinburgh, Appleton Tower, Crichton Street, Edinburgh EH8 9LE

☎ 0131 651 1239

E-mail: info@dcc.ac.uk Web: http://www.dcc.ac.uk

Funded by the JISC and the e-Science core programme, the Digital Curation Centre advises scientists, researchers and scholars at UK institutions on the storage, management and preservation of digital data, to help ensure their enhancement and continuing long-term use. Advice is offered on creating adequate documentation for the data, and dealing with problems of technology obsolescence and the fragility of digital media.

Digital Preservation Coalition
Innovation Centre, York Science Park, Heslington, York YO10 5DG

☎ 01904 435362

E-mail: info@dpconline.org Web: http://www.dpconline.org

The Digital Preservation Coalition was established in 2001 to foster joint action to address the urgent challenges of securing the preservation of digital resources in the UK and to work with others internationally to secure our global digital memory and knowledge base.

Digital Television Group (DTG)

c/o Babel PR, 5th Floor, 39-45 Shaftesbury Avenue,
London W1D 6AB
☎ 020 7434 5550
E-mail: office@dtg.org.uk Web: http://www.dtg.org.uk
The Digital Television Group is the industry association for digital television in the UK. The group is currently focussed on digital switchover and the rich media services and products it will help enable. Emerging consumer devices and experiences include high definition television, mobile television, video-on-demand, broadband television and television metadata.

Directors' and Producers' Rights Society (DPRS)

20-22 Bedford Row, London WC1R 4EB
☎ 020 7269 0677 **Fax:** 020 7269 0676
E-mail: info@dprs.org Web: http://www.dprs.org
The DPRS is the collecting society which represents British film and television directors. It collects and distributes money due to directors for the exploitation of their work. The Society is also a campaigning organisation, working to establish and protect directors' rights in the UK and abroad.

Directors Guild of Great Britain (DGGB)

4 Windmill Street, London W1 2TZ
☎ 020 7580 9131 **Fax:** 020 7580 9132
E-mail: guild@dggb.org Web: http://www.dggb.co.uk
The DGGB is an organisation representing directors in all media: film, television, theatre, radio, opera, commercials, corporate, multimedia and new technology.

DocHouse

Crisp Road, Hammersmith, London W6 9RL
☎ 020 8237 1220 **Fax:** 020 8237 1001
E-mail: info@dochouse.org Web: http://www.dochouse.org
DocHouse was formed to support and promote documentary in the UK. It aims to increase participation and develop new audiences for documentaries in the cinema, on television and emerging media; create faster and easier access to UK and international documentary; promote the use of documentary through education at all levels; and nurture and encourage new talent for the future.

DocSpace

Scottish Documentary Institute, 74 Lauriston Place, Edinburgh EH3 9DF
☎ 0131 221 6245/6125
E-mail: info@docspace.org.uk Web: http://www.docspace.org.uk
Docspace brings the power and art of documentary into the spotlight, forging partnerships with venues and digital technology. It works in the public domain, introducing new audiences to documentaries. It carries out research on audiences, and hosts master classes with feature documentary directors.

Documentary Filmmakers Group (DFG)

4th Floor, Shacklewell Studios, 28 Shacklewell Lane, London E8 2EZ
☎ 020 7249 6600
E-mail: info@dfgdocs.com Web: http://www.dfgdocs.com

DFG, founded in 2001, is an organisation providing a comprehensive resource for documentary filming. Its aim is to encourage, stimulate, promote and support the growth of a strong community of documentary filmmakers and film audiences. DFG's work falls into three main strands: training, the running of screenings, festivals and forums, and production.

EDINA

Causewayside House, 160 Causewayside, Edinburgh EH9 1PR
☎ 0131 650 3302 **Fax:** 0131 650 3308
E-mail: edina@ed.ac.uk Web: http://edina.ac.uk

EDINA, based at Edinburgh University Data Library, is one of the two JISC-funded national data centres. It offers the UK tertiary education and research community networked access to a library of data, information and research resources.

Educational Broadcasting Services Trust (EBS Trust)

12 Printing House Yard, Hackney Road, London E2 7PR
☎ 08450 523948
Web: http://www.ebst.co.uk

The EBS Trust is an independent trust company dedicated to the development of education at all levels using electronic technologies, principally those traditionally associated with broadcasting. The web site is undergoing significant restructuring in 2007 and will re-launch as ebs online.

Educational Recording Agency (ERA)

New Premier House, 150 Southampton Row, London WC1B 5AL
☎ 020 7837 3222 **Fax:** 020 7837 3750
E-mail: era@era.org.uk Web: http://www.era.org.uk

On behalf of its members, ERA operates a Licensing Scheme for educational use of copyright material. The scheme permits staff at educational establishments to record, for non-commercial educational purposes, broadcast output of ERA's members. Most educational establishments in the UK are covered by an ERA licence.

Entertainment Retailers Association (ERA)

Colonnade House, 1st Floor, 2 Westover Road, Bournemouth,
Dorset BH1 2BY
☎ 01202 292063 **Fax:** 01202 292067
E-mail: admin@eraltd.org Web: http://www.bardltd.org

The ERA is a UK trade organisation formed specifically to act as a forum for the retail and wholesale sectors of the music, video, DVD and multimedia products industry.

Equity

Guild House, Upper St Martins Lane, London WC2H 9EG
☎ 020 7379 6000 **Fax:** 020 7379 7001
Web: http://www.equity.org.uk

Equity is a trade union representing artists from across the entire spectrum of arts and entertainment including actors, singers, dancers, choreographers, stage managers, theatre directors and designers, variety and circus artists, television and radio presenters, walk-on and supporting artists, stunt performers and directors and theatre fight directors.

ESDS Qualidata

Economic and Social Data Service, UK Data Archive, University of Essex, Wivenhoe Park, Colchester, Essex CO4 3SQ

☎ 01206 873058 **Fax:** 01206 872003

E-mail: qualidata@esds.ac.uk Web: http://www.qualidata.essex.ac.uk

ESDS Qualidata is a specialist service of the ESDS led by the UK Data Archive at the University of Essex. The service provides access and support for a range of social science qualitative datasets, promoting and facilitating increased and more effective use of data in research, learning and teaching.

Federation Against Copyright Theft (FACT)

7 Victory Business Centre, Worton Road, Isleworth,
Middlesex TW7 6DB

☎ 020 8568 6646 **Fax:** 020 8560 6364

FACT is an investigative organisation funded by its members to combat video counterfeiting. It is a non-profit making organisation limited by guarantee.

Federation Against Software Theft (FAST)

1 Kingfisher Court, Farnham Road, Slough, Berkshire SL2 1JF

☎ 01753 527999 **Fax:** 01753 532100

E-mail: fast@fast.org Web: http://www.fast.org.uk

FAST was created in 1984 by the software industry to lobby parliament for changes to the copyright law. It works on behalf of the software industry, and addresses the misuse, overuse and theft of software intellectual property.

Federation of Commercial Audio-Visual Libraries (FOCAL)

Pentax House, South Hill Avenue, Northolt Road, South Harrow,
Middlesex HA2 0DU

☎ 020 8423 5853 **Fax:** 020 8933 4826

E-mail: info@focalint.org Web: http://www.focalint.org

FOCAL was formed in 1985 as an international, non-profit making, professional trade association limited by guarantee. It represents commercial film/audio-visual, stills and sound libraries as well as interested individuals such as facility houses, professional film researchers and producers working in the industry.

Film Archive Forum (FAF)

c/o Marion Hewitt (secretary), North West Film Archive,
Manchester Metropolitan University, Minshull House,
47-49 Chorlton Street, Manchester M1 3EU

Web: http://www.bufvc.ac.uk/faf

Established in 1987, the Film Archive Forum represents all of the public sector film and television archives which care for the UK's moving image heritage. It represents the UK's public sector moving image archives in all archival aspects of the moving image, and acts as the advisory body on national moving image archive policy.

Film Council See **UK Film Council**

Film Distributors' Association
22 Golden Square, London W1F 9JW
☎ 020 7437 4383 **Fax:** 020 7734 0912
E-mail: info@fda.uk.net Web: http://www.launchingfilms.com
FDA is the trade body for theatrical film distributors in the UK. Originally established in London in 1915, FDA liaises and works with many individuals, companies and organisations. FDA's Council, or board, comprising a senior representative of each member company, normally meets six times a year and considers only matters of generic interest to film distributors.

Film Education
21-22 Poland Street, London W1F 8QQ
☎ 020 7851 9450 **Fax:** 020 7439 3218
E-mail: postbox@filmeducation.org Web: http://www.filmeducation.org
Film Education is a registered charity funded by the film industry in the UK. Its aim is to encourage and promote the use of film and cinema within the National Curriculum.

Film London
Suite 6.10, The Tea Building, 56 Shoreditch High Street, London E1 6JJ
☎ 020 7613 7676 **Fax:** 020 7613 7677
E-mail: info@filmlondon.org.uk Web: http://www.filmlondon.org.uk
Film London is the capital's film and media agency. It supports the growth and development of all the screen industries based in the capital - film, television, video, commercials and new interactive media. Its aim is to sustain, promote and develop London as a major international film-making and film cultural capital.

Foundation for Information Policy Research (FIPR)

10 Water End, Wrestlingworth, Sandy, Bedfordshire SG19 2HA
☎ 01223 334733
E-mail: chair2006@fipr.org Web: http://www.fipr.org
The FIPR is the leading think tank for Internet policy in Britain. It studies the interaction between IT, Government, business and civil society. It researches policy implications and alternatives, and promotes better understanding and dialogue between business, Government and NGOs across Europe.

Free Culture UK

Web: http://www.freeculture.org.uk
Free Culture UK is a grassroots movement with an online network and locally-based groups of members working for an open, participatory culture, believing that individuals and communities should be empowered to be creative, and that this can be done by legal, social and political means by defending and promoting cultural spaces such as Free Software, Creative Commons and the public domain.

Grierson Trust

c/o Ivan Sopher & Co, 5 Elstree Gate, Elstree Way, Borehamwood, Hertfordshire WD6 1JD
Web: http://www.griersontrust.org
The Grierson Trust commemorates the pioneering Scottish documentary maker John Grierson and the man widely regarded as the father of the documentary. Each year the Trust recognises the best documentary filmmaking from Britain and abroad through the Grierson Awards. Throughout the year the Grierson Trust organises and collaborates in activities for the promotion and celebration of the best in documentary film and television production.

Incorporated Society of Musicians (ISM)

10 Stratford Place, London W1C 1AA
☎ 020 7629 4413 **Fax:** 020 7408 1538
E-mail: membership@ism.org Web: http://www.ism.org
The UK's professional body for musicians. The ISM promotes the art of music and the interests of professional musicians and aims to raise standards in the profession and give its members the best available advice on issues ranging from education to ethics, and from intellectual property to broadcasting.

Independent Cinema Office

3rd Floor, Kenilworth House, 79-80 Margaret Street, London W1W 8TA
☎ 020 7636 7120 **Fax:** 020 7636 7121
E-mail: info@independentcinemaoffice.org.uk
Web: http://www.independentcinemaoffice.org.uk
The Independent Cinema Office is a national organisation that aims to develop and support independent film exhibition throughout the UK. It works in association with independent cinemas, film festivals, film societies and the regional and national screen agencies.

Independent Film Parliament

Web: http://www.filmparliament.org.uk
Launched in July 2003, the IFP offers an opportunity for those involved in the production, distribution and exhibition of independent films to share ideas on structures and policy in an open, public forum.

Independent Television Commission See **Ofcom**

Industry Trust for IP Awareness
☎ 020 7079 6230
E-mail: info@piracyisacrime.co.uk Web: http://www.piracyisacrime.co.uk
In 2004 the major DVD distributors joined forces with retail and rental
outlets in the UK and formed the Industry Trust for IP Awareness to combat
DVD piracy.

Institute for Public Policy Research (IPPR)
30-32 Southampton Street, London WC2E 7RA
☎ 020 7470 6100 **Fax:** 020 7470 6111
Web: http://www.ippr.org.uk
The UK's leading progressive think tank, producing cutting edge research and
innovative policy ideas for a just, democratic and sustainable world.

Institute of Medical Illustrators (IMI)
29 Arboretum Street, Nottingham, NG1 4JA
☎ 020 7731 7962
Web: http://www.imi.org.uk
Founded in 1968 to bring together the several disciplines of medical
illustration, for over thirty years IMI has set and maintained standards for the
profession. For its membership, IMI provides a rich network of fellow
professionals, working together to improve and develop medical illustration
by means of conferences, courses and regional meetings.

Institute of Practitioners in Advertising (IPA)
44 Belgrave Square, London SW1X 8QS
☎ 020 7235 7020 **Fax:** 020 7245 9904
E-mail: info@ipa.co.uk Web: http://www.ipa.co.uk
The IPA is the industry body and professional institute for leading advertising,
media and marketing communications agencies in the UK.

International Broadcasting Trust See **3WE**

International Visual Communications Association (IVCA)
19 Pepper Street, Glengall Bridge, Docklands, London E14 9RP
☎ 020 7512 0571 **Fax:** 020 7512 0591
E-mail: info@ivca.org Web: http://www.ivca.org
The IVCA exists to promote effective business and public service communications of the highest ethical and professional standards. It aims to be a
centre of excellence for best communication practice and works with
production companies, freelancers, support service providers and clients of
the industry to represent their interests and help maximise their competitiveness and professionalism.

Internet Services Providers Association (ISPA)
28 Broadway, London SW1H 9JX
☎ 0870 050 0710 **Fax:** 0870 033 7205
E-mail: admin@ispa.org.uk Web: http://www.ispa.org.uk
ISPA UK is the UK's Trade Association for providers of Internet services. It
was established in 1995 and promotes competition, self-regulation and the
development of the Internet industry.

JANET UK

Lumen House, Library Avenue, Harwell Science and Innovation Campus, Didcot, Oxfordshire OX11 0SG
☎ 01235 822200 **Fax:** 01235 822399
Web: http://www.ja.net
JANET is the network dedicated to the needs of education and research in the UK. It connects the UK's education and research organisations to each other, as well as to the rest of the world through links to the global Internet. In addition, JANET includes a separate network that is available to the community for experimental activities in network development. Formerly known as UKERNA.

Joint Information Systems Committee (JISC)

JISC Secretariat, Northavon House, Coldharbour Lane, Bristol BS16 1QD
☎ 0117 931 7403 **Fax:** 0117 931 7255
E-mail: info@jisc.ac.uk Web: http://www.jisc.ac.uk
JISC's activities support education and research by promoting innovation in new technologies and by the central support of ICT services.

Kraszna-Krausz Foundation

c/o Angela English, 3 Downscourt Road, Purley, Surrey CR8 1BE
E-mail: info@k-k.org.uk Web: http://www.editor.net/k-k
The Kraszna-Krausz Awards, sponsored by the Kraszna-Krausz Foundation, are made annually, with prizes for books on still photography alternating with those for books on the moving image. Entries in each year cover books published in the previous two years. The winning books are those which make original and lasting educational, professional, historical, technical, scientific, social, literary or cultural contributions to the field.

Lecture Theatre Managers Group

Web: http://ltsmg.org.uk
The group consists of managers, technical supervisors and senior technicians within higher education. Responsible for managing and delivering audio visual facilities and equipment within lecture theatres and teaching space throughout higher education.

Libraries and Archives Copyright Alliance (LACA)

c/o CILIP, 7 Ridgmount Street, London WC1E 7AE
☎ 020 7255 0500 **Fax:** 020 7255 0501
E-mail: info@cilip.org.uk
Web: http://www.cilip.org.uk/professionalguidance/copyright
LACA monitors and lobbies in the UK and Europe about copyright and related rights on behalf of its member organisations and all users of copyright works through library, archive and information services.

MCPS-PRS Alliance

Copyright House, 29-33 Berners St, London W1T 3AB
☎ 020 7580 5544 **Fax:** 020 7306 4455
Web: http://www.mcps-prs-alliance.co.uk
Formed in 1997 by two royalty collection societies (MCPS and PRS), the MCPS-PRS Alliance exists to collect and pay royalties to its members when their music is recorded and made available to the public (MCPS); and when their music is performed, broadcast or otherwise made publicly available (PRS).

Media, Communication & Cultural Studies Association (MeCCSA)

Web: http://www.meccsa.org.uk

MeCCSA is the subject association for the field of media, communication and cultural studies in UK Higher education. Membership is open to all who teach and research these subjects in HE institutions, via either institutional or individual membership. The field includes film and television production, journalism, radio, photography, creative writing, publishing, interactive media and the web; and it includes higher education for media practice as well as for media studies.

Media Education Association (MEA)

c/o 2nd Floor, 21-22 Poland Street, London W1F 8QQ
E-mail: info@mediaedassociation.org.uk
Web: http://www.mediaedassociation.org.uk

Founded in June 2006 to provide media teachers in England and Wales with their own professional association to support media teachers, promote media literacy and work to raise the status of media education.

Media Literacy Task Force

☎ 020 8305 8006
E-mail: info@medialiteracy.org.uk Web: http://www.medialiteracy.org

The Media Literacy Task Force is an informal grouping of stakeholders, set up and supported by the Secretary of State for Culture, Media and Sport, which exists to help bring strategic cohesion to the development of media literacy in the UK. The founding members of the Media Literacy Task Force are the UK Film Council and Channel 4, the British Film Institute, the BBC and Skillset.

Media March

PO Box 244, Malvern WR14 9AT
☎ 020 8467 6452
Web: http://www.mediamarch.org.uk

A multi-faith protest movement, founded in 1999, to campaign for a strengthening of the country's obscenity laws, particularly through the organisation of marches. They fear the 'moral meltdown' in the media, particularly in broadcasting and on the Internet, is having a destructive influence and is contributing substantially to the breakdown of marriage and family life in the UK and to the increase in violent and sexual crime.

Media Society

Administrator, Dorothy Josem, Flat 1, 24 Park Road, London NW1 4SH
E-mail: Dorothy@themediasociety.co.uk
Web: http://www.themediasociety.co.uk

The Media Society stands for freedom of expression and the encouragement of high standards in journalism. The Society holds meetings and receptions through the year to discuss topics of current interest to its members, such as communications legislation, privacy and the press, the future of public service broadcasting, political reporting and the development of digital services.

Media Trust

3-7 Euston Centre, Regent's Place, London NW1 3JG
☎ 020 7874 7600 **Fax:** 020 7874 7644
E-mail: information@mediatrust.org Web: http://www.mediatrust.org

Media Trust's aim is to help charities communicate by providing an advice service, training courses on media production, and volunteering opportunities for media professionals.

mediawatch-UK

3 Willow House, Kennington Road, Ashford, Kent TN24 0NR
☎ 01233 633936
E-mail: info@mediawatchuk.org Web: http://www.mediawatchuk.org
Launched in 2002, mediawatch-UK is the successor to the National Viewers and Listeners Association, which was founded by Mary Whitehouse in 1965 with the purpose of putting pressure on the broadcasting authorities to improve their public accountability and to explain their policies on standards of taste and decency.

Mental Health Media

356 Holloway Road, London N7 6PA
☎ 020 7700 8171 **Fax:** 0171 686 0959
E-mail: info@mhmedia.com Web: http://www.mhmedia.com
The aim of Mental Health Media is to bring together media and the fields of mental health and learning difficulties to challenge discrimination. It works to help journalists print and broadcast the voices of people who have experienced mental health problems. Through video journalism training it helps people with learning difficulties record their own stories, wishes and demands.

MIMAS

Manchester Computing, Kilburn Building, University of Manchester, Oxford Road, Manchester M13 9PL
☎ 0161 275 6109
E-mail: info@mimas.ac.uk Web: http://www.mimas.ac.uk
MIMAS is a JISC- and ESRC-supported national data centre providing the UK higher education, further education and research community with networked access to key data and information resources to support teaching, learning and research across a wide range of disciplines. MIMAS also offers specialist support and training, and data sharing and gateway services.

Moving Image Society See **British Kinematograph, Sound & Television Society**

Museums, Libraries and Archives Council (MLA)

Victoria House, Southampton Row, London WC1B 4EA
☎ 020 7273 1444 **Fax:** 020 7273 1404
E-mail: info@mla.gov.uk Web: http://www.mla.gov.uk
MLA is the lead strategic agency for museums, libraries and archives. It is part of the wider MLA Partnership, working with the nine regional agencies to improve people's lives by building knowledge, supporting learning, inspiring creativity and celebrating identity.

Music Publishers Association (MPA)

6th Floor British Music House, 26 Berners Street, London W1T 5LR
☎ 020 7580 0126 **Fax:** 020 7637 3929
E-mail: info@mpaonline.org.uk Web: http://www.mpaonline.org.uk
The MPA looks after the interests of all music publishers based or working in the UK and exists to safeguard and improve the business and legal environment within which its members operate.

Musicians Union
National Office, 60-62 Clapham Road, London SW9 0JJ
☎ 020 7582 5566 **Fax:** 020 7582 9805
E-mail: info@musiciansunion.org.uk Web: http://www.musiciansunion.org.uk
The trade union for musicians in the UK.

The National Archives (TNA)
Kew, Richmond, Surrey, TW9 4DU
☎ 020 8876 3444
Web: http://www.nationalarchives.gov.uk
The National Archives is at the heart of information policy – setting standards and supporting innovation in information and records management across the UK, and providing a practical framework of best practice for opening up and encouraging the re-use of public sector information. The National Archives is also the UK government's official archive.

National Computing Centre (NCC)
Oxford House, Oxford Road, Manchester M1 7ED
☎ 0161 228 6333 **Fax:** 0161 242 2499
E-mail: info@ncc.co.uk Web: http://www.ncc.co.uk
NCC champions the effective deployment of IT to maximise the competitiveness of its members' business, and serves the corporate, vendor and government communities.

National Council on Archives (NCA)
Ruskin Avenue, Kew, Richmond, Surrey TW9 4DU
☎ 020 8392 5347 **Fax:** 020 8487 1987
E-mail: louise.ray@nationalarchives.gov.uk
Web: http://www.ncaonline.org.uk
The National Council on Archives was established in 1988 to bring together the major bodies and organisations, including service providers, users, depositors and policy makers, across the UK concerned with archives and their use. It aims to develop consensus on matters of mutual concern and provide an authoritative common voice for the archival community.

National Film & Television School (NFTS)
The Registry, Beaconsfield Studios, Station Road, Beaconsfield,
Buckinghamshire HP9 1LG
☎ 01494 671234 **Fax:** 01494 674042
E-mail: info@nfts.co.uk Web: http://www.nftsfilm-tv.ac.uk
The NFTS is one of the leading European centres for professional training in the screen entertainment and media industries. NFTS courses are predominantly practical and geared to the needs of people who plan to make their careers in the screen industries. The school's unique partnership with government and industry – both in funding and in liaison and consultation – ensures that its courses meet the present and future needs of the industry.

National Institute of Adult Continuing Education (NIACE)
Renaissance House, 20 Princess Road West, Leicester LE1 6TP
☎ 0116 204 4200/4201 **Fax:** 0116 285 4514
E-mail: enquiries@niace.org.uk Web: http://www.niace.org.uk
NIACE is the national, independent organisation for adult learning in England and Wales. As a registered charity, NIACE both represents and advances the

interests of all adult learners and potential learners – especially those who have benefited least from education and training.

National Media Museum
Bradford, West Yorkshire BD1 1NQ
☎ 0870 7010200 **Fax:** 01274 723155
Web: http://www.nationalmediamuseum.org.uk
The National Media Museum (formerly the National Museum of Photography, Film and Television) exists to engage, inspire and educate by promoting an understanding and appreciation of photography, film, television, radio and the web; using its collection and knowledge to deliver a cultural programme accessibly and authoritatively.

National Resource Centre for Dance (NRCD)
University of Surrey, Guildford, Surrey GU2 7XH
☎ 01483 259316 **Fax:** 01483 259500
E-mail: nrcd@surrey.ac.uk Web: http://www.surrey.ac.uk/NRCD
The NRCD is a non-profit national archive, centre for research, and information service for dance and movement. It aims to preserve the nation's dance heritage and enables, supports, and enhances the study, research, and teaching of dance.

National Student Television Association (NaSTA)
E-mail: nasta@warwicktv.co.uk Web: http://www.nasta.org.uk
NaSTA exists to bring together all the student television stations from across the UK, to help them communicate as a community and overcome problems, to offer advice, and to help new stations set up. It organises an annual conference and awards ceremony to showcase the best in student television, and raise the profile of student television in the industry.

New Producers Alliance (NPA)
7.03 Tea Building, 56 Shoreditch High Street, London E1 6JJ
☎ 020 7613 0440 **Fax:** 020 7729 1852
E-mail: queries@npa.org.uk Web: http://www.npa.org.uk
The NPA is the UK's national membership and training organisation for independent new producers and filmmakers.

Ofcom
2a Southwark Bridge Road, London SE1 9HA
☎ 020 7981 3000 **Fax:** 020 7981 3333
Web: http://www.ofcom.org.uk
Ofcom is the independent regulator and competition authority for the UK communications industries, with responsibilities across television, radio, telecommunications and wireless communications services. Ofcom has inherited the duties of the five previous regulators it replaced: the Broadcasting Standards Commission, the Independent Television Commission, Oftel, the Radio Authority and the Radiocommunications Agency.

Office of the Telecommunications Ombudsman (Otelo)
PO Box 730, Warrington WA4 6WU
☎ 0845 050 1614
E-mail: enquiries@otelo.org.uk Web: http://www.otelo.org.uk
Opened in January 2003, Otelo is a free, independent service designed to offer residential and small business consumers an alternative way to settle unresolved disputes with their telecommunications providers. It is currently

funded by eight member companies which have agreed to abide by the decisions of the Ombudsman on complaints referred to her by their customers.

Oftel See **Ofcom**

One World Broadcasting Trust (OWBT)

One World Broadcasting Trust, River House, 143-145 Farringdon Road, London EC1R 3AB

☎ 020 7239 1422 **Fax:** 020 7833 8347

E-mail: oneworld@owbt.org Web: http://www.owbt.org

Established in 1987, the Trust was set up to promote greater understanding between the developed and developing countries of the world through broadcasting and related educational activities. It aims, through encouraging the effective use of media, to promote a clear and balanced awareness of human rights and global development issues among the UK public – from poverty and debt to education and good governance.

Open Knowledge Foundation

37 Panton Street, Cambridge, CB2 1HL

☎ 07795 176 976

E-mail info@okfn.org Web: http://www.okfn.org

The Open Knowledge Foundation exists to promote more equitable access to knowledge, which has become a possibility due to the technological revolution.

Oral History Society

c/o Department of History, Essex University, Colchester C04 3SQ

☎ 020 7412 7405

E-mail: rob.perks@bl.uk Web: http://www.ohs.org.uk

The Oral History Society is a national and international organisation dedicated to the collection and preservation of oral history.

Performing Rights Society See **MCPS-PRS Alliance**

Phonographic Performance Limited (PPL)

1 Upper James Street, London W1R 3HG

☎ 020 7534 1000 **Fax:** 020 7534 1111

E-mail: info@ppluk.com Web: http://www.ppluk.com

PPL is a music industry organisation collecting and distributing airplay and public performance royalties in the UK on behalf of record companies and performers.

Press Complaints Commission (PCC)

Halton House, 20/23 Holborn, London EC1N 2JD

☎ 020 7831 0022 **Fax:** 020 7831 0025

E-mail: complaints@pcc.org.uk Web: http://www.pcc.org.uk

The Press Complaints Commission is an independent body which deals with complaints from members of the public about the editorial content of newspapers and magazines.

Producers Alliance for Cinema & Television (Pact)

Procter House, 1 Procter Street, Holborn, London WC1V 6DW

☎ 020 7067 4367

E-mail: enquiries@pact.co.uk Web: http://www.pact.co.uk

Pact is the UK trade association that represents and promotes the commercial interests of independent feature film, television, animation and interactive media companies.

Production Managers' Association (PMA)

Ealing Studios, Ealing Green, London W5 5EP

☎ 020 8758 8699

E-mail: pma@pma.org.uk Web: http://www.pma.org.uk

The PMA is a professional body of film, television, corporate and multi-media production managers, both freelance and permanently employed.

Publishers' Licensing Society (PLS)

37-41 Gower Street, London WC1E 6HH

☎ 020 7299 7730 **Fax:** 020 7299 7780

E-mail: pls@pls.org.uk Web: http://www.pls.org.uk

The PLS was established in 1971 by the UK publishing industry. Its role is to oversee a collective licensing scheme in the UK for book, journal, and magazine copying; stimulate innovation and good practice in rights management; clarify the relationship between traditional copyright management practices and those needed in the digital age.

Qualidata See **ESDS Qualidata**

Qualifications & Curriculum Authority (QCA)

83 Piccadilly, London W1J 8QA

☎ 020 7509 5555 **Fax:** 020 7509 6666

E-mail: info@qca.org.uk Web: http://www.qca.org.uk

QCA maintains and develops the national curriculum and associated assessments, tests and examinations; and accredits and monitors qualifications in colleges and at work.

Quality Improvement Agency (QIA)

Friars House, Manor House Drive, Coventry CV1 2TE

☎ 0870 1620 632 **Fax:** 0870 1620 633

Web: http://www.qia.org.uk

The Quality Improvement Agency (QIA) was set up to spark fresh enthusiasm for innovation and excellence in the adult and lifelong learning sector. It supports teachers, trainers and lecturers by running a series of programmes to inspire a culture of self-improvement.

Radio Academy

5 Market Place, London W1W 8AE

☎ 020 7927 9920

Web: http://www.radioacademy.org

The Radio Academy is a registered charity dedicated to the encouragement, recognition and promotion of excellence in UK broadcasting and audio production.

Radio Advertising Bureau See **The RadioCentre**

The Radio Authority See **Ofcom**

The RadioCentre

77 Shaftesbury Avenue, London W1D 5DU

☎ 020 7306 2603 **Fax:** 020 7306 2505

E-mail: info@radiocentre.org Web: http://www.radiocentre.org

The RadioCentre formed in July 2006 from the merger of the Radio Advertising Bureau (RAB) and the Commercial Radio Companies Association (CRCA). Its role is to maintain and build a strong and successful commercial radio.

Radiocommunications Agency See Ofcom

Radio Joint Audience Research (RAJAR)
Paramount House, 162-170 Wardour Street, London W1F 8ZX
☎ 020 7292 9040 **Fax:** 020 7292 9041
E-mail: info@rajar.co.uk Web: http://www.rajar.co.uk
Wholly owned by the RadioCentre and the BBC, RAJAR was established in 1992 to operate a single audience measurement system for the radio industry – BBC, UK licensed and other commercial stations.

Radio Society of Great Britain (RSGB)
Lambda House, Cranborne Road, Potters Bar, Hertfordshire EN6 3JE
☎ 0870 904 7373 **Fax:** 0870 904 7374
E-mail: postmaster@rsgb.org.uk Web: http://www.rsgb.org
Founded in 1913, the RSGB is the national membership organisation for amateur radio enthusiasts.

Raindance
81 Berwick Street, London W1F 8TW
☎ 020 7287 3833 **Fax:** 020 7439 2243
E-mail: info@raindance.co.uk Web: http://www.raindance.co.uk
Raindance is dedicated to fostering and promoting independent film in the UK and around the world, spanning the full spectrum of the art, craft and business of independent movies.

Research Information Network (RIN)
96 Euston Road, London NW1 2DB
☎ 020 7412 7946
Web: http://www.rin.ac.uk
The Research Information Network was set up in 2005 to lead and co-ordinate the provision of research information in the UK. Its ambition is to serve the research community by helping to cut paths through the ever-growing and increasingly-complex mass of information that underpins the work of all researchers.

The Royal Anthropological Institute (RAI)
50 Fitzroy Street, London W1P 5HS
☎ 020 7387 0455 **Fax:** 0 20 7388 8817
E-mail: admin@therai.org.uk Web: http://www.therai.org.uk
The Royal Anthropological Institute of Great Britain and Ireland (RAI) is the world's longest-established scholarly association dedicated to the furtherance of anthropology (the study of humankind) in its broadest and most inclusive sense. The RAI has a film and video library and organises an annual festival of ethnographic film.

The Royal Society
6 Carlton House Terrace, London SW1Y 5AG
☎ 020 7451 2500 **Fax:** 020 7930 2170
Web: http://www.royalsoc.ac.uk
The Royal Society is the independent scientific academy of the UK and the

Commonwealth dedicated to promoting excellence in science. The Society plays an influential role in national and international science policy and supports developments in science engineering and technology in a wide range of ways.

Royal Television Society (RTS)
5th Floor, Kildare House, 3 Dorset Rise, London EC4Y 8EN
☎ 020 7430 1000 **Fax:** 020 7430 0924
E-mail: info@rts.org.uk Web: http://www.rts.org.uk
The Royal Television Society is the leading forum for discussion and debate on all aspects of the television community.

Satellite and Cable Broadcasters Group (SCBG)
Gainsborough House, 81 Oxford Street, London W1D 2EU
☎ 0789 420 6515 **Fax:** 020 7637 0419
E-mail: info@scbg.org.uk Web: http://www.scbg.org.uk
The Satellite and Cable Broadcasters' Group is the trade association for satellite and cable programme providers.

Scottish Arts Council
12 Manor Place, Edinburgh EH3 7DD
☎ 0131 226 6051 **Fax:** 0131 225 9833
E-mail: help.desk.sac@artsfb.org.uk Web: http://www.sac.org.uk
The Scottish Arts Council is the lead body for the funding, development and advocacy of the arts in Scotland.

Scottish Screen
249 West George Street, Glasgow G2 4RB
☎ 0845 300 7300
E-mail: info@scottishscreen.com Web: http://www.scottishscreen.com
Scottish Screen is the national development agency for the screen industries in Scotland.

Screen Heritage Network
Attn. Michael Harvey, National Media Museum, Bradford,
West Yorkshire BD1 1NQ
☎ 01274 203374
E-mail: michael.harvey@nationalmediamuseum.ac.uk
Web: http://screenheritage.wordpress.com
The Screen Heritage Network was established in 2005 by the National Media Museum, the BUFVC, the BKSTS and the Film Archive Forum with start-up funding from the Museums Libraries and Archives Council. The Network is a group of national and regional museums and archives, educational institutions and organisations connected with the UK screen sector, interested in advancing the concept of screen heritage.

Shooting People
P.O. Box 51350, London N1 6XS
Web: http://www.shootingpeople.org
Shooting People is an online community of filmmakers, sharing resources, skills and experience. Members post to and receive daily e-mail bulletins covering all aspects of filmmaking. Members can also fill in online searchable profile cards.

EVISION

...entary history of TV',
...and Dr. VLADIMIR ZWORYKIN!

LEST WE FORGET!

Lenau," and "Flieger Am Feind" (A Nazi
...am that led to the verdicts, plus a film
...waffe. 35 minutes total.

...S OF THE RING

...film of some of the most
...of the century. 76 minutes total

...by MONTY

Skillset

Prospect House, 80-110 New Oxford Street, London WC1A 1HB
☎ 020 7520 5757 **Fax:** 020 7520 5758
E-mail: info@skillset.org Web: http://www.skillset.org
Skillset is the Sector Skills Council for the audio-visual industries (broadcast, film, video, interactive media and photo imaging). It exists to encourage the delivery of informed training provision so that the British broadcast, film, video and multimedia industry's technical, creative and economic achievements are maintained and improved. Skillset is a strategic, all-industry organisation and is supported by key employers and unions.

Society for Research into Higher Education (SHRE)

76 Portland Place, London W1B 1NT
☎ 020 7637 2766 **Fax:** 020 7637 2781
E-mail: srheoffice@srhe.ac.uk Web: http://www.srhe.ac.uk
SHRE is an independent society which aims to improve the quality of higher education through the encouragement of debate and publication on issues of policy, on the organisation and management of higher education institutions and on the curriculum, teaching and learning methods.

Society of Archivists

Prioryfield House, 20 Canon Street, Taunton, Somerset TA1 1SW
☎ 01823 327030 **Fax:** 01823 271719
E-mail: societyofarchivists@archives.org.uk Web: http://www.archives.org.uk
The Society of Archivists is the principal professional body for archivists, archive conservators and records managers in the United Kingdom and Ireland. The society exists to promote the care and preservation of archives and the better administration of archive repositories, to advance the training of its members and to encourage relevant research and publication.

Society of Authors

84 Drayton Gardens, London SW10 9SB
☎ 020 7373 6642 **Fax:** 020 7373 5768
Web: http://www.societyofauthors.net
A membership organisation serving the interests of professional writers, including academics and broadcasters, by offering business and legal advice, holding meetings, publishing a journal and administering a range of prizes.

Society of College, National and University Libraries (SCONUL)

102 Euston Street, London NW1 2HA
☎ 020 7387 0317 **Fax:** 020 7383 3197
E-mail: info@sconul.ac.uk Web: http://www.sconul.ac.uk
SCONUL promotes excellence in library services in higher education and national libraries across the UK and Ireland. All universities in the United Kingdom and Ireland are SCONUL members: so too are many of the UK's colleges of higher education.

Spoken Word Publishing Association See Audiobook Publishing Association

Staff & Educational Development Association (SEDA)

SEDA Administration Office, Woburn House, 20-24 Tavistock Square, London WC1H 9HF
☎ 020 7380 6767 **Fax:** 020 7387 2655
Web: http://www.seda.ac.uk
SEDA is the professional association for staff and educational developers in the UK, promoting innovation and good practice in higher education.

Standing Conference for Heads of Media Services (SCHoMS)

Selly Wick House, 59-61 Selly Wick Road, Selly Park, Birmingham B29 7JE
☎ 0121 415 6803 **Fax:** 0121 415 6809
E-mail: info@schoms.ac.uk Web: http://www.schoms.ac.uk
SCHoMS is the professional body for heads of media services working within UK Higher education. Its purpose is to provide a forum for discussion of strategic issues and a mechanism for the exchange of good practice.

Student Radio Association (SRA)

E-mail: chair@studentradio.org.uk Web: http://www.studentradio.org.uk
The association covers all aspects of student radio, producing publications and factsheets and presenting awards at their AGM.

TechDis

The Higher Education Academy, Innovation Way, York Science Park, York YO10 5BR
☎ 01904 717580
E-mail: helpdesk@techdis.ac.uk Web: http://www.techdis.ac.uk
TechDis aims to be the leading educational advisory service, working across the UK, in the fields of accessibility and inclusion. Its mission is to support the education sector in achieving greater accessibility and inclusion by stimulating innovation and providing expert advice and guidance on disability and technology.

Technical Advisory Service for Images (TASI)

Institute for Learning & Research Technology, University of Bristol, 8-10 Berkeley Square, Bristol BS8 1HH
☎ 0117 928 7091
E-mail: info@tasi.ac.uk Web: http://www.tasi.ac.uk
TASI is a service funded by the JISC set up to advise and support the academic community on the digital creation, storage and delivery of image-related information.

UK Data Archive

University of Essex, Wivenhoe Park, Colchester, Essex CO4 3SQ
☎ 01206 872143 **Fax:** 01206 872003
E-mail: help@esds.ac.uk Web: http://www.data-archive.ac.uk
The UK Data Archive (UKDA) is an internationally-renowned centre of expertise in data acquisition, preservation, dissemination and promotion. It is curator of the largest collection of digital data in the social sciences and humanities in the UK.

UK Film Council

10 Little Portland Street, London W1W 7JG
☎ 020 7861 7861 **Fax:** 020 7861 7862
E-mail: info@ukfilmcouncil.org.uk Web: http://www.ukfilmcouncil.org.uk

The UK Film Council is the Government-backed strategic agency for film in the UK. Its main aim is to stimulate a competitive, successful and vibrant UK film industry and culture, and to promote the widest possible enjoyment and understanding of cinema throughout the nations and regions of the UK.

UK Intellectual Property Office
Concept House, Cardiff Road, Newport, South Wales NP10 8QQ
☎ 0845 9 500 505 **Fax:** 01633 817777
Web: http://www.ipo.gov.uk
The official government body responsible for granting Intellectual Property (IP) rights in the United Kingdom. These rights include patents, designs, trade marks and copyright.

UK MEDIA
c/o UK Film Council, 10 Little Portland Street, London W1W 7JG
☎ 020 7861 7511 **Fax:** 020 7861 7950
E-mail: England@mediadesk.co.uk Web: http://www.mediadesk.co.uk
MEDIA is a support programme of the European Union to strengthen the competitiveness of the European film, television and new media industries and to increase the international circulation of European audio-visual product. MEDIA 2007 commenced on 1 January 2007 and will run to 31 December 2013. With a budget of 755 million (around £500 million) MEDIA 2007 supports professional training (screenwriting, business and new technologies), project development (single/slate), and the distribution and promotion of European audio-visual works.

UK Office for Library & Information Networking (UKOLN)
The Library, University of Bath, Bath BA2 7AY
☎ 01225 826580 **Fax:** 01225 826838
Web: http://www.ukoln.ac.uk
UKOLN is a national centre for support in network information management in the library and information communities. It provides awareness, research and information services.

United Kingdom Education & Research Networking Association (UKERNA) See **JANET (UK)**

Universities Collaboration in E-Learning (UCeL)
University of Cambridge, 16 Mill Lane, Cambridge CB2 1SB
☎ 01223 765363 **Fax:** 01223 765505
E-mail: info@ucel.ac.uk Web: http://www.ucel.ac.uk
UCeL was founded in March 2002 as a multi-institutional collective to collaboratively produce and share high quality interactive multimedia resources for health-professional education.

Universities UK
Woburn House, 20 Tavistock Square, London WC1H 9HQ
☎ 020 7419 4111 **Fax:** 020 7388 8649
E-mail: info@UniversitiesUK.ac.uk Web: http://www.universitiesuk.ac.uk
Universities UK is the university vice-chancellors' group which supports the work of universities and promotes their interests. It was previously the Committee of Vice-Chancellors and Principals of the Universities of the United Kingdom (CVCP).

Vega Science Trust
Sussex Innovation Centre, Science Park Square, Brighton BN1 9SB UK.
☎ 01273 678726 **Fax:** 01273 234645
E-mail: vega@vega.org.uk Web: http://www.vega.org.uk
The Vega Science Trust produces programmes for network television which treat science as cultural activity, so complementing present media coverage of science. It aims to bridge the gap between professional and public understanding of science by creating programmes in which the state-of-the-art understanding of our leading scientists is made more accessible.

Vera Media
30-38 Dock Street, Leeds LS10 1JF
☎ 0113 242 8646 **Fax:** 0113 242 8739
E-mail: vera@vera-media.co.uk Web: http://www.vera-media.co.uk
Vera Media is a video/multimedia production and training organisation. It produces programmes for education, arts, voluntary and public sector, and community documentaries with women's, youth and similar groups.

Video Performance Ltd (VPL)
1 Upper James Street, London W1F 9DE
☎ 020 7534 1400
E-mail: info@vpluk.com Web: http://www.vpluk.com
VPL is the collecting society set up by the record industry in 1984 to licence the broadcast and public performance of music videos on behalf of its members.

Video Standards Council (VSC)
Kinetic Business Centre, Theobald Street, Borehamwood,
Hertfordshire WD6 4PJ
☎ 020 8387 4020 **Fax:** 020 83874004
E-mail: vsc@videostandards.org.uk Web: http://www.videostandards.org.uk
Established 1989 as a non-profit making body to develop and administer a Code of Practice designed to promote high standards within the video industry. In 1993 its brief was expanded to include the computer games industry.

Voice of the Listener & Viewer (VLV)
101 King's Drive, Gravesend, Kent DA12 5BQ
☎ 01474 352835 **Fax:** 01474 351112
E-mail: info@vlv.org.uk Web: http://www.vlv.org.uk
The VLV is a non-profit-making society with the aim of supporting high standards in broadcasting. It has no political, sectarian or commercial affiliations and speaks for listeners and viewers on the whole range of broadcasting issues.

Writers & Scholars International
Lancaster House, 33 Islington High Street, London N1 9LH
☎ 020 7278 2313 **Fax:** 020 7278 1878
Web: http://www.indexonline.org
Writers and Scholars International publishes the magazine *Index on Censorship*. It aims to help the victims of censorship, to inform the world about the issues of censorship and freedom of expression, and to promote discussion and debate.

Writers Guild of Britain

15 Britannia Street, London WC1X 9JN

☎ 020 7833 0777 **Fax:** 020 7833 4777

E-mail: admin@writersguild.org.uk Web: http://www.writersguild.org.uk

The Writers' Guild of Great Britain is the trade union working on behalf of writers in television, radio, theatre, books, poetry, film and video games.

ORGANISATIONS – INTERNATIONAL

This is a small selection of international organisations working in audio-visual media in a broadly educational context. Most either have associations with the BUFVC or share in one or other of its interests. A number belong to the International Association for Media in Science (IAMS), of which the BUFVC is a founder member.

Action Coalition for Media Education (ACME)
2808 El Tesoro Escondido NW, Albuquerque, NM 87120, USA
☎ +1 505 893 9702 **Fax:** + 1 505 828 3142
Web: http://www.acmecoalition.org
ACME is a US-based, independent strategic network linking media educators, health advocates, media reformers, independent media makers, community organisers and others.

La Asociación Española de Cine Científico (ASECIC)
C/Vitruvio, 8, 28006 Madrid, Spain
☎/**Fax:** +34 91 564 69 12
Web: http://www.asecic.org
ASECIC was founded in 1966 by Dr Guillermo Fernandez Zúñiga. Since then it has promoted the work of audio-visual Spanish scientists and scientific cinema internationally, and promotes the use of scientific film as an educational tool.

Association of Moving Image Archivists (AMIA)
E-mail: amia@amianet.org Web: http://www.amianet.org
A US-based non-profit professional association established to advance the field of moving image archiving by fostering co-operation among individuals and organisations concerned with the acquisition, preservation, exhibition and use of moving image materials.

Audiovisueel Centrum Vrije Universiteit (AVC)
V.d. Boechorststraat 7-9, 1081 BT Amsterdam, The Netherlands
☎ +31 20 59 89161 **Fax:** +31 20 598 9160
E-mail: avc@dienst.vu.nl Web: http://www.audiovisueelcentrum.nl
The audio-visual services department of Vrije Universiteit, Amsterdam, specialising in videoconferencing, webcasting, streaming video services, video lectures, and medical imaging.

AVNet
K.U.Leuven, Kapeldreef 62, B-3001 Heverlee (Leuven), Belgium
☎ +32 16 32 82 00 **Fax:** +32 16 32 82 70
E-mail: info@avnet.kuleuven.be Web: http://www.avnet.kuleuven.be
AVNet is the name of a new structure incorporating K.U.Leuven Audiovisual Services AVdienst, eLink, and the Open University Study Centre. For several years K.U.Leuven has been a major player in the field of ICT and media-supported higher education, through projects implemented at the university as well as in an international context. AVNet acts as a central department for educational support, provided more specifically by using audio-visual media and interactive multimedia in education, in networked e-learning and distance education.

Centre nationale de la recherche scientifique (CNRS)

E-mail: webcnrs@cnrs-dir.fr Web: http://www.cnrs.fr

CNRS is a government-funded research organisation, under the administrative authority of France's Ministry of Research. Founded in 1939 by governmental decree, CNRS has the following missions: to evaluate and carry out all research capable of advancing knowledge and bringing social, cultural, and economic benefits for society; to contribute to the application and promotion of research results; to develop scientific information; to support research training; to participate in the analysis of the national and international scientific climate and its potential for evolution in order to develop a national policy.

CERIMES (Centre de ressources et d'information sur les multimédias pour l'enseignement supérieur)

6, avenue Pasteur 92170 Vanves, France

☎ +33 1 41 23 08 80 **Fax:** +33 1 45 29 10 99

E-mail: info@cerimes Web: http://www.cerimes.education.fr

CERIMES exists to facilitate access for teachers, researchers and students to audio-visual resources suitable for use in higher education. It locates, describes and distributes such materials, with particular emphasis on resources produced by higher education and research institutions. Previously known as Service du film de recherche scientifique (SFRS).

Coalition for Networked Information (CNI)

21 Dupont Circle, Suite 800, Washington, DC, 20036, USA

☎ +1 202 296 5098 **Fax:** +1 02 872 0884

E-mail: info@cni.org Web: http://www.cni.org

The Coalition for Networked Information is an organisation dedicated to supporting the transformative promise of networked information technology for the advancement of scholarly communication and the enrichment of intellectual productivity. Some 200 institutions representing higher education, publishing, network and telecommunications, information technology, and libraries and library organisations make up CNI's members.

DiMA – the Digital Media Association

1029 Vermont Ave, NW, Suite 850, Washington, DC 20005, USA

☎ +1 202 639 9509

Web: http://www.digmedia.org

The Digital Media Association promotes pro-consumer competitive opportunities that will contribute to the growth, production and enjoyment of digital content; supports the development and use of responsible measures to protect intellectual property rights underlying digital media, and the payment of fair and reasonable royalties associated with such rights; and opposes technical and legal barriers that inhibit innovation or adoption of new digital technologies, products and services.

DIVERSE

Web: http://www.diverse-video.net

DIVERSE stands for Developing Innovative Video Resources for Students Everywhere. It began life as a Teaching and Learning Technology Programme Phase 3 project, funded by the UK government through the Higher Education Funding Council for England. It has developed to become an international community of international practitioners in both video production and videoconferencing, with an annual conference. The focus is on developing alternative modes of learning and teaching to complement the asynchronous text-based formats that predominate within e-learning.

EuroDoc

4, rue Astruc, BP 2060, F- 34025, Montpellier Cedex 1, France
☎ +33 4 67 60 23 30
E-mail: eurodoc@wanadoo.fr Web: http://www.eurodoc-net.com
EURODOC is a training programme designed for European professionals in the documentary field developing a specific project, either independent producers of documentary projects with international potential, or commissioning editors from the documentary departments of the broadcasters or from partners in the sector, bankers, distributors etc.

European Audiovisual Observatory

76 Allée de la Robertsau, 67000 Strasbourg, France
☎ +33 3 88 14 44 00 **Fax:** +33 3 88 14 44 19
E-mail: obs@obs.coe.int Web: http://www.obs.coe.int
Set up in December 1992, the purpose of the European Audiovisual Observatory is to gather and circulate information on the audio-visual industry in Europe. The Observatory is a European public service body with thirty-six member States and the European Community, represented by the European Commission.

European Broadcasting Union (EBU)

L'Ancienne-Route 17A, CH-1218 Grand-Saconnex, Switzerland
☎ + 41 22 717 2111 **Fax:** + 41 22 747 4000
E-mail: ebu@ebu.ch Web: http://www.ebu.ch
The European Broadcasting Union is the largest professional association of national broadcasters in the world. It negotiates broadcasting rights for major sports events, operates the Eurovision and Euroradio networks, organises programme exchanges, stimulates and coordinates co-productions, and provides a full range of other operational, commercial, technical, legal and strategic services.

European Bureau of Library Information and Documentation Associations (EBLIDA)

PO Box 16359, NL-2500 BJ The Hague, The Netherlands
☎ +31 70 309 05 51 **Fax:** +31 70 309 05 58
E-mail: eblida@debibliotheken.nl Web: http://www.eblida.org
An independent umbrella association of national library, information, documentation and archive associations and institutions in Europe. EBLIDA concentrates on European information society issues, including copyright and licensing, culture and education and EU enlargement. EBLIDA promotes unhindered access to information in the digital age and the role of archives and libraries in achieving this goal.

European Digital Media Association (EDiMA)

☎ +32 2 626 1990
E-mail: infor@europeandigitalmedia.org
Web: http://www.europeandigitalmediaassociation.org
EDiMA is an alliance of digital media and technology companies that distribute audio and audio visual content online. The main business of EDiMA revolves around two different areas: the formation of EU legislation and the licensing regime in the EU for the distribution of content online. The association is involved in developments relating to copyright issues, music licensing, competition law, taxation of digital music sales and a range of other market and legislative issues which impact on the way in which online content distributors do business in the EU.

European Television History Network (ETHN)

E-mail: Sonja.deLeeuw@let.uu.nl
Web: http://www.birth-of-tv.org/birth/pages/static/research/Research.jsp
The ETHN, founded in April 2005 by the Media Studies department of Utrecht University, is a European network of academics and institutions active in the field of European television history which aims to facilitate international research co-operation. The ETHN has a dedicated section on the BIRTH web site which disseminates information, hosts a discussion forum and provides space for academics to post their CVs and research interests.

Fédération Internationale des Archives du Film (FIAF)

1 Rue Defacqz, B-1000 Brussels, Belgium
☎ +32 2 538 3065 **Fax:** +32 2 534 4774
E-mail:info@fiafnet.org Web: http://www.fiafnet.org
The International Federation of Film Archives, brings together institutions dedicated to rescuing films both as cultural heritage and as historical documents. Founded in Paris in 1938, FIAF is a collaborative association of the world's leading film archives whose purpose has always been to ensure the proper preservation and showing of motion pictures. Today, more than 120 archives in over sixty-five countries collect, restore, and exhibit films and cinema documentation spanning the entire history of film.

FIAT/IFTA

c/o Oesterreichischer Rundfunk, Documentation & Archives, Wuerzburggasse 30, A-1136 Wien, Austria
☎ +43 1 87878 12380 **Fax:** +43 1 87878 12739
E-mail: office@fiatifta.org Web: http://fiatifta.org
The International Federation of Television Archives is an international professional association established to provide a means for co-operation

amongst broadcast and national audio-visual archives and libraries concerned with the collection, preservation and exploitation of moving image and recorded sound materials and associated documentation.

Institut für den Wissenschaftlichen Film (IWF)

Nonnenstieg 72, D-37075 Göttingen, Germany
☎ +49 551 5024 0 **Fax:** -400
E-mail: iwf-goe@iwf.de Web: http://www.iwf.de

IWF – Knowledge and Media is the German federal and states' service facility for multimedia communication in a scientific context. It promotes science and education through its development and transfer services in the field of audio-visual media. Its core task is to acquire scientific audio-visual media, to optimise it and to make it available for teaching and research in the long-term.

International Association for Media and History (Iamhist)

Box 1216, Washington, CT 06793, USA
E-mail: info-contact@iamhist.org
Web: http://www.iamhist.org

The International Association for Media and History is an organisation of filmmakers, broadcasters, archivists and scholars dedicated to historical inquiry into film, radio, television, and related media. It encourages scholarly research into the relations between history and the media as well as the production of historically informed documentaries, television series, and other media texts.

International Association for Media in Science (IAMS)

c/o CERIMES, 6, avenue Pasteur 92170 Vanves, France
☎ +33 1 41 23 08 80 **Fax:** +33 1 45 29 10 99
E-mail: lievre@cerimes Web: http://iams.cerimes.fr

Established in 1992 as the successor to the International Scientific Film Association, IAMS promotes the production, documentation, preservation, distribution and use of audio-visual media and materials for the growth and communication of knowledge in the natural and human sciences, technology and medicine. Its members come from the major national associations for scientific media, numerous audio-visual centres of universities, production houses, and individual experts from all over the world.

International Association of Sound & Audiovisual Archives (IASA)

Web: http://www.iasa-web.org

IASA was established in 1969 in Amsterdam to function as a medium for international co-operation between archives that preserve recorded sound and audio-visual documents. The organisation is concerned with the development of good practice and the dissemination of information on collection development and access, documentation and metadata, copyright and ethics, and conservation and preservation.

Internet2

1000 Oakbrook Drive, Suite 300, Ann Arbor MI 48104, USA
☎ +1 734 913 4250 **Fax:** +1 734 913 4255
E-mail: info@internet2.edu Web: http://www.internet2.edu

Internet2 is the foremost US advanced networking consortium. Led by the research and education community since 1996, Internet2 promotes the missions of its over 300 members by providing both leading-edge network capabilities and unique partnership opportunities that together facilitate the development, deployment and use of revolutionary Internet technologies.

Motion Picture Association

1600 Eye Street, NW, Washington, DC 20006, USA
☎ +1 202 293 1966 **Fax:** +1 202 296 7410
Web: http://www.mpaa.org
The Motion Picture Association of America (MPAA) and its international counterpart, the Motion Picture Association (MPA), serve as the voice and advocate of the American motion picture, home video and television industries, domestically through the MPAA and internationally through the MPA. Main areas of concern to the association are educating young people about copyright theft, promoting copyright protection, and working with the technology sector to find innovative ways of delivering entertainment.

National Science Foundation (NSF)

201 Wilson Boulevard, Arlington, Virginia 22230, USA
☎ +1 703 292 5111
Web: http://www.nsf.gov
The National Science Foundation is an independent federal agency created by Congress in 1950 'to promote the progress of science; to advance the national health, prosperity, and welfare; to secure the national defense ...' With an annual budget of about $5.91 billion, it is the funding source for approximately twenty percent of all federally supported basic research conducted by America's colleges and universities. In many fields such as mathematics, computer science and the social sciences, NSF is the major source of federal backing.

Online/More Colour in the Media (OLMCM)

PO Box 672, 3500 AR Utrecht, The Netherlands
☎ +31 30 239 9035 **Fax:** +31 30 230 2975
E-mail: info@olmcm.org Web: http://www.olmcm.org
Online/More Colour in the Media is a network of minority organisations and multicultural NGOs, local and national broadcast media, training institutes and media education organisations, aiming to improve the representation of ethnic minorities in the media.

SURFfoundation

Hojel City Center, building D (5th floor), Graadt van Roggenweg 340, 3531 AH Utrecht, The Netherlands
☎ + 31 30 234 66 00 **Fax:** + 31 30 233 29 60
E-mail: info@surf.nl Web: http://www.surffoundation.nl
SURF is the collaborative organisation for higher education institutions and research institutes aimed at breakthrough innovations in ICT. SURF provides the foundation for the excellence of higher education and research in the Netherlands.

University Film and Video Association (UFVA)

University of Illinois Press, 1325 South Oak Street Champaign, Illinois 61820-6903, USA
☎ +1 217 244 0626 **Fax:** +1 217 244-9910
E-mail: berryks@gwm.sc.edu Web: http://www.ufva.org

An association for universities – predominantly but not exclusively American and Canadian – with an interest in the making and teaching of film and video.

Video Active

Kromme Nieuwegracht 29, 3512 HD Utrecht, Netherlands
☎ +31 (0)30 2536526
E-mail: Sonja.deLeeuw@let.uu.nl Web: http://www.videoactive.eu
A consortium of archives, academic institutions and ICT developers whose aim is to create access to television archives across Europe. Video Active is funded by the eContentPlus programme of the European Commission.

Video Development Initiative (ViDe)

Web: http://www.vide.net
The Video Development Initiative is an international professional organisation built around the development and deployment of digital video and collaborative technologies. ViDe is open to all people studying or engaged in digital video or collaborative research and services within the education community, government agencies, and non-profit organisations.

World Association of Medical and Health Films (WAMHF)

E-mail: WAMHF@ammonite.nl Web: http://www.ammonite.nl/WAMHF.htm
The WAMHF was founded in 1990 in Spain, on the occasion of the 6th International Medical and Health Film Festival (Videomed) of Badajoz. Its objectives are: to promote medical and health audio-visual media; to promote the circulation and distribution of medical and health audio-visual productions throughout the world; to develop an approved index of all medical films so as to facilitate and stimulate exchanges among the producers of audio-visual health media; to develop an international data bank of medical and health films, available to all the members of the Association from anywhere in the world; to facilitate co-operation among existing festivals by encouraging the organisers to compare their experiences; to defend and harmonise copyright laws in the medical and health fields.

World Intellectual Property Organisation (WIPO)

34, Chemin des Colombettes, 1211 Geneva, Switzerland
☎ +41 22 338 91 11
Web: http://www.wipo.int/about-wipo/en/what_is_wipo.html
WIPO, founded in 1967, is a specialised agency of the United Nations. It is dedicated to developing a balanced and accessible international intellectual property system, which rewards creativity, stimulates innovation and contributes to economic development while safeguarding the public interest.

PODCASTING

Podcasts are digital media files available over the Internet, which can be downloaded for later use through an iPod or computer. Podcasts can be audio or video (vodcasts). The BUFVC's Moving Image Gateway (http://www.bufvc.ac.uk/gateway) includes podcasting and vodcasting services in its classified listing of web sites relating to moving images and sound for use in higher education. Below is a small selection of the rapidly growing number of relevant sites which offer podcasts, with an emphasis on those available from universities. For information on the use of podcasting for UK higher education, see these two articles available from the BUFVC's free online journal, Media Online Focus:

Nick Townend, 'Podcasting in Higher Education' (issue 22, December 2005)
Web: http://www.bufvc.ac.uk/publications/mediaonlineissues/mof22_vf61.pdf

Dave Jobbings, 'Exploiting Podcasting in Educational Settings' (issue 26, December 2006)
Web: http://www.bufvc.ac.uk/publications/mediaonlineissues/mof26_vf65.pdf

Arizona Health Science Library – Medical Podcasts
Web: http://www.ahsl.arizona.edu/weblinks/Medical_podcasts.cfm
A useful listing of some key podcasting services for medical professionals.

Bath Pod
Web: http://www.bath.ac.uk/podcast
Podcasts from the University of Bath's public lecture series where leading names from the worlds of science, humanities and engineering talk about the latest research in their field.

BBC News
Web: http://news.bbc.co.uk/1/hi/programmes/4977678.stm
The BBC online news service is offering a wide range of audio podcasts, including: TODAY PROGRAMME; WORLD NEWS BULLETIN; NEWS-NIGHT ('without the inconvenience of pictures'); WORLD TODAY SELECT (interviews and features from the BBC World Service's flagship news programme); TODAY IN PARLIAMENT; FROM OUR OWN CORRES-PONDENT; IN BUSINESS; FILE ON 4; DOCUMENTARY ARCHIVE; DIGITAL PLANET.

The BBC's video podcasts underwent a year's trial, ending July 2007, and are no longer available. Those that were produced were: TEN WEEKLY (a weekly presentation of the best of BBC news from the 10 O'CLOCK NEWS team); NEWSNIGHT (video highlights from the BBC's flagship television news and current affairs programme); STORYFix ('the week at high velocity'); BBC BREAKFAST TAKEAWAY; and BBC QUESTION TIME.

Berkeley Groks Science Show
Web: http://www.ocf.berkeley.edu/~clgroks
Berkeley Groks Science Show is a weekly science programme broadcast on radio stations throughout the USA. Each programme provides an in-depth look at recent developments in the world of science and technology and examines the effects of these discoveries on our daily lives. Each new show is available as a podcast and past episodes are archived as MP3 files on the Internet Archive (http://www.archive.org).

Biz/ed
Web: http://www.bized.co.uk/homeinfo/podcasting.htm
Biz/ed broadcasts regular podcasts for students and educators in business studies, economics, accounting, leisure, sport and recreation, and travel and tourism in the UK.

CUSP-BlueSci Podcasts
Web: http://www.bluesci.org/content/view/471/401
Popular science broadcasts produced by Cambridge University's *BluSci* science magazine, including the Darwin Lectures series from 2006 and 2007.

DEEP (Digital Education Enhancement Project)
Web: http://www.open.ac.uk/deep/Public/web/about/deepBriefings.html
The Open University's DEEP project is a research and development programme investigating the use of new information and communications technology (ICT) for teaching and learning, working in schools serving disadvantaged communities in different parts of the world. Its 'DEEP Briefings' are podcasts giving quick introductions to the ideas, contexts and practices of the project.

ECS Video Podcasts
Web: http://www.ecs.soton.ac.uk/about/podcasts.php
Electronics and Computer Science (ECS), University of Southampton, was the first academic institution in the UK to offer a video podcast news service, providing coverage of a wide range of activities in the School.

Education Podcast Network
Web: http://epnweb.org
Mainly American schools-oriented directory of podcast programming that may be helpful to teachers looking for content to teach with and about, and to explore issues of teaching and learning in the 21st century.

EduPodder
Web: http://www.edupodder.com
Advocacy site, with a well-established blog on research into the use of podcasting in education.

Enlightenment in the 21st Century
Web: http://www.ed.ac.uk/explore/av/enlightenment2006
In partnership with ScottishPower, the University of Edinburgh is hosting a series of speakers who will seek to examine aspects of the Enlightenment's legacy in the context of our own fraught and hectic times.

Every Object Tells a Story
Web: http://www.everyobject.net
Every Object Tells a Story is collecting an online archive of stories about objects that people value. It is produced by the Victoria & Albert Museum, with Ultralab and Channel 4, and commissioned by Culture Online. It offers audio and video podcasts of museum and gallery curators discussing objects in their collections.

Glasgow University Podcasts
Web: http://podlearn.arts.gla.ac.uk/podcasts.html
Lecture podcasts from Glasgow University, on such themes as consciousness, cultural and heritage informatics, Kant, and 2D digitisation.

Imperial College London – Public Lectures
Web: http://www3.imperial.ac.uk/aboutimperial/events/onlinelectures
Video podcasts of public lectures from Imperial College London, including guest lecturers such as Trevor Phillips, Professor Sir Harry Kroto and Lord Robert Winston.

Institute for Public Policy Research (IPPR)
Web: http://www.ippr.org/podcasts
The IPPR launched a podcasting programme in March 2007 to provide information on the organisation's latest research developments and events programmes, as well as web reports, books and broadcast media. The IPPR is the UK's leading progressive think tank, producing cutting edge research and innovative policy ideas for a just, democratic and sustainable world. Topics include prison populations in the UK, the failings of ASBOs, and Home Office reform.

MicrobiologyBytes
Web: http://www.microbiologybytes.com/podcasts/help.html
The latest news on microbiology, from the University of Leicester, with detailed supporting textual information.

Nova
Web: http://www.pbs.org/wgbh/nova/rss/podcasting.html
Wide range of podcasts and vodcasts on the world of science, from the US science television channel.

Open2.net
Web: http://www.open2.net
The online learning portal from the Open University and the BBC has several podcasts available, including discussion coming out of the series THINGS WE FORGOT TO REMEMBER, TALKING LANGUAGES and EVER WONDERED ABOUT FOOD?

Podcats
Web: http://www.podcats.co.uk
Professional service providing podcasts for charities and commercial organisations. Clients (whose podcasts are available from the Podcats site) include the Royal Shakespeare Company, the Royal Society for the Protection of Birds, and the Philharmonia Orchestra.

Podcasts for Educators, Schools and Colleges
Web: http://recap.ltd.uk/podcasting
A UK-based directory of podcasts for education, predominantly those aimed at children and young people at school, but including some suitable for universities and colleges. Includes a section on video podcasts. Provides an RSS feed, weblog and educators' tips.

Public Service Reform Interviews
Web: http://www.bris.ac.uk/Depts/CMPO/audio/main.htm
Series of interviews from the University of Bristol's Centre for Market and Public Organisation.

Research at Chicago
Web: http://research.uchicago.edu/highlights
Audio and video interviews with staff at the University of Chicago on a variety of research topics.

The Royal Society
Web: http://www.royalsoc.ac.uk/page.asp?id=1110
This extensive resource offers lectures and podcasts on a broad range of scientific subjects including Biology, Climate Science, Chemistry, Geology, Mathematics and Physics. The lecturers include David Attenborough, Bill Bryson, Ben Okri and Tim Berners-Lee.

Scientific American Podcasts
Web: http://www.sciam.com/podcast
A weekly audio report by Steve Mirsky discussing the latest developments in science and technology through interviews with leading scientists and journalists. The service began in February 2006 and is available by podcast or online download.

ShakespeareCast.com
Web: http://www.shakespearecast.com
A project which aims eventually to provide the complete works of William Shakespeare, podcast act by act. Recordings made by the Antioch Classical Theatre Company, Los Medanos College, and Antioch High School in the USA.

Snowmail
Web: http://www.channel4.com/news/watchlisten/more4snowmail.jsp
Channel 4 News presenter Jon Snow's alternative take on the news, broadcast every Saturday on More4 and available online or via iTunes.

Songwriting
Web: http://www.stevecooperband.co.uk/songwriting/Home.html
A series of podcasts on songwriting techniques, from the University of Wolverhampton.

The South Bank Show
Web: http://www.itv.com/page.asp?partid=2380
The long-running ITV arts programme's site gives information on recent and upcoming programmes, some interesting facts about the programme's history and its most popular broadcasts, and information on the South Bank Show Awards. There is now a podcasting feature, with exclusive interviews taken from the interviews for recent programmes. It also includes some good quality vodcasts of extracts from recent editions with more promised from the archives in the future.

Stanford on iTunes U
Web: http://itunes.stanford.edu
Provides access to a wide range of Stanford-related digital audio content via iTunes. The public site includes Stanford courses, faculty lectures, event highlights, music, sports, etc.

Teachers' TV
Web: http://www.teachers.tv/help/podcasting
Video podcasts of selected programmes from Teachers' TV, the UK digital television channel for teachers.

University Channel
Web:
http://uc.princeton.edu/main/index.php?option=com_frontpage&Itemid=1
A collection of public affairs lectures, panels and events from academic institutions across the world. Participating universities contribute video and audio recordings of lectures, seminars, panels and interviews to a virtual pool of academic content; these are made available as podcasts and vodcasts, as downloadable MP3 or MP4 files, or as streaming audio/video.

University of Ulster Public Affairs Audio Archive
Web: http://www.publicaffairs.ulster.ac.uk/podcasts
Audio files from the life and work of the University of Ulster, its staff, students, partners and visitors.

Warwick Podcasts
Web: http://www2.warwick.ac.uk/newsandevents/audio
University of Warwick experts commenting on important issues, their research and events. Includes Will@Warwick, featuring academic thoughts on William Shakespeare (http://www2.warwick.ac.uk/newsandevents/audio/more/will).

Z-Axis: History of Animation in Court
Web: http://podcasts.zaxis.com/pac
A continuing series of video podcasts of some of the computer animations that have been used in USA courtrooms over the last twenty years. Z-Axis Corporation was a pioneer in the creation of animated trial exhibits in the late 1980s and has continued to develop new ways to present visual information to judges and juries. This collection includes some of the landmark cases to use computer animation over the years as well as other less famous, but still innovative and interesting applications of computer graphics.

REGIONAL SUPPORT CENTRES

JISC RSCs (Regional Support Centres) exist to advise the learning providers of designated sectors in the deployment of Information and Communications Technologies (ICT) to achieve their organisational mission. The various RSCs are based regionally across the UK, with staff usually located within host institutions, although some operate on a distributed model. RSCs give advice to key contacts within the learning providers that they support. Usually such contacts comprise a senior management contact, a teaching and learning contact, a learning resources contact and an IT technical contact. The overall aim of the RSCs is to advise, with customers then responsible for any actions taken.

JISC RSC UK
2nd Floor Beacon House, Queens Road, Clifton, Bristol, BS8 1QU
☎ 0117 9545067
Web: http://www.jisc.ac.uk/rsc

JISC RSC Eastern
Anglia Ruskin University, CU House, Southernhay, Basildon, Essex SS14 1EZ
☎ 01268 273277 **Fax:** 01268 293145
E-mail: support@rsc-eastern.ac.uk Web: http://www.rsc-eastern.ac.uk

JISC RSC East Midlands
Loughborough College, Radmoor Road, Loughborough LE11 3BT
☎ 01509 618110
E-mail: support@rsc-em.ac.uk Web: http://www.rsc-east-midlands.ac.uk

JISC RSC London
University of London Computing Centre, 20 Guilford Street,
London WC1N 1DZ
☎ 020 7692 1637 **Fax:** 020 7692 1601
E-mail: admin@rsc-london.ac.uk Web: http://www.rsc-london.ac.uk

JISC RSC Northern
Sunderland Enterprise Park West, Wessington Way (A1231), Colima Avenue, Sunderland SR5 3XB
☎ 0191 515 3456
E-mail: http://www.rsc-northern.ac.uk/feedback.asp
Web: http://www.rsc-northern.ac.uk

JISC RSC Northern Ireland
Queen's University Belfast, Riddel Hall, 185 Stranmillis Road, Belfast, BT9 5EE
North West Institute of Further and Higher Education, Strand Road, Londonderry BT48 7AL
☎ 028 9097 5611 **Fax:** 028 9097 4264
E-mail: m.peoples@rsc-ni.ac.uk Web: http://www.rsc-ni.ac.uk

JISC RSC Northwest
12A Darwin Court, Hawking Place, Blackpool, FY2 0JN
☎ 01253 503180 **Fax:** 01253 503182
E-mail: support@rsc-northwest.ac.uk Web: http://www.rsc-northwest.ac.uk

JISC RSC Scotland North & East
Edinburgh's Telford College, 350 West Granton Road, Edinburgh EH5 1QE
☎ 0131 559 4112
E-mail: http://www.rsc-ne-scotland.ac.uk/contact.php
Web: http://www.rsc-ne-scotland.ac.uk

JISC RSC Scotland South & West
1 Todd Campus, West of Scotland Science Park, Acre Road, Glasgow G20 0XA
☎ 0141 585 0022/0023 **Fax:** 0141 585 0020
E-mail: support@rsc-sw-scotland.ac.uk
Web: http://www.rsc-sw-scotland.ac.uk

JISC RSC South East
Darwin College, University of Kent, Canterbury, Kent CT2 7NY
☎ 01227 827091 **Fax:** 01227 824078
E-mail: support@rsc-southeast.ac.uk Web: http://www.rsc-southeast.ac.uk

JISC RSC South West
University of Plymouth, Babbage Room 316, Drake Circus, Plymouth PL4 8AA
☎ 01752 23 38 99
E-mail: rsc-advice@rsc-south-west.ac.uk
Web: http://www.rsc-south-west.ac.uk

JISC RSC Wales
Regional Support Centre Wales, Library and Information Services, Swansea University, Singleton Park, Swansea, SA2 8PP
☎ 01792 295959
E-mail: support@rsc-wales.ac.uk Web: http://www.rsc-wales.ac.uk

JISC RSC West Midlands
Technology Centre, Wolverhampton Science Park, Stafford Road, Wolverhampton WV10 9RU
☎ 01902 322001 **Fax:** 01902 824345
E-mail: support@rsc-wm.ac.uk Web: http://www.rsc-westmidlands.ac.uk

JISC RSC for Yorkshire and Humber
University of Leeds, 44 Clarendon Road, LS2 9PJ
☎ 0113 343 1000 **Fax:** 0113 343 4652
E-mail: support@rsc-yh.ac.uk Web: http://www.rsc-yh.ac.uk

UNIVERSITY AUDIO-VISUAL CENTRES

This is a listing of the main universities which promote their audio-visual production facilities as being central services, rather than simply supporting particular academic courses in media production. Details of videoconferencing facilities are also included, where known. Some universities make these services available for commercial hire by users outside the university, and details are generally given on the unit's web site.

University of Aberdeen: Department of Medical Illustration
Polwarth Building, Foresterhill, Aberdeen AB25 2ZD
☎ 01224 553813 **Fax:** 01224 274484
E-mail: i.harold@abdn.ac.uk Web: http://www.abdn.ac.uk/diss/avu
Provides photographic, graphic and television/audio-visual services for the Medical School and Aberdeen Royal Hospital Trusts and other departments within the university. Services include programme planning and production for clinical and non clinical applications; standards conversion; video and audio dubbing; video editing; voice-over recording/editing; live interactive video for teaching/symposia within the medical faculty; teaching room equipment servicing within the medical faculty.

University of Abertay Dundee: Information Services
Bell Street, Dundee, DD1 1HG
☎ 01382 308816
E-mail: itdesk@abertay.ac.uk
Web: http://www.abertay.ac.uk/About/Facilities/IT.cfm
Television and video equipment and a videoconferencing studio are available for use by outside clients as well as within the university.

Anglia Ruskin University: Communications & IT Services
East Road, Cambridge CB1 1PT
☎ 0845 271 3333 ex 2221
E-mail: cits-support@anglia.ac.uk
Web: http://www.anglia.ac.uk/ruskin/en/home/central/cits.html
The Media Production team provides a full range of audio-visual, media production and graphic design services across the university. It also provides videoconferencing facilities and classroom support.

Aston University: Aston Media
Birmingham B4 7ET
☎ 0121 204 4237 **Fax:** 0121 359 6427
E-mail: media@aston.ac.uk
Web: http://www.aston.ac.uk/from-business/business-services/astonmedia/index.jsp
Aston Media provides multimedia production, equipment and expertise within the university and also to private and public sector clients. It offers a full range of services including production management, studio and location video recording, post-production editing, graphic design, multimedia authoring, web design and streamed video delivery, as well as audio-visual technical support.

University of Bath: Audio Visual Unit
Audio Visual Unit, Claverton Down, Bath BA2 7AY
☎ 01225 384846
E-mail: a.v.bookings@bath.ac.uk Web: http://www.bath.ac.uk/bucs/avu

Provides audio-visual equipment to assist with all university activities. The Audio Visual service is normally free of charge to University of Bath staff and students, but some services are open to external customers for a fee. The recording studio is equipped with three high quality Sony 3 chip colour cameras, lighting grid and an assortment of radio and floor microphones. Video and audio post production facilities and portable audio and video recording equipment for location work are also available.

University of Birmingham: Media Centre
Edgbaston, Birmingham B15 2TT
☎ 0121 414 3344 **Fax:** 0121 414 3971
E-mail: comtempdagger@adf.bham.ac.uk
Web: http://www2.bham.ac.uk/landing_page.asp?section=0001000100090214
The Media Centre has comprehensive studio facilities and offers a full script to screen service. The editing suite has a full range of facilities – editing, duplication, caption generation and audio production and the studio is fully equipped with state-of-the-art cameras, microphones and lighting. The studio and equipment are available for hire by internal and external users, with technical advice being available. Radio broadcast facilities enable live radio interviews to be held directly from the university. Multimedia programmes are also produced, from simple text and graphics CD-ROMs with simple step-through instructions, to video, audio and animation with more complicated search and option facilities.

Bournemouth University: Media Services
Library and Learning Centre, Talbot Campus, Poole Dorset BH12 5BB
☎ 01202 965515 **Fax:** 01202 966955
E-mail: itservicedesk@bournemouth.ac.uk
Web: http://www.bournemouth.ac.uk/itservices/staff/media.html
Media Services looks after the media equipment for lecture theatres and centrally booked teaching rooms on both campuses. Staff and students are able to borrow from an extensive range of media equipment including: DV cameras, digital stills cameras, projectors, analogue and digital audio recording devices.

University of Bradford: Learner Support Services
Bradford, West Yorkshire BD7 1DP
☎ 01274 233343
E-mail: lsshelp@bradford.ac.uk
Web: http://www.brad.ac.uk/lss/guide/facilities.php#ilc
The Interactive Learning Centre provides students and staff with a large room with multimedia networked PCs, all with DVD players and CD writers; three study rooms for group work or quiet study all with video playback facilities; audio-visual teaching and learning equipment, video-editing facilities and scanner. Other services provided include CD-ROM writing and videoconferencing.

University of Brighton: Media Centres
Information Services, Moulescombe Media Centre, Brighton BN2 4GJ
☎ 01273 642767
E-mail: mcm9@brighton.ac.uk
Web: http://www.brighton.ac.uk/is/cms/index.php?option=
com_content&task=section&id=9&Itemid=246

A range of media services is available at each site for staff and students including audio, video and IT equipment for loan, as well as video editing suites and media conversion facilities, an animation suite and a television studio. The media streaming service can convert video and audio materials into appropriate digital formats and serve them via the web from centrally-managed servers for delivery to students via the VLE or other web pages. The video and audio studios and editing suites are available for outside hire when not in use by students and staff. Duplication of videotapes and DVDs is also available to non-members of the university.

Brunel University: Media Services
Computer Centre, John Crank Building, Kingston Lane, Uxbridge UB8 3PH
☎ 01895 274 000 **Fax:** 01895 255614
E-mail: colin.burgess@brunel.ac.uk
Web: http://www.brunel.ac.uk/life/study/computing/media
Media Services provides a range of services and facilities to support teaching, learning and research: supplying audio-visual presentation facilities in lecture rooms; offering creative and technical expertise to produce photographic, video and multimedia projects; teaching video and radio production modules within the university's degree programme; providing a central off-air recording service (television and radio, including satellite/digital) to enable staff to use broadcast material for teaching purposes.

Cambridge University Science Productions (CUSP)
E-mail: enquiries@bluesci.org
Web: http://www.bluesci.org/content/view/471/401
Cambridge University Science Productions is a society founded by students and members of the University of Cambridge with the aim of helping people who are interested in science communication, in all media. It produces multimedia packages such as podcasts and webcasts, and training in science communication and 'how the media works' for all its members. CUSP produces webcasts for the annual BA Festival of Science and a regular science magazine entitled *BlueSci*.

Cardiff University: Media Resources Centre
University Hospital of Wales (UHW Unit), Block A-B link corridor, Cardiff University, Heath Park, Cardiff CF14 4XN
☎ 029 2074 3305
E-mail: Med-Res@cardiff.ac.uk
Web: http://www.cardiff.ac.uk/insrv/graphicsandmedia/mediaresources
Responsible for the design, production and provision of media and resources to support teaching, research and clinical documentation in the Wales College of Medicine, Biology, Life and Health Sciences and the Cardiff and Vale NHS Trust, Heath Park Cardiff. The Video Unit is based at the Media Resources Centre, in the University Hospital Wales building. The Video Unit also offers professional advice on procurement and production.

University of Chester: Media Services
Learning Resources, Parkgate Road, Chester CH1 4BJ
☎ 01244 375444
E-mail: david.evans@chester.ac.uk
Web: http://www.chester.ac.uk/lr/media.html
Provides a range of services to support academic staff and students. These services include: audio-visual support; graphic design; photography; printing

and reprographics; video production; video streaming – video compression archiving and transfer service for broadcast (webcast) over the Intranet or Internet (copyright-enabled).

City University: Audio-Visual Services
Computing Services, Northampton Square, London EC1V OHB
☎ 020 7040 8181
E-mail: response-centre@city.ac.uk
Web: http://www.city.ac.uk/client_services/avs
Responsible for: equipment loans; a studio equipped with a two-camera Panasonic system controlled via a vision and audio production mixer, fed into an industrial SVHS video recorder, autocue and talk-back facilities; audio and video transfers; digital editing facilities consisting of a non-linear G4 Macintosh editing system running Adobe Premiere Software. Analogue editing room facilities consist of two Panasonic industrial SVHS linear editing systems and a title generator.

University of Dundee: Video Production Service
Information & Communication Services, Computing Centre, Park Place, Dundee DD1 4HN
☎ 01382 384140 **Fax:** 01382 385505
E-mail: avsupport@dundee.ac.uk
Web: http://www.dundee.ac.uk/ics/services/videoprod
Services include production of television (video) material for teaching, promotional and other purposes; a digital non-linear video editing suite; consultancy in video production; specialist services in the video area; transfer of video between different formats; titling, music and voice-over services for video editing; tape to DVD service; production of clips for VLE Blackboard. These services are also available for outside commercial use.

Durham University: Audio Visual Service
Information Technology Services, Old Elvet, Durham DH1 3HP
☎ 0191 334 1185
E-mail: it-av@durham.ac.uk
Web: http://www.dur.ac.uk/its/services/audio_visual
There are two professional videoconferencing rooms based on the Sony and Polyspan equipment which gives excellent audio and video quality (up to 384 Kbps on ISDN6 and up to 1024 Kbps on the campus network). There is a video editing PC containing a Pinnacle DV500 Plus video capture card and a copy of Adobe Premiere 6.0. Audio-visual/IT equipment and technical support are available for occasional hire for external meetings and conferences.

University of East Anglia: Audio Visual Services
Norwich NR4 7TJ
☎ 01603 592488
E-mail: C.Browne@uea.ac.uk
Web: http://www1.uea.ac.uk/cm/home/services/units/is/services/teaching/avs
AVS supports four main activities within the university: television studio and video production, lecture room support, and videoconferencing. Production services include studio recording, video and audio copying, video standards conversion, location audio recording, voice-over recording, off-air recording, media training, post production facilities and equipment hire. Videoconferencing is provided by Access Grid. The facilities are available for hire by outside clients.

University of East London: Learning Resource Centres
Docklands Campus, 4-6 University Way, London E16 2RD
☎ 020 8223 3434
E-mail: hamilton@uel.ac.uk
Web: http://www.uel.ac.uk/students/being_student/lrc.htm
There are six Learning Resource Centres across the university's different campuses. Video playback machines for individual and group viewing are provided in all LRCs. In the Barking LRC there are video production and editing suites. A range of equipment can be borrowed including camcorders, cameras and audio cassette recorders.

Edge Hill University: Learning Services
St Helens Road, Ormskirk Lancs L39 4QP
☎ 01695 584286
Web: http://www.edgehill.ac.uk/Sites/LearnServ/EquipFac/mediafac.htm
Learning Services provides a range of presentation and media equipment within its resource centres for use by students and staff. Media facilities include a fully equipped television studio, linear and non-linear editing, sound production and off-air recording facilities.

University of Essex: Audiovisual & Media Services
Wivenhoe Park, Colchester, Essex CO4 3SQ
☎ 01206 873220 **Fax:** 01206 872523
E-mail: avmserv@essex.ac.uk Web: http://www.essex.ac.uk/avms
AVMS advises University of Essex staff and technical staff at other HE institutions on the use of multimedia and audio-visual technologies for teaching and learning. AVMS is also responsible for audio-visual equipment in seminar and lecture rooms and hire of portable equipment. For videoconferencing, the university has a centrally provided system (Tandberg 990) in the Multi Media Centre that uses digital telephone lines (ISDN 6) or an Internet connection (IP). Staff of the university and external users can book the service.

University of Exeter: IT Services
North Park Road, Exeter, Devon EX4 4QE
☎ 01392 264344
E-mail: avsqueens@exeter.ac.uk Web: http://www.its.ex.ac.uk/services
Provides technical support for audio-visual facilities in centrally-bookable teaching and meeting rooms; co-ordination of audio-visual facilities throughout the university; support for videoconferencing in teaching and meeting rooms; support for desktop videoconferencing systems; management of the ongoing programme for upgrade/replacement of audio-visual equipment and infrastructure in centrally-bookable teaching and meeting rooms. Audio-visual support is available for external clients using university facilities for conferences and events.

University College Falmouth: Media Centre
Tremough Campus, Penryn TR10 9EZ
☎ 01326 370400
Web: http://www.falmouth.ac.uk/index.php?option=com_content&task=view&id=299&Itemid=138
The Media Centre houses industry-standard facilities including a recording studio, a well-equipped newsroom with an IRN news feed and forty-five workstations with professional scriptwriting and editing software, a talk studio with three radio control rooms, four dedicated Pro-Tools audio post-produc-

tion rooms with 5.1 surround sound capability and a new animation studio. Other facilities include a television studio, fourteen AVID edit suites, a well-stocked equipment store with a range of cameras and related items, an IT Suite with audio editing and graphics software, and a 106-seat cinema. The facilities are available for use by local businesses.

University of Glamorgan: Media Services
Learning Resources Centre, Pontypridd CF37 1DL
☎ 01443 482608
E-mail: msparks@glam.ac.uk
Web: http://www.glam.ac.uk/lrc/about/media.php
Media Services supports the effective use of audio and visual media in teaching, learning and research by providing facilities, equipment, production services, advice and training. It assists staff in producing and acquiring audio-visual content and in delivering it in the classroom or online. It helps with the production of video, audio and photographic materials to support teaching, learning, and research. Media Services has two fully equipped videoconferencing studios, which are part of the Welsh Video Network that supports over eighty similar studios throughout the Welsh HE and FE sectors.

University of Glasgow: Learning & Teaching Centre
Southpark House, 64 Southpark Avenue G12 8LB
☎ 0141 330 4864/3870
E-mail: learn@admin.gla.ac.uk
Web: http://www.gla.ac.uk/services/learningteaching/mediaproduction
The media production team provide innovative and cost-effective teaching aids, mixed media, consultancy and training. They offer a comprehensive service from script development to completed programme, plus creative preparation of materials for multi-format delivery. Production facilities include top of the range filming and editing crews and equipment, well equipped television studio, sound suite, video transfers between all major professional formats, video encoding, DVD and CD authoring, VHS, CD and DVD duplication, and off-air recording.

Glasgow Caledonian University: Audio-Visual Services
William Harley Building, Cowcaddens Road, Glasgow G4 0BA
☎ 0141 273 1234
E-mail: ithelp@gcal.ac.uk Web: http://www.learningservices.gcal.ac.uk/avs
Audio-Visual Services provide a range of support for teaching and learning within the university, including videoconferencing, off-air recording, classroom resources, audio-visual equipment hire, sound and video production facilities and expertise. There is broadcast-quality camera and editing equipment, a fully-equipped sound studio, and open-access video editing facilities for use by staff and students.

University of Hull: AudioVisual Service
Computing Services, Applied Science 3 Building, Cottingham Road, Hull HU6 7RX
☎ 01482 466116
E-mail: helpdesk@hull.ac.uk Web: http://www.hull.ac.uk/comp/av_service
The camera and sound recording team are available to make short videos for academic staff for use in teaching. They also offer advice and facilities for video editing in Avid Edit suites. The unit has equipment for playing most types of video tape and can make single or multiple copies of video tapes, audio tapes

and CDs (copyright permitting). Video can be digitised for streaming on university web sites or inclusion in PowerPoint presentations. Stills can be captured from video and conversion can be done between the video standards of different countries.

University of Hull: Hull Immersive Visualization Environment (HIVE)

Cottingham Road, Hull HU6 7RX
☎ 01482 465016 **Fax:** 01482 465823
E-mail: hive@hull.ac.uk Web: http://www.hive.hull.ac.uk
HIVE provides state-of-the-art visualisation, interaction and computing technology and related support for both university departments and industry. Facilities include stereoscopic vision (using immersive workwall or desktop PCs); virtual and augmented reality; virtual prototyping; collaborative design reviews; development of virtual environment trainers; simulation of urban development and terrain; scientific and medical visualisation scene capture and reverse engineering using stereo cameras, motion tracking, CMM; haptic interaction with visualisations; high performance computing.

University of Keele: Media and Communications Centre

Chancellors Building, Keele, Staffordshire ST5 5BG
☎ 01782 583377 **Fax:** 01782 714832
E-mail: Media@keele.ac.uk and info@mediaandcomms.co.uk
Web: http://www.keele.ac.uk/depts/md and http://www.mediaandcomms.co.uk
The Centre has a large range of audio visual equipment for hire; purpose built studio space with the latest Tandberg videoconferencing equipment; multimedia and video facilities including video production and digital edit suites, CD, VHS and DVD duplication and standards conversion, and television and radio off-air recording. The facilities are available for commercial hire by organisations outside of the university.

University of Kent: Audio Visual Services

Computing Services, Cornwallis South Building, Canterbury CT2 7NF
☎ 01227 824666
E-mail: avs@kent.ac.uk Web: http://www.kent.ac.uk/is/computing/avs
Audio Visual Services aims to enhance learning and teaching through the use of interactive and digital technology. It provides videoconferencing facilities for internal and external use, lecture recording in web-ready format for putting online so that students can download and listen to them, an off-air recording service, and equipment loan for use in lecture rooms.

Lancaster University Television

Round House, Lancaster University, Lancaster LA1 4YW
☎ 01524 593984
E-mail: lutv@lancaster.ac.uk Web: http://www.lancs.ac.uk/users/lutv
LUTV provides a wide range of television and video production services to staff and students at Lancaster University. Most of these services are also available to commercial companies, organisations and government agencies in the UK and overseas. Services range from 'off-air' recording and multiple copying to high quality programme production and the provision of 'production skills' workshops. LUTV is able to produce and distribute video materials on DVD, VHS, MPEG files for use in PowerPoint presentations and web video for streaming media servers.

University of Leeds: Media Services
Roger Stevens Building, Leeds LS2 9JT
☎ 0113 3432668
E-mail: mediaservices@leeds.ac.uk Web: http://mediant.leeds.ac.uk/A2a.html
Media Services supports the academic, student and administrative communities at the university with a full range of audio-visual and print solutions. It offers a full script-to-screen service and has a purpose-built multi-camera studio, broadcast quality location recording unit, graphic design unit, linear and non-linear editing suites, and a sound studio. There are also facilities for producing 2D and 3D graphics and images, webcasting, video and audio copying and off-air recording. Many of the unit's video productions are available for sale to other institutions.

Leeds Metropolitan University: Technology Services
Room C520 Civic Quarter, Leeds LS1 3HE
☎ 0113 812 5965
E-mail: j.lynch@leedsmet.ac.uk
Web: http://helpzone.leedsmet.ac.uk/staff_video_recording.htm
Video recordings can be made in the television studios or on location in classrooms, lecture theatres, labs and off campus. The Media Production Support Service (http://helpzone.leedsmet.ac.uk/media_production_support. htm) offers video recording and video editing support for students working on media projects. Camcorders and audio recorders are available for loan and there are edit suites on both campuses.

Leeds Trinity & All Saints: Media Services
Brownberrie Lane, Horsforth, Leeds, West Yorkshire LS18 5HD
☎ 01132 283 7249
E-mail: a.clifford@leedstrinity.ac.uk
Web: http://www.leedstrinity.ac.uk/services/media_services
The Media Centre is housed in purpose-built accommodation offering television and radio production and training services. Studio facilities and a wide range of production equipment allow realistic broadcasting, recording and editing to take place. Both domestic and broadcast quality video and audio equipment is available for loan from the Media Centre.

University of Leicester: Audio Visual Services
PO Box 138, Medical Sciences Building, University Road, Leicester LE1 9HN
☎ 0116 252 2910
E-mail: nsp@le.ac.uk Web: http://www.le.ac.uk/avs
AVS provides facilities and expertise to support the presentation needs of the university, as well as undertaking some outside work. Equipped to broadcast standards, it produces video, audio and multimedia materials for teaching, promotion and research. A complete range of services is offered from copying, digitising and editing to full production facilities. Equipment support, video and telephone conferencing, and television/radio off-air recording are also undertaken.

Liverpool Hope University: Library, Learning & Information Services (LLIS)
Hope Park, Liverpool L16 9JD
☎ 0151 291 2041
E-mail: itshelp@hope.ac.uk Web: http://www.hope.ac.uk/llis

LLIS supports the learning, teaching, research and administrative activities of the university. Its responsibilities include IT and AVA support and videoconferencing.

Birkbeck, University of London: Estates and Facilities

Malet Street, Bloomsbury, London WC1E 7HX

☎ 020 7631 6271 **Fax:** 020 7631 6019

E-mail: roombookings@bbk.ac.uk

Web: http://www.bbk.ac.uk/ef/roombookings/audiovisual/index.shtml

Recently refurbished lecture theatres and meeting rooms with state-of-the-art technology are available for external hire as well as internal use. This service also includes video and audio editing.

Goldsmiths, University of London: Media Services Centre

The Library, New Cross, London SE14 6NW

☎ 020 7919 7622

E-mail: media-services@gold.ac.uk   Web: http://www.gold.ac.uk/infos/media

The Media Services Centre provides materials, facilities, support and services to help with all media requirements from video to audio, and from photography to photocopying. There are non-linear digital 'Casablanca' suites with opportunities for special effects; a linear tape-to-tape suite for quicker tasks; multi-format video-copying facilities with capacity for making high quality video stills; equipment for fast and real-time audio copying and simple audio mixing.

Imperial College, University of London: Media Services

Level 3, Faculty Building, South Kensington Campus, London SW7 2AZ

☎ 020 7594 8135 or 020 7594 8136

E-mail: c.grimshaw@imperial.ac.uk or m.sayers@imperial.ac.uk

Web: http://www3.imperial.ac.uk/ict/services/
databasewebsiteandmediaservices/mediaservices

Media Services provide professional video and DVD production and web streaming services to Imperial College and external clients. They offer location recording, post-production and VHS and DVD duplication as well, using high end computer technology to encode video content for storing on the server and streaming out onto the Internet.

Institute of Education, University of London: Information Services

20 Bedford Way, London WC1H 0AL

☎ 020 7612 6700

E-mail: media.enq@ioe.ac.uk

Web: http://ioewebserver.ioe.ac.uk/ioe/cms/get.asp?cid=8869&8869_0=9580

The Media section of IS provides facilities and help with the creation of print, audio and video materials; facilities for audio and video copying/editing in a variety of analogue and digital formats; a playback area for viewing multimedia materials.

King's College, University of London: Audio Visual Services

Information Services & Systems, Room 23B, Main Building, The Strand, London WC2R 2LS

☎ 020 7848 2386 **Fax:** 020 7848 2790

E-mail: rod.wilkinson@kcl.ac.uk Web: http://www.kcl.ac.uk/iss/av

Provides audio-visual support for lectures and conferences and also carries out the following work for both staff and students within the college and external clients: videoconferencing; video and audio recording of events and lectures; video and audio dubbing; digital video editing; off-air and satellite recording. There is a small television studio equipped for basic video recording onto DV or mini-DV tape. This can then be edited on PC using a range of video editing software. Captions and voice-overs etc can be added and the edit written to DVD disk. The filmed material can also be processed by ISS staff for web streaming etc. Audio Visual Services also has location equipment including portable DV and mini-DV digital camcorders, audio mixer, microphones etc.

Royal Holloway, University of London: Audio Visual Service
Room AG 01 Arts Building, Egham Hill, Egham TW20 0EX
☎ 01784 443319/443232
E-mail: audiovisual@rhul.ac.uk
Web: http://www.rhul.ac.uk/Information-Services/Audio-Visual
The Audio Visual Service is responsible for providing teaching room support; satellite and television off-air recording; language lab support; videoconferencing; video and audio duplication; maintaining and running the video codec and associated equipment which provides the Livenet interactive video network links to other colleges in the University of London.

Royal Veterinary College, University of London: Electronic-media Unit
Room F17, Royal College Street, London NW1 0TU
☎ 020 7468 5175 **Fax:** 020 7383 0615
E-mail: nshort@rvc.ac.uk
Web: http://www.rvc.ac.uk/AboutUs/Services/eMedia/Index.cfm
The e-Media Unit was set up to develop multimedia learning resources, and staff have experience of graphics, video, animation, instructional design and web development. The Unit's activities include: filming, editing and streaming all college digital videos; developing podcasts, wikis and blogs including collaborative projects with other institutions; developing and supporting the Blackboard Academic Suite VLE; providing technical and pedagogic support to the RVC e-CPD programme.

St George's, University of London: Television Production Unit
4th Floor Hunter Wing, Cranmer Terrace, London SW17 0RE
☎ 020 7825 5087 **Fax:** 020 8725 0075
E-mail: television@sgul.ac.uk
Web: http://www.sgul.ac.uk/depts/academic-services/tv.cfm
The Television Production Unit is responsible for video programme development, multi-camera production, digital and slide imaging, fully equipped studio and editing facilities, off-air broadcast recording, video duplication, audio production. In terms of television graphics it offers: 3-D modelling for animated sequences and still frames, anatomical 'wire-frame' library, titling and special effects. Some of the programmes produced by St George's Media Services are available for sale for patient or medical staff education, and the CLINICAL SKILLS ONLINE series of videos has been developed for web distribution by the e-learning Unit at St George's. An advanced video-conferencing unit is available for use in various locations.

University College London: Media Resources
Windeyer Building, Cleveland Street London W1T 4JF
☎ 020 7679 9257
E-mail: c.nalty@ucl.ac.uk Web: http://www.ucl.ac.uk/mediares/av
Media Resources comprises Multimedia and Production Units, the Audiovisual Centre, Photography and Illustration Units. The Audiovisual Centre supports the audio-visual facilities in UCL's teaching spaces. The Multimedia Unit is responsible for the provision and support of video communications, networked multimedia and the development of multimedia applications and imaging in the support of teaching and learning across all of UCL. Video production has a fully equipped studio and post-production facilities including broadcast quality editing suite, digital dubbing and an audio effects library.

London Metropolitan University: Media Services
166-200 Holloway Rd, London N7 8DB
☎ 020 7133 2315
E-mail: d.coles@londonmet.ac.uk
Web: http://www.londonmet.ac.uk/services/sas/media-services/
media_home.cfm
Media Services offers advice, resources and production facilities in various media to enhance and support teaching and learning. Among these are equipment and technical support for teaching and presentations in classrooms and lecture theatres; creative facilities, assistance and advice on the production of teaching materials; off-air recording service for radio and television broadcasts; photographic services for the production of teaching aids, promotional work and publications.

Loughborough University: Media Services
Loughborough, Leicestershire LE11 3TU
☎ 01509 222190 **Fax:** 01509 610813
E-mail: mediaservices@lboro.ac.uk
Web: http://www.lboro.ac.uk/mediaservices
Among the services offered are linear and non-linear video editing, production and encoding; web site development; CD-ROM mastering and duplication; videoconferencing; video transfer and standard conversions. The Video Production Service offers a professional service from initial concepts and storyboards, location or studio filming, to a final high-quality master in a choice of formats.

Manchester Metropolitan University: Media Services
Ormond Building, Lower Ormond Street, Manchester M15 6BX
☎ 0161 247 3414
E-mail: a.fraser@mmu.ac.uk Web: http://www.mediaservices.mmu.ac.uk
Services include multimedia and video production and editing; video-conferencing; television and radio off-air recording; supply and maintenance of audio-visual equipment. Full length video productions or short sequences can be produced for use on VHS, DVD, CD-ROM or incorporated into a web site.

University of Manchester: Media Centre
☎ 0161 275 2521
E-mail: media-centre@manchester.ac.uk
Web: http://www.estates.manchester.ac.uk/Groups/SupportServices/
Mediacentre/AudioVideo.html

The Media Centre has a pool of equipment for short term loan to members of staff and students to use in programme production; well-equipped television and sound studios; ten edit suites all offering Avid Xpress Pro, Adobe Premiere and Adobe Encore DVD software and one is dedicated to subtitling. The Media Centre also offers Avid Media Composer and Avid Xpress suites and media copying. The Audio Visual Support section provides equipment and technical support for teaching and off-air recording of terrestrial television programmes.

Middlesex University: Learning Resources

Information and Learning Resources, Cat Hill Campus, Barnet EN4 8HT
☎ 020 8411 5798
E-mail: p.dade@mdx.ac.uk Web: http://www.lr.mdx.ac.uk
Audio-visual facilities include videoconferencing, television and photographic studios, darkrooms, video editing suites and various kinds of equipment for loan, such as cameras and camcorders.

University of Newcastle upon Tyne: Television Services

William Leech Building, The Medical School, Framlington Place, Newcastle upon Tyne NE2 4HH
☎ 0191 222 6633
E-mail: urwin.wood@ncl.ac.uk Web: http://www.ncl.ac.uk/iss/tvservices
Television Services provides a comprehensive range of audio, video and film services to both internal and external clients, including: research and script writing; broadcast quality camera recording; analogue/digital broadcast editing; DVD authoring; digital conversion of audio and video files; off-air recording of Freeview television programmes; ISDN and IP videoconferencing; broadcast quality radio interview recording; video streaming.

Northumbria University: IT Services

Room 128, Northumberland Building, Newcastle upon Tyne NE1 8ST
☎ 0191 232 6002 ext 4242
E-mail: it.helpline@northumbria.ac.uk
Web: http://northumbria.ac.uk/sd/central/its/staff_info/audio_visual_info
IT Services provide fixed audio-visual equipment in classrooms, lecture theatres and meeting rooms, including PCs with connection to the network, LCD projectors and screens; loan of equipment to staff for use on university premises; portable videoconferencing facilities; streaming media service.

Nottingham Trent University: Video Services

IS Learning Team, Kings Meadow Campus, Lenton Lane, Nottingham NG7 2NA
☎ 0115 846 7809
E-mail: IS-Video-Production-Group@nottingham.ac.uk
Web: http://www.nottingham.ac.uk/is/services/video/index.phtml
Offers a complete broadcast quality production service to internal and external clients, including filming (location and studio); creation of video 'still' images as well as MPEG, AVI and QuickTime movies; offline and online video editing; sound recording and editing; live event coverage; media streaming – live and on-demand; digital media encoding/compression (video, audio and stills); DVD authoring/production; CD/DVD duplication and printing; videotape duplication and standards conversion; off-air recording; video archive; audio broadcasting; equipment loan/hire; advice and consultancy; videoconferencing.

Oxford Brookes University: Audio Visual Production

F1/17 Harcourt Hill Campus, Oxford OX2 9AT
☎ 01865 48 8382
E-mail: avharcourthill@brookes.ac.uk
Web: http://www.brookes.ac.uk/avproduction
Provides a service for recording lectures, studio or location filming, video editing in PC-based suites, tape copying and international standards conversion, off-air recording, and making training videos. Advice and consultancy is offered in matters concerning video production, from concept through to duplication. All these services can be hired by external customers, subject to availability. Audio-visual equipment loan and facilities in teaching rooms are handled by Audio Visual Services.

University of Oxford: Media Production Unit

Oxford Public Affairs Directorate, 37 Wellington Square, Oxford OX1 2JF
☎ 01865 270526
E-mail: lisa.wiggins@admin.ox.ac.uk
Web: http://www.ox.ac.uk/publicaffairs/mpu
The Media Production Unit has the facility to produce broadcast quality video. The crew can be hired to produce programmes to support teaching and to promote university or college activities, or for commercial activities outside the university. The unit offers professional digital editing as well as an iMac suite where customers may edit their own video footage, tape duplication and standards conversion, and videoconferencing facilities for up to 100 people. There is a small amount of audio-visual equipment for hire.

University of Paisley: ICT Media Services

High Street, Paisley PA1 2BE
☎ 0141 848 3824
E-mail: charlie.hunter@paisley.ac.uk
Web: http://www.paisley.ac.uk/schoolsdepts/students/media/index.asp
Facilities include a colour television studio, videoconferencing suite, television and radio off-air recording from all the UK national terrestrial networks plus the majority of satellite channels broadcast in the western hemisphere, tape duplication, and loan of a range of media services equipment to students and staff.

University of Plymouth: Television and Broadcast Services

Information & Communication Systems, Drake Circus, Plymouth PL4 8AA
☎ 01752 233640
E-mail: l.portman@plymouth.ac.uk
Web: http://www.plymouth.ac.uk/pages/view.asp?page=2525
Services include live television broadcasting; satellite services supporting broadcasting and research experiments; video production; television presentation training; video recording of lectures; location recording; specialist graphic facilities; video editing; videoconferencing ISDN2 and ISDN6 for meetings and specialist lectures; advice on all aspects of television production; satellite installation site surveys and advice; video-transfer; web streaming. Technical advice, facilities hire and video production are also available to external clients.

University of Portsmouth: e-Learning Centre

Town Mount, Hampshire Terrace, Portsmouth PO1 2QG
☎ 023 9284 6510
E-mail: richard.hackett@port.ac.uk
Web: http://www.elearning.port.ac.uk/services
The Media Production Team is part of the e-Learning Centre which draws together the university's central resources for e-learning, media production (including video streaming and podcasting) and editorial print-based publishing. The Media Production team can guide colleagues through the production process and advise on using different techniques or the many pedagogical issues that may arise. Services offered include: script development; location filming; television studio production; blue screen; post-production/editing; media encoding; podcasting; recording of lectures; videoconferencing.

Queens University Belfast: Media Services

Information Services Learning & Teaching Division, Science Library, Chlorine Gardens, Belfast BT9 5EQ
☎ 028 90974293
E-mail: avs@qub.ac.uk Web: http://www.qub.ac.uk/is/MediaServices
In addition to teaching room support, Media Services is responsible for portable videoconferencing facilities; photographic and graphic design services; video and audio digitisation for PowerPoint, multimedia or web streaming applications; video duplication and systems conversion. Video production at all levels is supported, from 'self-drive' VHS and digital editing for staff and students, to broadcast quality recording and post production. A multimedia production service is available for producing digital files for use in PowerPoint presentations, media streaming or CD-ROM format.

University of Reading: Media Production

IT Services Centre, Whiteknights P.O. Box 220 Reading RG6 6AF
☎ 0118 378 8771
E-mail: its-media@reading.ac.uk
Web: http://www.reading.ac.uk/its/info/services/media.htm
Media Production provides low cost, quality digital and traditional media components for teaching, learning, and research, including: single camera video (digital); video digitisation and encoding; basic video editing (digital and traditional); VHS and digital video copying; off-air terrestrial and satellite recordings; audio recording and copying (digital and traditional); 35mm and medium format stills photography; slide digitisation.

Robert Gordon University: Educational Media Services (EMS)

Department for the Enhancement of Learning, Teaching and Assessment (DELTA), Blackfriars Building, Schoolhill, Aberdeen AB10 1FR
☎ 01224 263349
E-mail: s.merrakech@rgu.ac.uk
Web: http://www2.rgu.ac.uk/celt/ems/index.html
EMS supports learning and teaching needs across the university through the provision of video and multimedia production, digital photography and imaging, and audio-visual hardware. It offers a comprehensive range of services including educational DVD video production; digital video encoding; interactive multimedia design and production; audio programmes production; audio-visual presentation programmes; graphic design; digital media files; screen graphics design; still video animation; video frame capture; CD/DVD replication; media production training.

Roehampton University: Television Roehampton (TVR)

Information Services, Television Centre, Digby Stuart, Roehampton Lane, London SW15 5PH
☎ 020 8392 3590
E-mail: tvr@roehampton.ac.uk
Web: http://www.roehampton.ac.uk/media/TelevisionRoehampton.asp
The facilities of TVR include four studios (a small presentation studio, a sound studio for audio recording, interviews and voice-overs, and two small production studios); VHS, digital, linear and non-linear editing; location and studio-based production; off-air recording from terrestrial and satellite broadcasts. The Multimedia section of Media Services provides and supports the facilities for sound editing from audio cassette, VHS and CD digitised to computer, edited and transferred to audio cassette or CD in conjunction with TVR voice recordings, as well as video editing for multimedia projects.

St Andrews University: SALTIRE

91 North Street, St. Andrews, Fife KY16 9AJ
☎ 01334 462141
E-mail: learning@st-andrews.ac.uk Web: http://www.st-andrews.ac.uk/saltire
SALTIRE was established to enhance the development of traditional as well as innovative approaches to learning and teaching. One of SALTIRE's six main areas of activity is supporting the delivery of study skills. This includes assisting Schools to create and maintain learning and teaching materials in order to enhance teaching via both traditional and innovative methods, including online approaches using a virtual or managed learning environment (VLE or MLE). The Psychology Department provides audio and video production and editing services, as well as off-air recording, video copying and standards conversion.

University of Salford: Audio Visual Services

Information Services Division, Chapman Building, Salford, Greater Manchester M5 4WT
☎ 0161 2955000
E-mail: avs-cars@salford.ac.uk Web: http://www.isd.salford.ac.uk/audiovisual
AVS supports the teaching and learning environment across the university campus. It provides audio, video and DVD duplication and transfer, and a broadcast quality filming, editing and DVD authoring service. Facilities and services are available to users outside the university via the Conference Office.

University of Sheffield: Learning Development and Media Unit

5 Favell Road Sheffield S3 7QX
☎ 0114 222 0400
E-mail: ldmu@shef.ac.uk Web: http://www.shef.ac.uk/ldmu
LDMU has a skilled production team comprising designers, programmers and educational advisers that work with academic staff to produce high quality resources to support student learning. Their involvement ranges from offering advice at the beginning of projects and allowing staff to produce their own material using the DIY facilities Suite, providing equipment and a television studio, to producing bespoke videos as stand-alone programmes or as video clips embedded into a larger learning resource, and to producing large interactive multimedia teaching packages and networked learning courses for WebCT. Other services offered include media conversion and copying, off-air recording and standards conversion.

University of Southampton: e.media

Information Systems Services, Building 35-3003, Highfield SO17 1BJ
☎ 023 8059 7626
E-mail: tjor@soton.ac.uk Web: http://www.soton.ac.uk/iss/mediadesign
e.media is the university's specialist multimedia production team for interactive CD-ROMs, DVDs, web sites and videos. Services offered include video and audio encoding and streaming; video duplication and off-air recording. e.media also provides a complete range of media production services, from the straightforward videoing of lectures or demonstrations, to writing, filming, editing and bulk-copying promotional material for schools and producing complete educational packages.

University of Strathclyde: Learning Services

Alexander Turnbull Building, 155 George Street, Glasgow G1 1RD
☎ 0141 548 2712
E-mail: learningservices@strath.ac.uk
Web: http://www.learningservices.strath.ac.uk
The video production service produces resources ranging from simple lecture recordings to complex projects produced in studio or in other locations, for delivery via the web, CD-ROM, DVD and use in PowerPoint presentations. A campus-wide 24/7 video streaming service is provided as well as live video streaming to provide enhanced access to lectures and conference presentations. Learning Services also provides teaching room audio-visual equipment, support for the VLE and e-learning, IT training, special needs IT support, design, Internet copyright clearance and multimedia production.

University of Sunderland: Audio Visual Team

Learning Development Services, Room 008, Prospect Building, Sir Tom Cowie campus at St. Peter's, St. Peters Way, Sunderland SR6 0DD
☎ 0191 515 2280/3192
E-mail: paula.devlin@sunderland.ac.uk
Web: http://my.sunderland.ac.uk/web/services/lds/daudio-visual?daudio-visual
The audio-visual team is responsible for equipping the theatres and managing the audio-visual facilities; promoting the use of new equipment and technology; evaluating new and emerging audio-visual technology and equipment; WebCT support; offering audio-visual support, advice and expertise to special events.

University of Surrey: UniS Television

Guildford, Surrey GU2 7XH

☎ 01483 879991

E-mail: b.johnson@surrey.ac.uk Web: http://www.surrey.ac.uk/tv

UniS Television offers professional production and facilities house services including two fully equipped studios, DVC Pro and Betacam Edit Suite, DVC pro and Betacam SP ENG facilities, AVID online suite, SVHS Edit Suite, voice-over recording and a sound booth. It also offers video copying and industrial standards conversion that can master from DVC pro, DVCAM, Umatic and VHS formats via TBC and VDA ADA distribution amps to quality Panasonic HiFi VHS machines. Audio-visual equipment support for teaching rooms is provided by the Audio Visual Services section of IT Services.

University of Sussex: Media Services Unit

Education Development Building, EDB 252, Falmer, Brighton BN1 9RG

☎ 01273 678022

E-mail: msu@sussex.ac.uk Web: http://www.sussex.ac.uk/its/msu

Multimedia services include providing audio-visual equipment and staff for teaching rooms and conferences, and a consultancy service for advice on purchase and installation; audio and video copying and standards conversion; digital video editing using industry-standard Avid DV Xpress and digital audio editing using Adobe Audition software; professional-quality audio and video programme production and post-production facilities for academic and commercial clients; a videoconferencing facility using ISDN and other technologies on other networks via the JVCS service.

University of Ulster: Media Technology Support

IT User Services, South Building, Cromore Road, Coleraine BT52 1SA

☎ 028 9036 6777

E-mail: helpdesk@ulster.ac.uk Web: http://www.ulster.ac.uk/isd/itus/media

Services include teaching and space support; a range of room-based, roll-about and personal videoconferencing systems; video streaming; video and sound production team to enable staff to create, edit and produce video and audio recordings on video cassette, CD-ROM and DVD for incorporation into lectures and tutorials or digitisation for online learning via download or on-demand video streaming.

University of Wales, Aberystwyth: See3D

Visualisation Centre, Llandinam Building, Penglais Campus, Aberystwyth, Ceredigion SY23 3DB

☎ 01970 628428

E-mail: info@see3d.co.uk Web: http://www.see3d.co.uk

See3D uses a Silicon Graphics Prism machine for developing specialist visualisations and software, providing motion tracking, stereo 3D, and true perspective imagery. The facilities are available for use by outside academic and commercial institutions as well as by staff at Aberystwyth. Videoconferencing, off-air recording, lecture recording, video streaming, and video duplication and conversion services within the university are provided by Media Services (http://www.inf.aber.ac.uk/mediaservices).

University of Wales, Bangor: Media Centre

Hen Goleg, College Road, Bangor, Gwynedd LL57 7PX

☎ 01248 382412

E-mail: R.P.Wood@bangor.ac.uk

Web: http://www.bangor.ac.uk/itservices/av/mediacentre.php.en
The Media Centre houses radio and television facilities, together with video and audio editing suites. It has a range of portable video and audio equipment for use by staff and students, a broadcast radio studio with analogue and digital facilities, video editing facilities, television studio, and three videoconferencing studios.

University of Wales, Newport: Audio Visual Services

Library and Information Services, Room C1A41 Lodge Road, Caerleon Newport NP18 3NT
☎ 01633-432172 ext. 2172
E-mail: rob.hyde@newport.ac.uk Web: http://lis.newport.ac.uk/av
The television studio can produce with up to five cameras and record on to S-VHS video tape or semi-professional Mini-DV format. The Control Room has the facility for caption camera, a video playback machine and audio playback. The studio has a Panasonic vision and effects mixer, which provides a range of luminance and 'chroma-keying' facilites. A videoconferencing suite, with facilities to conference by both IP and ISDN, is available for university and external use. Other services include off-air recording, equipment loan and teaching room support.

University of Wales, Swansea: Media Resources

Room 15 Keir Hardie Building, Singleton Park, Swansea SA2 8PP Wales
☎ 01792 295010
E-mail: aamedia@swan.ac.uk
Web: http://www.swan.ac.uk/acu/MediaResources
Media Resources is a central service providing a wide range of facilities to the university, some of which include television and video, language laboratory, audio-visual facilities and videoconferencing.

University of Wales Institute, Cardiff: Audio Visual Support

Howard Gardens Campus, Cardiff CF24 0SP
☎ 029 2041 7107
E-mail: AVsupportHG@uwic.ac.uk Web: http://www.uwic.ac.uk/avsupport
Audio-visual offices are situated at all four teaching sites. The core functions of the service are: provision of audio-visual support services to general teaching areas; equipment loan service; supporting a videoconferencing facility.

University of Warwick: Audio Visual Centre

IT Services Building, Gibbett Hill Road, Coventry CV4 7AL
☎ 024 76573737
E-mail: audio-visual@warwick.ac.uk
Web: http://www2.warwick.ac.uk/services/its/servicessupport/av
The multimedia production service offers analogue and digital copying between formats, and basic editing. The filming service provides digital camera recording of lectures given in centrally timetabled teaching rooms. The Audio Visual Centre also supports the equipment needs of teaching rooms; operates a short-term equipment loan scheme for staff; provides videoconferencing facilities; and runs the off-air recording scheme.

University of Westminster: Computing and Audio Visual

E-mail: mrav@wmin.ac.uk Web: http://www.wmin.ac.uk/sabe/page-942
Each of the four campuses provides a range of audio-visual equipment from data projectors, cameras and video camcorders to flip chart stands and

microphones for use by staff and students. Audio-visual equipment, a CCTV studio and video editing suite, together with technical support, are available for outside hire from the university's Estates and Facilities Department (http://www.wmin.ac.uk/page-6661).

University of Winchester: IT & Communication Services Department

Winchester SO22 4NR
☎ 01962 841515
E-mail: ITCentre@winchester.ac.uk
Web: http://www.winchester.ac.uk/?page=7856

ITCS provides a wide range of equipment and support for IT, audio, video and photographic activities. A loan service offers photographic, video, lighting and audio equipment, supported by advice on its choice and use. Staff also provide training and support in the use of the video editing suites and video copying facilities which are available for post-production work.

University of Worcester: Digital Arts Centre

Henwick Grove, WR2 6AJ
☎ 01905 855392
E-mail: p.hazell@worc.ac.uk Web: http://www.worc.ac.uk/digitalmedia

Offers studio facilities, consultancy, courses and content creation to the local community as well as students attending courses at the university. Users are able to draw on a central bank of digital multimedia facilities such as computers running industry-standard digital media software and smaller spaces for digital media experimentation, research, production and development work. There is a 48-track digital recording studio, a digital video production studio with full lighting rig and blue screen technology, digital video editing facilities and web servers.

University of York: Audio-Visual Centre

Directorate of Facilities Management, Heslington, York YO10 5DD
☎ 01904 43 3031
E-mail: rw8@york.ac.uk
Web: http://www.york.ac.uk/campusservices/avcentre

Responsible for providing equipment and technical staff to support teaching in term-time and conference business in vacation. The Centre consists of colour television and sound studios, control room and full editing suite for the production of high band video recordings. It can also offer a three-camera outside recording unit. The university has a closed circuit television network capable of transmitting four programmes simultaneously across the campus. The videoconferencing facility is equipped with a Tandberg 990 MXP unit and can use either ISDN channels providing from 128Kbs (ISDN 2) to 384Kbs (ISDN 6) bandwidth, or a network connection to provide IP connectivity up to 2Mbps.

WEB SITES

All of these web sites, and over 900 more, can be found on the BUFVC's Moving Image Gateway (http://www.bufvc.ac.uk/gateway). The MIG collects together sites that relate to moving images and sound and their use in higher and further education. The sites are classified by academic discipline, some forty subjects from Agriculture to Women's Studies, collected within the four main categories of Arts & Humanities, Bio-Medical, Social Sciences and Science & Technology. Each site is evaluated and described by the BUFVC's Information Service. The selection of sites given below all offer video or audio content, and is an indication of the great variety of specialist sites delivering audio-visual materials online.

Acoustics and Vibration Animations
Web: http://www.kettering.edu/~drussell/demos.html
An imaginative and extensive use of animations to visualise concepts concerning acoustics and vibration, constructed by Dr. Dan Russell at Kettering University, Flint, Michigan, using Mathematica software. The animations and other, static diagrams accompany informative texts illustrating such topics as Basic Wave Phenomena, Sound Waves and Radiation from Sources, Room Acoustics, Vibrational Modes of Continuous Systems, Optical Ray Tracing, and Matter Rays. Among the delights are the acoustics of baseball bats, and vibrational modes of an electric and acoustic guitar. The site also contains GIF animations and brief movies (using RealPlayer), including the celebrated Tacoma Narrows Bridge, 'when engineers don't account for resonance when designing structures.'

AdForum.com
Web: http://www.adforum.com
An advertising industry portal, boasting links to over 20,000 agencies, and with an impressively orderly and informative database of nearly 80,000 adverts (magazine, radio, Internet, television etc.), searchable by type, agency, production company, brand, country, business sector and credits (including performers). Access to the advertisements themselves is no longer free but exists under a variety of subscription plans, including educational.

American Memory
Web: http://memory.loc.gov/ammem/amhome.html
The incomparable American Memory section of the vast Library of Congress site includes a Performing Arts section, with playscripts, theatre bills, sound recordings and motion pictures, notably the *American Variety 1870-1920* section which includes a wide selection of early film productions, usefully categorised by theme, and with excellent supporting catalogue information.

Apollo Lunar Surface Journal
Web: http://history.nasa.gov/alsj
The Apollo Lunar Surface Journal is a record of the lunar surface operations conducted by the six pairs of astronauts who landed on the Moon from 1969 through 1972. The Journal is intended as a resource for anyone wanting to know what happened during the missions and why. It includes a corrected transcript of all recorded conversations between the lunar surface crews and Houston. The Journal also contains extensive, interwoven commentary by the editor and by ten of the twelve moonwalking astronauts. There are extensive

downloadable videoclips (QuickTime, Real and MPEG) for Apollos 11 to 17, including the first Moon landing, with supporting metadata.

Archival Sound Recordings

Web: http://sounds.bl.uk

12,000 selected audio recordings of music, spoken word, and human and natural environments. Anyone can search or browse the information. For copyright reasons, only people in licensed UK higher and further education institutions, or in the BL's reading rooms, can play the recordings. Downloading is available in licensed institutions. The collections include popular music tracks (mostly British bands from the 1930s to 1990s), African Writers' Club, Art and design interviews, Beethoven String Quartets, David Rycroft Africa recordings, Klaus Wachsmann Uganda recordings, Oral history of jazz in Britain, Records and record players, Sony Radio Awards – drama (every short-listed play 1986-1997), Soundscapes and St Mary-le-Bow public debates. The project has been funded as part of the JISC Digitisation Programme.

ARKive

Web: http://www.arkive.org

ARKive is a centralised digital library of films, photographs and sound recordings on species, created by the Wildscreen Trust and launched in May 2003. ARKive describes itself as a 'virtual conservation effort – finding, sorting, cataloguing and copying the key records of species, and building them into a comprehensive and enduring audio-visual record.' Its ultimate aim is to provide an audio-visual record of 11,000 endangered species. There is a mixture of still and moving image records, and sound recordings – the moving images are available in downloadable QuickTime, and in streaming format for Real (modem and broadband) and Windows Media Player (modem and broadband).

AthenaWeb

Web: http://www.athenaweb.org

Launched in the spring of 2005, AthenaWeb is a video portal and workspace for European audio-visual communication professionals in the areas of science and scientific information. Contributors and users of the service include institutions, universities, labs, corporations, not-for-profit organisations, and the television and film industries. It has a library of freely-accessible videos (QuickTime), classified by subject discipline.

BBC Audio Interviews

Web: http://www.bbc.co.uk/bbcfour/audiointerviews

Hundreds of audio extracts from the BBC archives can be accessed here using Real Player, and feature a wide range of personalities, including Siegfried Sassoon, Alfred Hitchcock, Roald Dahl, George Bernard Shaw, Stevie Smith and dozens of others. It is possible to search alphabetically by name or by professions such as: actors, architects, cartoonists, composers, dancers, film directors, musicians, painters, photographers, poets, religious thinkers, sculptors, sports and writers. The individual clips are supplemented with biographical notes.

BBC On This Day

Web: http://news.bbc.co.uk/onthisday

Video and audio from the BBC news archive from 1950 onwards, made available through RealPlayer, with plenty of textual support. The entire database can be searched by month, day and theme, and there is an eye-witness accounts section.

BBC Training & Development: Free Online Courses

Web: http://www.bbctraining.com/onlineCourses.asp

A range of free online modules and guides on production techniques for television and radio. Some use audio (Real) or Flash animation and others are print-based. They were originally designed for BBC staff and the online versions have not been re-edited. This is because they are primarily aimed at anyone who is working for, with or alongside the BBC, so the modules still contain some specific references to BBC procedures, methods and services. Topics covered include shooting and lighting for digital video; post and pre-production; BBC News style guide; interviewing, minidisc and microphones for radio.

BBC Video Nation

Web: http://www.bbc.co.uk/videonation

Inspired by the Mass-Observation movement of the 1930s onwards, the BBC Video Nation site has grown out of its Video Diaries programmes of the 1990s, where people were given Hi-8 video cameras and invited to record their lives for a year. Video Nation Online was launched in 2001 with 250 of the original shorts. The site has expanded to some 750 films, with strong English regional coverage. The films are classified by theme, special features, localities and contributor.

BIRTH

Web: http://www.birth-of-tv.org/birth

The BIRTH Television Archive is one of the major results an EU-funded project within the MEDIA+ programme. It is a rich multimedia, multilingual web portal giving access to audio-visual and textual material (programme schedules, articles etc) on the early days of European television. The archive was built up by five major European television archives: the BBC, Österreichischer Rundfunk (ORF), Nederlandse Instituut voor Beeld and Geluid, Radio Télévision Belgique Française (RTBF) and Südwestrundfunk (SWR).

British Pathe

Web: http://www.britishpathe.com

British Pathe, with New Opportunities Fund money, has made its whole newsreel film library (3,500 hours) available online with downloadable copies available for free at low resolution, covering the period 1896-1970. Higher resolution copies for broadcast or lecture presentations are available for a fee. Searches can be limited by date, range of years, keyword and type of film. In April 2003 management of British Pathe was taken over by the ITN Archive (now ITN Source).

Clinical Skills Online

Web: http://www.elu.sgul.ac.uk/cso

Clinical Skills Online provides online videos demonstrating core clinical skills common to a wide range of medical and health-based courses. The video content is available in QuickTime or Windows Media Player. Users must be aged over 18 (or 21, depending on location), and content can be selected by user description. The downloadable videos are freely available to anyone using them for educational, personal and non-commercial purposes only (Creative Commons licence). CSO is produced by St George's, University of London, and has been funded by the Higher Education Academy Subject Centre for Medicine, Dentistry and Veterinary Medicine.

Conversations with History

Web: http://globetrotter.berkeley.edu/conversations

A series of video interviews with politicians, economists, historians, journalists, diplomats, educationalists, writers and others, covering a wide range of political, economic, military, legal, cultural, and social issues, with a focus on the individual and their ideas. The series is produced at the Institute of International Studies at the University of California at Berkeley, and began in 1982. The collection comprises over 380 interviews, including Linus Pauling, J.K. Galbraith, Kofi Annan, Wole Soyinka, Oliver Stone and Neil Kinnock. Recent additions to the collection are available as podcasts.

Creative Club

Web: http://www.creativeclub.co.uk

This commercial site provides a useful archive of several years' worth of advertisements which can be searched by brand or company, including items produced for television, radio, cinema and print. These can be purchased from the site and made available on VHS, U-matic, CD and audio tape. The JISC has entered into an agreement with Creative Club to allow access for HE and FE institutions in the UK at special rates.

Ethics Updates

Web: http://ethics.sandiego.edu

Site dedicated to ethics and the study of ethics, particularly providing updates on current literature through Internet links to both texts and video resources. Its section on ethics videos provides an extensive range of videos of public fora, interviews, conferences and round-table discussions on such themes as the Human Genome Project, ethics in medicine, business, computing and religion, ethical theory, and a public forum event from the University of San Diego on terrorist violence given the day after the terrorist attacks of 11 September 2001.

Étienne-Jules Marey: Movement in Light

Web: http://www.expo-marey.com

An ingenious 'online exhibition,' constructed along panoramic lines, on the life and work of French chronophotographer Étienne-Jules Marey, who made a detailed study of human and animal motion in the late nineteenth century, and whose experiments were influential in the development of film. Extensively illustrated, with some QuickTime animations. In French and English.

Findsounds

Web: http://www.findsounds.com

A search engine for sounds. Sounds can be accessed via a simple search or by searching from sound types. Audio files can be downloaded as AIFF, AU and WAVE. Sound types are divided into various categories, including Birds, Animals, Mayhem and Nature. The sound files within these are extensive: for example, there are eight volcano sound files, twenty-five sound files of didgeridoos, eleven examples of thunder, and five kookaburra recordings. All searches link the user to audio files hosted by external web sites.

FORA.tv
Web: http://fora.tv
FORA.tv is an online television station delivering discourse, discussions and debates on the world's most interesting political, social and cultural issues. The programmes (chiefly interviews and speeches) are divided into Arts and Culture, Business, Education, Environment, Politics, Religion, Science and Health, and Technology. Viewers are able to add comments and subject tags, and the programmes are chaptered with word-searchable synchronised transcripts. The videos can be downloaded in MPEG-4 format.

Gaumont Pathé Archives
Web: http://www.gaumontpathearchives.com
The combined archives of the Gaumont, Éclair and French Pathé news archives, with news material going back to 1896. There are a substantial number of streamed video copies of the Gaumont newsreels, making this site one of the leading sources of online historical news footage in the world. The videos use RealPlayer, for connections from 56K to T1, and the quality of the encodings is high. The catalogue is available in French and English, the latter appearing to have been produced using a translation programme, which has produced some quaint results.

Health Library Online Video Collection
Web: http://med.stanford.edu/healthlibrary/resources/videos.html
The Health Library and Stanford University provide over fifty streamed videos on common health topics in six categories: Cancer Supportive Care, Health and Society, Women and Health, Stanford Hospitals and Clinics, Jonathan King Lectures and Health Matters. The videos are between thirty and sixty minutes long and are offered in up to six different bandwidths.

HubbleSite
Web: http://hubblesite.org
Produced by the Space Telescope Science Institute's Office of Public Outreach to explain the findings of the Hubble Space Telescope. There is an extensive video news section which includes all video content released as part of its news service, categorised by theme (cosmology, nebula, galaxy, star cluster etc) and type (interview, webcast, illustrative etc). The videos are available in QuickTime and MPEG formats, for low and high bandwidth.

Laparoscopy.com
Web: http://www.laparoscopy.com/fr_movies.html
As the introduction states, 'this web-site provides an interactive enjoyable multimedia database to inform about the advancing technology of laparoscopic surgery and other micro-invasive techniques.' There is a picture gallery and a movie gallery (using Real Audio G2), each subdivided by the categories of abdomen, complications, urology, gynaecology, thorax, endoscopy, vascular and miscellaneous.

Living Room Candidate
Web: http://livingroomcandidate.movingimage.us
An online exhibition containing 183 television commercials, from every American presidential election from 1952 to 2004. The ads can be accessed chronologically or by theme. For each election year there is a selection of commercials, an analysis of each major party's advertising campaign, and a map showing the election results. Hosted by the American Museum of the Moving Image.

Microbiology Video Library

Web: http://www.microbiologybytes.com/video

The University of Leicester's Department of Microbiology & Immunology offers both extracts from its video productions and over 300 dedicated web movies (all using QuickTime) offering such subjects as bacterial photosynthesis, microbiology laboratory procedures, how penicillin kills cells, and the human head louse.

Molecular Expressions Digtal Video Library

Web: http://micro.magnet.fsu.edu/moviegallery/index.html

Collection of short animated videos from the photomicrograph collections of Florida State University, being 'time-lapse digital image sequences that explore the effect of rotating polarisation, sample rotation, and crystallisation as it actually appears under the microscope.' The videos can be streamed using Real Player to suit low or high bandwidths (from 14.4K up to T1 or DSL connections), with a selection of uncompressed digital videos available as AVI downloads. The videos are available in four galleries: Chemical Crystals, Pond Life, the QX3 Microscope Time-Lapse Movie Gallery, and the Nikon MicroscopyU Digital Movie Gallery, and each comes with supporting descriptions.

Moving History

Web: http://www.movinghistory.ac.uk

An online guide to the UK's public sector moving image archives, designed to encourage the use of such archives for scholarly research. The site contains 100 film clips, arranged by archive or by theme, in-depth descriptions of the archives, and guidelines for researchers. The site includes **Films from the Home Front** (http://www.movinghistory.ac.uk/homefront), featuring films of life on the home front in Britain during the Second World War.

Newsfilm Online
Web: http://www.bufvc.ac.uk/newsfilmonline
Newsfilm Online will offer access to 3,000 hours of television news content to users throughout UK higher and further education. The newsfilm will be delivered in downloadable form, meaning that users may retain and reuse copies long term under a sub-licence agreement. All of the ITN material encoded for Newsfilm Online is being made available to UK higher and further education 'in perpetuity.' Nearly 100 downloadable stories are currently freely available to all from this demonstrator site, with a full web service planned for early 2008.

Old Time Radio (OTR)
Web: http://www.otr.com
A nostalgia site for American radio which is wide-ranging and informative, including useful sections on radio news (commentators, major stories and series such as THE MARCH OF TIME, science fiction, private eyes, comedy and mystery. Its radio links page with short, helpful descriptions is valuable. It now offers podcasts of archive radio programmes, include FLASH GORDON episodes.

OpenLearn
Web: http://openlearn.open.ac.uk
The Open University's OpenLearn web site provides free and open educational resources for learners and educators around the world. OpenLearn offers online free learning material taken from Open University courses, state-of-the-art learner support, tools connecting learners with learners and educators, and learning media and technologies on a large scale. It is not necessary to be a student of the OU to use the resources, but OpenLearn does not of itself grant degrees or award credits. There is substantial video content included (Flash).

Open Video Project
Web: http://www.open-video.org
The Open Video Project is being developed by the Interaction Design Laboratory at the University of North Carolina. It is building up a library of downloadable video segments in MPEG-1, MPEG-2, MPEG-4, and so far includes materials predominantly from the Carnegie Mellon University Informedia Project on geology, geography and oceanography; the University of Maryland Human-Computer Interaction Lab; and particularly the Prelinger Archives on everyday life in America.

Parliamentlive.tv
Web: http://www.parliamentlive.tv
Proceedings from the British parliament have been streamed live since February 2002. The service is available using Windows Media Player or RealPlayer, and offers live webcasts of the House of Commons, the House of Lords, Westminster Hall, and Select Committees. A schedule shows what sessions are coming up over the week, and which of these will be audio or video streamed.

Poetry Archive
Web: http://www.poetryarchive.org
Spearheaded by the Poet Laureate Andrew Motion, this audio resource (RealOne is required) collects recordings of dozens of poems read by their

authors. It can be searched by author name and by title as well as theme and form. The authors included cover a wide range, from Margaret Atwood to W.B. Yeats, and many have links to CDs of the recordings which are available for sale. In addition there are useful biographical essays on the poets themselves.

Public Information Films
Web: http://www.nationalarchives.gov.uk/films
Public information films, produced by the Central Office of Information 1946-2006. There is useful contextual material, both on the films and on the historical reasons for their production. Titles include COUGHS AND SNEEZES, THE BRITISH POLICEMAN, an example of the THIS WEEK IN BRITAIN cinemagazine, SUEZ IN PERSPECTIVE, CLUNK CLICK, PROTECT & SURVIVE and AIDS MONOLITH. The films are available in Windows Media Players and QuickTime formats (high and low quality), with five titles available for download to iPods.

ResearchChannel
Web: http://www.researchchannel.com
ResearchChannel is a webcaster and an audio-visual library of over 3,000 streamed lectures on the arts, engineering, law, medicine, sciences, social sciences and other topics. Through cable and satellite distribution, ResearchChannel is available to more than 25 million US households. The channel is also available on select academic networks in the United States and other countries.

Research-TV
Web: http://www.research-tv.com
Research-TV was created by the University of Warwick to provide broad-casters with a regular news feed of stories about cutting-edge research. It divides its programmes up into Health, Technology, Society, Science and Nature, Business, and Creative and Cultural. Each comes with synopsis, transcript, links, and the programme in narrowband or broadband options (using Windows Media Player). All stories are made available to broadcasters free of charge through the APTN service, on local ends for UK broadcasters and London-based foreign correspondents, with additional tape distribution upon request. All stories are available for preview online.

Roland Collection
Web: http://www.roland-collection.com
The Roland Collection consists of more than 640 films and videos on art available for sale worldwide for institutional and individual use. These are now available on a pay-per-view basis, either streamed or download. Owing to rights management issues, the collection is currently not available to Apple Mac users.

ScienceLive
Web: http://www.sciencelive.org
ScienceLive is an initiative delivering popular science video (discussions, lectures, interviews) to online users. It is an initiative between Cambridge University Science Productions, the British Association for the Advancement of Science, and the Cambridge Science Festival. The video archive is divided into Movies, Lectures and Interviews. All video content is streamed, using Real Player.

Scitalks

Web: http://www.scitalks.com

Portal offering free science video recordings and lectures from around the world; essentially a YouTube for science and scientists. The videos are classified under scientific field, and as Academic, Broadcast or Corporate.

SCRAN

Web: http://www.scran.ac.uk

Scran contains 360,000 multimedia resources (pictures, reconstructions, audio, video and virtual reality) representing material culture and human history from the media, museums, galleries, archives, libraries and universities (over 300 UK partners but predominantly in Scotland). There are over 5,000 video clips in the collection. It maintains a fully searchable online resource bank and registered users may download copyright cleared resources for teaching and learning. Key subject areas are Arts (Art & Design, Architecture, Language and Literature), Social Sciences (History, Geography, Archaeology) and Education.

Screenonline

Web: http://www.screenonline.org.uk

This British Film Institute resource is aimed at media studies students. It includes biographies of British film and television personnel, including actors, writers, directors, producers and composers, searchable by name or via an alphabetical list. A vast amount of material can be viewed on the site, much of which comes from the BFI National Archive. This is only available to schools, colleges and public libraries on their premises and not elsewhere. The streamed material is viewable via QuickTime, Real and Windows Media Player but cannot be downloaded.

Speech Accent Archive

Web: http://accent.gmu.edu

This George Mason University site examines the accented speech of speakers from many different language backgrounds reading the same sample paragraph. Ninety-one national origins are covered from Afrikaans to Zulu. Details of nationality, age, sex, residence and the means by which they learned English are given. The paragraph each person reads has been chosen for containing most of the consonants, vowels, and clusters of standard American English. The audio files use QuickTime.

Spoken Word Services

Web: http://www.spokenword.ac.uk

Spoken Word Services is based in the Saltire Centre at Glasgow Caledonian University. Its core aim is to enhance and transform educational experience through the integration of digitised spoken word audio and video into learning and teaching. It is attempting to make a substantial portion of the BBC's radio archive accessible online for educational use. Other audio content includes audio recordings from the Glasgow Centre for Population Health events and Glasgow Caledonian University Archives Witness Seminars. Users need to sign up for an Educational Users Account, and then can download content or link to a stable web address.

Stagework

Web: http://www.stagework.org.uk

Stagework has been developed by the Culture Online programme to open up innovative theatre practice at the National Theatre and selected regional partners in England to new and existing audiences. It goes behind the scenes to reveal the various stages of the production process, using video content throughout, and a wealth of curriculum resources based upon key productions for teachers and learners of English and Drama, Citizenship, and other subjects.

Television News Archive Vanderbilt University

Web: http://tvnews.vanderbilt.edu

Outstanding collection of American broadcast news, from 1968 to the present day. The database supports a collection of more than 30,000 individual network evening news broadcasts and more than 9,000 hours of special news-related programming, all of which are available as video loans. Searches can be narrowed down by year and give a basic, official description of each story within the news broadcast. There is a premium subscription service for educational institutions (including the UK) enabling them to have access to online video streams from the Archive's collection of CNN material.

theatreVOICE

Web: http://www.theatrevoice.com

Stylishly-designed online 'audio-driven' forum for debate about theatre in London and beyond. Its archive includes forum discussions of plays, interviews, reviews and debates, including contributions from Michael Billington and Richard Eyre. Technical support is provided by the Theatre Museum. There are a few transcriptions available.

To Fly is Everything

Web: http://invention.psychology.msstate.edu/air_main.shtml

A 'virtual museum' on the invention of the aeroplane, including a collection of articles from Leonardo da Vinci to Wilbur Wright, lists of patents, 3D models of aircraft, and a gallery of photographs and films from the earliest years of powered flight. The latter come from the National Air and Space Museum, and include Wilbur Wright in Europe, a film taken from a Wright Flyer in flight, Santos-Dumont's *Demoiselle* and *14 bis*, Henry Farman with passenger, and film of Theodore Roosevelt in a Wright Flyer. The films all require QuickTime.

United States Holocaust Memorial Museum

Web: http://www.ushmm.org

The United States Holocaust Memorial Museum is located in Washington. Its well-organised, informative and attractively laid out site provides a good introduction to its collections, and features video and audio clips (using Real), online exhibitions, oral history material, documents, and resources for students and families, covering Jewish life before, during and after the Holocaust. There is also access to the Museum's library database, including the records of its film and video archive.

University of Newcastle – School of Neurology, Neurobiology and Psychiatry

Web: http://www.ncl.ac.uk/nnp/teaching/video

Videos produced for use in the School of Neurology, Neurobiology and Psychiatry. They are in two main groups: psychopathology clips, which are .avi files, and higher quality Real Media streaming video, used to illustrate common disorders. The clips are based on Stage 3 Cases as used in Newcastle University undergraduate medical course. All the clips are role-playing fictional scenarios using clinical staff and actors. No real patients are included. The clips may be re-used under a Creative Commons licence.

Vega Science Trust
Web: http://www.vega.org.uk
The Vega Science Trust aims to support and promote the science and technology communities through the use of television and the Internet. It produces television programmes, many of which have been broadcast on BBC2's *Learning Zone*. The site contains details of the programmes, searchable by series, subject and speaker, which can be ordered online. There are also video clips (in QuickTime and MPEG formats), complete audio lectures (using RealAudio), complete video lectures by Harry Kroto, and a useful set of links to science video and related sources.

videolectures.net
Web: http://videolectures.net
Hundreds of video lectures and tutorials from some of the world's leading scientists, on a wide variety of topics, as well as interviews with such luminaries as Sir Tim Berners Lee and Noam Chomsky. Windows Media Player is required to view. Copies of the relevant PowerPoint presentations have sometimes been included.

Videography for Educators
Web: http://ali.apple.com/ali_sites/ali/exhibits/1000019
The Videography for Educators exhibit features tips and techniques to assist in the creation of quality video products. The exhibit provides sample planning documents and video examples to illustrate concepts and skills. The content assumes you are already learning the mechanics of iMovie 3 or Final Cut Pro, are familiar with the fundamentals of operating your camcorder, and are ready to learn the art of videography. The concepts, skills, and examples are presented in a manner relevant to classroom teachers. Part of the Apple Technology Showcase.

Virtual Chemistry
Web: http://www.chem.ox.ac.uk/vrchemistry
The University of Oxford's Virtual Chemistry site links to its Chemistry Film Studio (using QuickTime 4) illustrating popular experiments, mainly for use in schools, including 'The Non-Burning £5 Note' and 'The Properties of Liquid Oxygen.' Other resources include LiveChem, an online video library of nearly 300 titles of transition metal salt reaction, and Chemistry QuickTime TV. Also includes a number of streamed lectures.

Visual Cognition Lab
Web: http://viscog.beckman.uiuc.edu/djs_lab/demos.html
The Visual Cognition Lab of the University of Illinois has created a number of videos that show the limits of perception, attention, and awareness. The videos come from Professor Daniel Simons' experiments on visual awareness, and demonstrate how different viewers will see different things in seemingly simple actions. The videos include A PERSON CHANGE VIDEO, CHANGES ACROSS CUTS IN A MOTION PICTURE, and A SUBJECT IN A REAL-WORLD PERSON CHANGE EVENT. All require QuickTime or Java. A famous Simons experiment, the 'basketball' video, is available as a Java applet.

Wochenschau-Archive

Web: http://www.wochenschau-archiv.de

The Federal Film Archives, Berlin, are digitising the DEUTSCHE WOCHESCHAU newsreel collection of German newsreels from 1949 and making them freely available over the Internet. Over 6,000 stories have been issued so far, for lowband (56K) or broadband (250K) connections, using Windows Media Player. The latter requires registration. Each clip comes with 'storyboard' and background information, and searching is by freetext, or by topic, personality, date or location. There are English language and German language versions of the site, but catalogue descriptions are in German only. The commentaries on the newsreels are, of course, in German.

World's Earliest Television Recordings

Web: http://www.tvdawn.com

Dedicated to recordings of the earliest British television broadcasts, many of them taken from disc recordings. There are fleeting glimpses of John Logie Baird experiments from 1927-28, the Paramount Astoria Girls on the BBC in 1933, and a recreation of Pirandello's THE MAN WITH THE FLOWER IN HIS MOUTH, the first television play (1930). Plus plenty of background information concerning Baird and the earliest experimental BBC broadcasts.

World Wide Internet TV

http://wwitv.com

Portal to live and on-demand online television programmes worldwide, covering over 2,300 channels from 137 countries. It also categorises channels by type, including Business News, Educational, Entertainment and Government, plus teletext/videotext, webcam streams, and P2P television.

INDEX

01zero-one, the Creative Learning Lab 103
100.4 SmoothFM 93
102.2 Smooth FM 87
10secfilmfest 122
2 entertain 112
3C 93, 97, 101
3WE 157
4 Learning 112
4Talent 103
96.3 Rock Radio 97

A

ABC1 58
Acorn Media UK 112
Acoustics and Vibration Animations 225
Action Coalition for Media Education 191
AdForum.com 225
Adult Channel 58
Adventure One 58
Advertising Association 157
Advertising Standards Authority 157
Africa in Motion 122
AHDS See Arts & Humanities Data Service
AHRC See Arts & Humanities Research Council
Ahead Training 103
All Party Parliamentary Group on Telecommunications 157
All Party Parliamentary Internet Group 157–158
Alliance Against IP Theft 158
ALT See Association for Learning Technology
Alternative Film Guide 53
American Memory 225
AMIA See Association of Moving Image Archivists
Angel Film Festival 122
Anglia Ruskin University: Communications & IT Services 205
Anglia See ITV1
Animal Planet 58

Animation Research Centre 158
Apollo Lunar Surface Journal 225
Archival Sound Recordings 226
Archives 43–46
Arizona Health Science Library – Medical Podcasts 198
ARKive 226
ARLIS-Link 108
Art Design Media Subject Centre 131
Art Libraries Society (ARLIS) 158
Artificial Eye Film Company 112
Arts & Humanities Data Service (AHDS) 53, 108, 158
Arts & Humanities Research Council (AHRC) 158
Arts Council of England 158–159
Arts Council of Northern Ireland 159
Arts Council of Wales 159
Artsworld See SkyArts
ARY Digital 58
Asia 1 TV 58
AsiaNet 59
Aslib – the Association for Information Management 159
Asociación Española de Cine Científico 191
Assessment of the Market Impact of the BBC's New Digital TV and Radio Services 145
Associate Parliamentary Media Literacy Group 159
Association for Database Services in Education & Training 159
Association for Learning Technology (ALT) 159
Association for Measurement and Evaluation of Communication 159–160
Association for the Study of Medical Education 160
Association of Commonwealth Universities 160
Association of Moving Image Archivists (AMIA) 108, 191
Association of UK Media Librarians 160

Aston University: Aston Media 205
AthenaWeb 226
Audiobook Publishing Association
 160
*Audiovisual Archiving: Philosophy and
 Principles* 146
Audio-Visual Association 160
Audio-visual centres 205–224
*Audiovisual Media Services Without
 Frontiers* 155
Audiovisueel Centrum Vrije
 Universiteit 191
Aurora Festival 122
Authors' Licensing and Collecting
 Society 160–161
AV Festival 122
AVNet 191
AVP 112
Awards 47–51

B

BAF Awards 47
BAFTA *See* British Academy of Film
 and Television Arts
Bangla TV 59
Bath Pod 198
Bay, The 94
BBC
Channels: BBC1 56, BBC1 regions
 59–61, BBC 1Xtra 85, BBC2 56,
 BBC2 regions 61–62, BBC3 57,
 BBC4 57, BBC4 World Cinema
 Awards 47, BBC 6 music 85, BBC
 7 86, BBC Asian Network 86,
 BBC London 94.9 87, BBC News
 24 59, BBC Parliament 59, BBC
 Radio 1 84, BBC Radio 2 84, BBC
 Radio 3 84, BBC Radio 4 84, BBC
 Radio 5 Live 85, BBC Radio 5
 Live Sports Extra 85, BBC Radio
 Berkshire 89, BBC Radio
 Cornwall 91, BBC Radio Cymru
 100, BBC Radio Derby 96, BBC
 Radio Devon 91, BBC Radio
 Foyle 101, BBC Radio Guernsey
 91, BBC Radio Lancashire 94,
 BBC Radio Leeds 95, BBC Radio
 Merseyside 94, BBC Nan
 Gaidheal 97, BBC Radio
 Newcastle 93, BBC Radio
 Orkney 97, BBC Radio Oxford

89, BBC Radio Scotland 97, BBC
 Radio Sheffield 95, BBC Radio
 Shetland 97, BBC Radio Solent
 89–90, BBC Radio Somerset
 Sound 91, BBC Radio Swindon
 91, BBC Radio Ulster 101, BBC
 Radio Wales 100, BBC Radio York
 95, BBC Southern Counties
 Radio 90, BBC World Service
 Radio 85, CBBC 64, CBeebies 64
Other: BBC Active 112, BBC Radio
 Collection 113, BBC Training 103,
 227, blogs 53, podcasts 198,
 websites 226
*BBC High Definition Television Channel
 Public Value Test* 155–156
BBC History 108
*BBC Independent Television
 Commissioning* 153
BBFC *See* British Board of Film
 Classification
Beat 106 *See* XFM Scotland
BECTa *See* British Educational
 Communications & Technology
 Agency
Belfast Film Festival 122
Berkeley Groks Science Show 198
Betting on Shorts 47
Beyond TV 123
BFFS *See* British Federation of Film
 Societies
BFI *See* British Film Institute
Bid TV 62
Bill Curtis Associates 104
BioethicsBytes 53
Biography Channel 63
Bioscope, The 53
Birds Eye View Film Festival 123
Birkbeck, University of London:
 Estates and Facilities 214
BIRTH 227
BISA *See* British and Irish Sound
 Archives Forum
Biz/ed 199
BKSTS *See* British Kinematograph,
 Sound & Television Society
Blogs 53–55
Bloomberg TV 63
Bollywood 4U 63
Bolton Digital Television Trial 151
Boomerang 63
Border *See* ITV1

Bournemouth University: Media Services 206
Bradford Animation Festival 123
Bradford International Film Festival 123
Bravo 63
BritDoc 123
British Academy 161
British Academy of Film and Television Arts (BAFTA) 47, 161
British Advertising Clearance Centre 161
British and Irish Sound Archives Forum (BISA) 108, 161
British Animation Awards 47–48
British Archaeological Awards 48
British Association of Picture Libraries and Agencies 161–162
British Board of Film Classification (BBFC) 162
British Broadcasting Corporation See BBC
British Computer Society 162
British Copyright Council 162
British Council 162
British Educational Communications & Technology Agency (BECTa) 162–63
British Educational Supplies Association 163
British Eurosport 63
British Federation of Film Societies (BFFS) 47, 163
British Film Industry, The: HCP 667–I: Sixth Report of Session 2002–03 141
British Film Industry Government Response to the Select Committee Report on the British Film Industry Session 2002–2003 CM 6022 142
British Film Institute (BFI) 163
BFI Distribution 113, BFI National Archive 43, BFI Video 113, Screenonline 233
British Independent Film Awards 48
British Interactive Media Association 48, 113
British Interactive Multimedia Association 163
British Internet Publishers Alliance 163

British Kinematograph, Sound & Television Society (BKSTS) 104, 164
British Library 164
British Library Sound Archive 113, 164
British Literary and Artistic Copyright Association 164
British Music Rights 164
British Pathe 227
British Phonographic Industry 164–165
British Screen Advisory Council 165
British Silent Cinema Festival 123
British Universities Film & Video Council (BUFVC) 165
contacts 13, courses 5, 104, discussion lists 108, 110–111, distribution 113, history 14–18, Learning on Screen 11, 52 membership 11–12, publications 7–10, services 1–10
British Video Association 165
Broadband Stakeholder Group 165
Broadcast Awards 48
Broadcast Digital Channel Awards 48–49
Broadcast Journalism Training Council 165–166
Broadcasters 56–102
Television channels recorded by the BUFVC 56–57, Other television channels listed on TRILT 59–84, Radio stations listed on TRILT: East Midlands 96–97, Eire 102, London 87–89, National 84–87, North East 93–96, Northern Ireland 101–102, Scotland 97–100, South East 89–90, South West 91–93, Wales 100–101, West Midlands 104, Yorkshire and Humberside 102–104
Broadcasters' Audience Research Board (BARB) 165
Broadcasting, Entertainment & Cinematograph Technicians Union (BECTU) 166
Broadcasting in Transition 142
Broadcasting Standards Commission See Ofcom
Broadcasting Trust 166

Brunel University: Media Services
207
BUFVC *See* British Universities Film
& Video Council
BUFVC/CBA Committee for
Audiovisual Education (CAVE)
166
*Building a Sustainable UK Film
Industry* 139
Business, Management, Accountancy
and Finance Centre 131
Buzz 97.1 *See* Wirral's Buzz 97.1

C

Cambridge Film Festival 123
Cambridge University Science
Productions (CUSP) 199, 207
Campaign for Digital Rights 166
Campaign for Press and
Broadcasting Freedom 166
Capital FM 87
Capital Gold 87
Cardiff University: Media Resources
Centre 207
*Caring for Our Collections: Culture,
Media and Sport Committee, Sixth
Report of Session 2006–07* 156
Carlton *See* ITV1
Carlton Cinema 64
Carlton West Country *See* ITV1
Cartoon Network 64
CAVE *See* BUFVC/CBA Committee
for Audiovisual Education
CBBC *See* BBC
CBeebies *See* BBC
Center for Independent
Documentary 53
Central FM 98
Centre for Bioscience, The 131
Centre for Education in the Built
Environment 131
Centre nationale de la recherche
scientifique (CNRS) 192
CERIMES 192
Challenge 64
Channel 64
Channel 4 57
Channel 5 *See* Five
Chartered Institute of Library and
Information Professionals (CILIP)
166–167

Choice FM 88
CILIP *See* Chartered Institute of
Library and Information
Professionals
CILT – The National Centre for
Languages 167
Cimtech 167
Cinema Exhibitors Association *See*
Independent Cinema Office
Cinenova 113
Cinephoto 108
City University: Audio-Visual
Services 209
Civilisation 65
Classic Gold 666/954 91
Classic Gold Marcher 1260AM
100
Classic Gold Plymouth 1152 91
Classroom Video 113
Clickandgovideo 108
Clinical Skills Online 227–228
Clyde 1 FM/2 AM 98
CNBC 65
CNI *See* Coalition for Networked
Information
CNNI 65
CNRS *See* Centre nationale de la
recherche scientifique
CNX *See* Toonami
Coachwise 114
Coalition for Networked
Information 192
Commercial Radio Companies
Association *See* Radiocentre
Commonwealth Broadcasting
Association 49, 167
Commonwealth Institute 167
Communications Act 2003 141
*Communications: Fourth Report of
Session 2001–2002: Vol. 1 – Report
and Proceedings of the Committee
– Culture Media and Sport
Committee* 138
*Communications: Government
Response to the Fourth Report of
the Culture, Media and Sport Select
Committee Session 2001–2002
(Cm 5554)* 138
Community Channel 65
Community Media Association 167
Community TV Trust 168
Concord Media 114

Construction Industry Training
  Board 114
*Consultation on Revised Ofcom
  Guidance for Broadcasters on Codes
  of Practice* 155
Consultation on the Future of Radio
  155
Contemporary Arts Media 114
Contender Entertainment 114
Conversations with History 228
Cool FM 102
Co-production Agreements 138
*Copyright, etc. and Trade Marks
  (Offences and Enforcement) Act
  2002* 139
Copyright Licensing Agency 168
Council for British Archaeology 168
County Sound Radio 90
Courses 103–107
CPH:DOX Copenhagen
  International Documentary Film
  Festival 125
Creative Club 228
Creativity-in-Education 108
C-SAP 135
*Cultural Test for British Films: Final
  Framework* 148
CUSP-BlueSci Podcasts 199
Cyfle 104, 168

D

Dance Books 114
DAVA – Digital Audiovisual
  Archiving 53
David Bordwell 54
DD Home Entertainment 114
*Decision no. 676/2002/EC on a
  Regulatory Framework for Radio
  Spectrum Policy in European
  Community (Radio Spectrum
  Decision)* 138
DEEP (Digital Education
  Enhancement Project) 199
Department for Children, Schools
  and Families (DCSF) 168
Department for Innovation,
  Universities and Skills (DIUS) 169
Department of Culture, Media and
  Sport (DCMS) 169
Descartes Prize for Science
  Communication 48

Design and Artists Copyright
  Society 169
Digital Content Forum 169
Digital Curation Centre 169
Digital Dividend Review 154
Digital Ethnography 54
Digital Preservation Coalition
  169–170
*Digital PSB – Public Service
  Broadcasting Post Digital Switchover*
  154
*Digital Switchover (Disclosure of
  Information) Act 2007 (c.8)* 156
Digital Television Group 170
DIMA – the Digital Media
  Association 192
*Directive 2001/29/EC: Copyright and
  Related Rights in the Information
  Society: Harmonisation of Certain
  Aspects* 137
*Directive 2002/19/EC of the European
  Parliament and of the Council on
  access to, and interconnection of,
  electronic communications networks
  and associated facilities (Access
  Directive)* 139
*Directive 2004/48/EC of the
  European Parliament and of the
  Council on the Enforcement of
  Intellectual Property Rights*
  144
Directors' and Producers' Rights
  Society 170
Directors Guild of Great Britain
  170
Discovery 65–66
Discussion lists 108–111
Disney Channel 66
DIVERSE 192–193
DocHouse 170
DocSpace 170
Document 5 International Human
  Rights Documentary Film Festival
  125
Documentary Blog, The 54
Documentary Educational
  Resources 114
Documentary Filmmakers Group
  105, 171
DOCUSUR 125
DOK.FEST 125
Downtown Radio 102

Durham University: Audio Visual Service 209
DV Talent 105

E

E4 67
E4 + 1 67
Earthstation1.com 115
East Anglian Film Archive 43
Eat Our Shorts 125
EBS Trust *See* Educational Broadcasting Services Trust
Economic Contribution of the UK Film Industry, The 147
Economic Impact of the UK Screen Industries, The 147–148
Economics Network, The 132
Economics of Delivering Local Digital Audio-visual and Interactive Services, The 147
ECS Video Podcasts 199
Edge Hill University: Learning Services 210
EDINA 171
Edinburgh International Film Festival 125
Edinburgh International Television Festival 125
Education Podcast Network 199
Educational Broadcasting Services Trust 115, 171
Educational Recording Agency (ERA) 19–22, 171
EduPodder 199
Einstein Network 115
Elearning 109
Emerging Themes 145
Encounters Short Film Festival 126
Engineering Subject Centre 132
English Subject Centre 132
Enlightenment in the 21st Century 199
Entertainment Retailers Association 171
Equity 171–172
ERA *See* Educational Recording Agency
ESCalate 132
ESDS Qualidata 172
Ethics Updates 228
Ethnographic Film Awards 49

Étienne-Jules Marey: Movement in Light 228
EuroDoc 193
European Audiovisual Observatory 193
European Broadcasting Union 193
European Bureau of Library Information and Documentation Associations 194
European Charter for the Development and Take Up of Film Online 151
European Convention for the Protection of the Audiovisual Heritage 137
European Digital Media Association 194
European Television History Network 194
Eurosport 67
Every Object Tells a Story 199
Exposures National Student Film Awards 49
Exposures UK Student Film Festival 126

F

Fantasy Channel *See* Television X
Federation Against Copyright Theft 172
Federation Against Software Theft 172
Fédération Internationale des Archives du Film (FIAF) 194
Federation of Commercial Audio-Visual Libraries (FOCAL) 49, 105, 181
Fenman Training 115
Festivals 122–130
FIAF *See* Fédération Internationale des Archives du Film
FIAT/IFTA 194–195
Film Archive Forum 172
Film Council *See* UK Film Council
Film Council: Improving Access to, and Education about, the Moving Image through the British Film Institute 142
Film Design International 105
Film Distributors' Association 173
Film Education 115, 173

Film London 173
Filmbank Distributors 115
FilmFour 67
Film-Philosophy 109
Films for the Humanities & Sciences 115
Films from the Home Front 230
Film-Screening 109
Final Report: Study on Co-Regulation Measures in the Media Sector 154
Findsounds 228
First Light Movies Awards 49
Five 57
FOCAL *See* Federation of Commercial Audio-Visual Libraries
FORA.tv 229
Forth One/Two 98
Foundation for Information Policy Research 174
Fox Kids 67
FREDDIE Awards 49
Free Culture UK 174
Front Row 67
FT2 105
FTN 68
Future of European Regulatory Audiovisual Policy, The: Communication from the Commission to the Council, the European Parliament, the European Economic and Social Committee and the Committee of the Regions COM(2003)784 141

G

Galaxy 101 *See* Kiss 101
Gaumont Pathé Archives 229
GEES Subject Centre 133
Gemini FM 97.0 92
German Film Festival 126
Glasgow Caledonian University: Audio-Visual Services 211
Glasgow Film Festival 126
Glasgow University Podcasts 199
Goldsmiths, University of London: Media Services Centre 214
Government Response to the Creative Industries Forum on Intellectual Property 148

Government's Response to the Report of the Joint Committee on the Draft Communications Bill (Cm 5646) 139
Gower Publishing 115
Gowers Review of Intellectual Property: Call for Evidence 151
Gowers Review of Intellectual Property: Final Report 151
Grampian *See* Scottish
Granada 68 *See also* ITV1
Grant and Cutler 116
Grierson Trust 49, 174
Guide to Digital Television and Digital Switchover, A 149
GWR 92

H

Hallmark 68
HE Academy subject centres 131–136
Health and Safety Executive Videos 116
Health Library Online Video Collection 229
Health Sciences & Practice Subject Centre 133
Heart 100.7 96
Heart 106.2 88
Heat 86
H-Film 109
Hidden Treasures: The UK Audiovisual Archives Strategic Framework 142
Higher Education Academy Physical Sciences Centre 135
Higher Education Academy Psychology Network 135
Higher Education Academy Subject Centre for Medicine, Dentistry and Veterinary Medicine (MEDEV) 135
History 68
History-Digitisation 109
Hospitality, Leisure, Sport & Tourism Network 133
Hotdocs 126
HTV Wales *See* ITV1
HTV West *See* ITV1
HubbleSite 229
Human Kinetics Europe 116

Human Rights Watch International Film Festival 126
HWD Radio 95

I

i2010 Digital Libraries Communication (COM 2005) 465 final 148
Iamhist *See* International Association for Media and History
IAMS *See* International Association for Media in Science
I.A. Recordings 116
IASA *See* International Association of Sound and Audiovisual Archives
Ideal World 68
Illuminations 116
Image et Science 126
Images of Black Women Film Festival 127
Imperial College London – Public Lectures 200
Imperial College, University of London: Media Services 214
Imperial War Museum
distribution 116, Film and Video Archive 43, Student Film Awards 49, Student Film Festival 127
Incorporated Society of Musicians 174
Independent Cinema Office 174
Independent Film Parliament 174
Independent Review of BBC Online 145
Independent Review of the BBC's Digital Radio Services 144
Independent Review of the BBC's Digital Television Services 144–145
Independent Television Commission *See* Ofcom
Industry Trust for IP Awareness 175
Information Aesthetics 54
Information and Computer Sciences 133
Institute for Public Policy Research 175, 200
Institute of Education, University of London: Information Services 214

Institute of Medical Illustrators 175
Institute of Practitioners in Advertising 175
Institut für den Wissenschaftlichen Film (IWF) 195
Institution of Civil Engineers 116
Intellectual Property; A Balance 151–152
International Association for Media and History (Iamhist) 49, 195
International Association for Media in Science (IAMS) 109, 195
International Association of Sound & Audiovisual Archives (IASA) 109, 195
International Broadcasting Trust 116 *See also* 3WE
International Festival of Ethnographic Film 127
International Science Film Festival 127
International Visual Communications Association (IVCA) 50, 175
Internet Services Providers Association 175
Internet2 195–196
Intute-Announce 109
Island FM 92
ITN News Channel Radio 86
ITV
ITV1 Anglia 70, Border 70, Carlton Central 70, Carlton West Country 70, Granada 70, London 57, Meridian 71, Tyne Tees Television 71, Wales 71, West of England 71, Yorkshire 71, ITV2 71, ITV3 71, ITV4 72, ITV News 70, ITV Sports Channel 70
IWF *See* Institut für den Wissenschaftlichen Film

J

JANET UK 176
Jazz FM 100.4 *See* 100.4 SmoothFM
JISC *See* Joint Information Systems Committee
John Brabourne Awards 50
Joint Information Systems Committee (JISC) 54, 109, 176, 203–204

K

Kerrang! Radio 86
Kestrel FM 90
Key 103FM 94
Kick FM 90
Kingdom FM 99
King's College, University of London: Audio Visual Services 214–215
Kiss 100 FM 88
Kiss 101 91, 100–101
Kix 96 See Touch FM
Kraszna-Krausz Foundation 50, 176

L

Lancaster University Television 212
Lantern 96.2 FM 91
Laparoscopy.com 229
Learning on Screen 11, 50
Lecture Theatre Managers Group 176
Leeds Animation Workshop 117
Leeds International Film Festival 127
Leeds Metropolitan University: Technology Services 213
Leeds Trinity & All Saints: Media Services 213
Leeds Young People's Film Festival 127
Legislative Proposal for an Audiovisual Media Directive: Towards a Modern Framework for Audiovisual Content 153
Legislative Proposal for an Audiovisual Media Services Directive: Towards a Modern Framework for Audiovisual Content (COM(2005)646final) 147
Liberty TV 72
Libraries and Archives Copyright Alliance 176
LIS-Link 109
LIS-MMIT 110
Listening to the Past, Speaking to the Future: Report of the Archives Task Force 142
Liverpool Hope University: Library, Learning & Information Services 213–214
Living 72

Living Room Candidate 229
London Film Festival See The Times BFI London Film Festival
London International Animation Festival 128
London International Documentary Festival: A Conversation in Film 128
London Mathematical Society 117
London Metropolitan University: Media Services 216
London's Screen Archives: The Regional Network 44
LondonScreenArchives 110
Loughborough University: Media Services 216
Lux 117
LWT See ITV1

M

Magic 105.4 88
Magic 1152 93
Magic 1548 94
Magic 828 95
Manchester Metropolitan University: Media Services 216
Manx Radio 94
Marcher Gold See Classic Gold Marcher 1260AM
Maths, Stats & OR Network (MSOR) 135
MCPS-PRS Alliance 176
MECCSA See Media, Communication & Cultural Studies Association
Media Archive for Central England 44
Media, Communication & Cultural Studies Association (MECCSA) 110, 177
Media Diversity in Europe 138
Media Education Association 177
Media Education Foundation 117
Media legislation and reports 137–56
Media Literacy Task Force 177
Media March 177
Media Resources Center 54
Media Society 177
Media Trust 177–178
Medialib 110
Media-Support-Services 110

mediawatch-UK 178
Men and Motors 72
Mental Health Media 117, 178
Meridian *See* ITV1
MFM 103.4 101
Michael Geist 54
Microbiology Video Library 230
MicrobiologyBytes 200
Middlesex University: Learning Resources 217
MIMAS 178
Minster FM 96
Mission Staff Working Document; Media Pluralism in the Member States of the European Union, Sec(2007)32 154
MLA *See* Museums, Libraries and Archives Council
Molecular Expressions Digital Video Library 230
Money Channel, The 72
Moray Firth Radio 99
More4 72
More4 + 1 72
Motion Picture Association 196
Moving History 230
Moving Image Society *See* British Kinematograph, Sound & Television Society
MTV 73
Munich International Short Film Festival 128
Museums, Libraries and Archives Council (MLA) 110, 178
Music Factory, The 73
Music Publishers Association 178
Musicians Union 179
MUTV 73

N

National Archives, The 179
National Computing Centre 179
National Council on Archives 179
National Film & Television School 179
National Geographic 73–74
National Institute of Adult Continuing Education (NIACE) 179–180
National Media Museum 180

National Resource Centre for Dance 181
National Science Foundation 196
National Screen and Sound Archive of Wales 44
National Student Television Association (NaSTA) 180
New Approach to Public Service Content in the Digital Media Age: The Potential Role of the Public Service Publisher 154–155
New Entrants Animation Scheme (NEATS) 106
New Producers Alliance 180
Newsfilm Online 231
Nick Jr. 74
Nickelodeon 74
Northern Region Film and Television Archive 44
Northsound One/Two 99
Northumbria University: IT Services 217
North West Film Archive 44
Nottingham Trent University: Video Services 217
Nova 200

O

Ocean FM 90
Ofcom 180
Ofcom's Decision on the Future Regulation of Broadcast Advertising 144
Office of Communications Act 2002 139
Office of the Telecommunications Ombudsman (Otelo) 180–181
Oftel *See* Ofcom
Old Pond Publishing 117
Old Time Radio 231
One World Broadcasting Trust 181
Onedotzero 128
One World International Human Rights Film Festival 128
Oneword 86
Online/More Colour in the Media 196
Onsport1/2 74
Open2.net 200
Open Knowledge Foundation 181

Open University Worldwide – Learning Resources 117
Open Video Project 231
OpenLearn 231
Oral History Society 181
Orchard FM 92
Organ Grinder 54
Organisations – UK 157–190
Organisations – international 191–197
Otelo See Office of the Telecommunications Ombudsman
Oxfam Publishing 117
Oxford Brookes University: Audio Visual Production 218
Oxford Educational Resources 118

P

Pact See Producers Alliance for Cinema & Television
Pakistani Channel See ARY Digital
PALATINE 132
Panda Awards 50
Paradise FM 88
Paramount Comedy Channel 74
Parliamentlive.tv 231
Pavilion Publishing 118
Peak 107FM 96
Performance 74
Performing Rights Society See MCPS-PRS Alliance
Phoenix CNE 75
Phonographic Performance Limited 181
Pidgeon Digital 118
Pirate FM 92
Planning Options for Digital Switchover 149
Playboy TV 75
Play UK 75
Podcasting 198–202
Podcasting (discussion list) 110
Podcasts for Educators, Schools and Colleges 200
Podcats 200
Poetry Archive 231–232
Praxis Films 106
Prelinger Library Blog 54
Premier Christian Radio 88
Press Complaints Commission 181

Producers Alliance for Cinema & Television (Pact) 105–106, 181–182
Production Managers' Association 182
Progress Towards Achieving Digital Switchover – A BBC Report to the Government 145
Projection Box Essay Award 50
Proposals for a Co-regulatory System for Training and the Development of Skills in Television and Radio 146
Provision of Current Affairs, The – Report on: The Current Affairs Audit 2005, Current Affairs Qualitative Viewer Research and Ofcom's Symposium on the Future of Current Affairs 152
Public BBC, A 146
Public Information Films 232
Public Innovation: Intellectual Property in a Digital Age 153
Public Service for All, A: The BBC in the Digital Age (Cm 6763) 149–150
Public Service Reform Interviews 200
Publishers' Licensing Society 182
Pulse, The 96

Q

Q Radio 86
Q102.9FM 102
Q96 FM See 96.3 Rock Radio
Qualidata See ESDS Qualidata
Qualifications & Curriculum Authority 182
Quality Improvement Agency 182
Quantum Leap 118
Queens University Belfast: Media Services 219
Quiz Call 75
QVC 75

R

Racing Channel 75
Radio 2CRFM 90
Radio Academy 182
Radio Advertising Bureau See RadioCentre
Radio Airedale 96

Radio Atlantic 252 87
Radio Authority *See* Ofcom
Radio Borders 93, 99
Radio City 96.7 94
Radio Joint Audience Research
　(RAJAR) 183
Radio – Preparing for the Future:
　Phase 2 Implementing the
　Framework 149
Radio Royal 99
Radio Society of Great Britain 183
Radio Tay AM/FM 99
Radio Victory *See* Ocean FM
Radiocommunications Agency *See*
　Ofcom
RadioCentre, The 182–183
Radio-Studies 110
Raidio Na Gaeltachta 102
Raindance 106, 128, 183
Rapture TV 75
Real Radio 100
Real to Réel 128
Red Dragon FM 101
Red Hot 75
Reform of Film Tax Incentive, The:
　Promoting the Sustainable
　Production of Culturally British Film
　148
Regional Support Centres
　203–204
Regulatory Impact Assessment: BBC
　Charter Review 150
Report into Digital Rights
　Management 152
Report of the Inquiry into the
　Circumstances Surrounding the
　Death of Dr David Kelly (HCP 247)
　145–146
Report of the Joint Committee on the
　Draft Communications Bill 138–139
Research at Chicago 201
Research Information Network
　(RIN) 183
ResearchBuzz 55
ResearchChannel 232
Research-TV 232
Response from the Department of
　Culture Media and Sport to the
　Communication from the
　Commission i2010: Digital Libraries
　150
Restoration Tips & Notes 55

Review of ITV Networking
　Arrangements 149
Review of the BBC Value for Money
　and Efficiency Programmes 150
Review of the BBC's Royal Charter:
　Draft Royal Charter and Framework
　Agreement 150
Review of the Television Production
　Sector: Consultation Document 150
Robert Gordon University:
　Educational Media Services 220
Rock FM 95
Roehampton University: Television
　Roehampton 220
Roland Collection 118, 232
Royal Anthropological Institute
　(RAI) 118, 183
Royal Holloway, University of
　London: Audio Visual Service 215
Royal Society, The 183–184, 201
Royal Television Society (RTS) 184
Royal Veterinary College, University
　of London: Electronic-media Unit
　215

S

S4C/S4C2 76
Safety Media 118
St Andrews University: SALTIRE 220
St George's, University of London:
　Television Production Unit 215
Satellite and Cable Broadcasters
　Group 184
SCHoMS *See* Standing Conference
　for Heads of Media Services
Science 76
ScienceLive 232
Scientific American Podcasts 201
Sci-Fi 76
Scinema Festival of Science Film 129
Scitalks 233
SCONUL *See* Society of College,
　National and University Libraries
Scot FM *See* Real Radio
Scottish 76
Scottish Arts Council 184
Scottish Screen 184
Scottish Screen Archive 45
Scottish Screen New Entrants
　Training Scheme (NETS)
　106–107

Scottish Students on Screen 50
SCRAN 233
Screen07 129
Screen Archive South East 45
Screen Heritage Network 184
Screenonline 233
Screenshop 76
SCUDD 110
SEE: The Brighton Documentary
    Film Festival 129
ShakespeareCast.com 201
Shaksper 110
Sheffield Doc/Fest 129
Shooting People 184
Shop! 77
Simply Money77
Skillset 107, 186
Sky
SkyArts 77, Sky Box Office Events
    77, Sky cinema 77, Sky Movies
    77–79, Sky News 79, Sky One
    79–80, Sky Premier 80, Sky
    Sports 80, Sky Three 80, Sky
    Travel 80
Smash Hits Radio 87
Snowmail 201
Society for Research into Higher
    Education 186
Society of Archivists 186
Society of Authors 186
Society of College, National and
    University Libraries (SCONUL)
    186
Songwriting 201
Sony Radio Academy Awards 51
South Bank Show 201
South Hams Radio 93
South West Film and Television
    Archive 45
Spectrum 558 AM 88
Speech Accent Archive 233
Spoken Word Publishing Association
    See Audiobook Publishing
    Association
Spoken Word Services 233
Staff & Educational Development
    Association 187
Stagework 234
Standing Conference for Heads of
    Media Services (SCHoMS)
    187
Stanford on iTunes U 201

*Statutory Instrument 2001 No. 223:
    The Broadcasting (Limit on the
    Holding of Licences to Provide
    Television Multiplex Services) Order
    2001* 137
*Statutory Instrument 2001 No. 2378:
    The Broadcasting (Subtitling) Order
    2001* 137
*Statutory Instrument 2003 No. 187:
    The Copyright (Certification of
    Licensing Scheme for Educational
    Recording of Broadcasts) (Open
    University) Order 2003* 140
*Statutory Instrument 2003 No. 1672:
    The Broadcasting (Independent
    Productions) (Amendment) Order
    2003* 140
*Statutory Instrument 2003 no. 1901:
    The Advanced Television Services
    Regulations 2003* 141
*Statutory Instrument 2003 No. 2498:
    The Copyright and Related Rights
    Regulations 2003* 140
*Statutory Instrument 2003 No. 3299:
    The Media Ownership (Local Radio
    and Appointed News Provider)
    Order 2003* 141
*Statutory Instrument 2004 no. 1944:
    The Community Radio Order 2004
    144 Statutory Instrument 2005 No.
    222: The Copyright (Certification of
    Licensing Scheme for Educational
    Recording of Broadcasts)
    (Educational Recording Agency Ltd)
    Order 200* 146
*Statutory Instrument 2006 No. 18: The
    Performances (Moral Rights, etc.)
    Regulations 2006* 149
Stephen's Web 55
Strategy for UK Screen Heritage 156
Streaming 111
Street Anatomy 55
*Strong BBC, Independent of
    Government, A* 146
Student Radio Association 51, 187
Subject Centre for History, Classics
    and Archaeology 133
Subject Centre for Languages,
    Linguistics and Area Studies 134
Subject Centre for Philosophical
    and Religious Studies 135
Sunrise Radio 89

SURFfoundation 196
SWAP HE Academy Subject Centre 136

T

TASI *See* Technical Advisory Service for Images
TCM 80
TCM/WCW 81
Teachers' TV 81, 118, 202
TechDis 29–33, 187
Technical Advisory Service for Images (TASI) 55, 107, 187
Television Access Services: Review of the Code and Guidance 151
Television Archiving 55
Television Content in the Digital Age 140
Television News Archive Vanderbilt University 234
Television Production Sector Review: A Survey of TV Programme Production in the UK 148
Television X 81
Televisual Intelligent Factual Festival 129
theatreVOICE 234
Thomas Cook TV 81
Times BFI London Film Festival 129
To Fly is Everything 234
Toonami 81
Touch FM 96
Trace the Noble Dust 55
Training 103–107
Training and Performance Showcase (TAPS) 107
Travel & Living 81
Trouble 81
Trumedia 119
Trust for the Study of Adolescence 119
Turbo 82
.TV 82
TV Choice 119
Tyne Tees Television *See* ITV1

U

UCB Christian Radio 89, 97
UK and International Film Co-production Agreements, The: A Policy Paper DCMS/UK Film Council 147
UK Centre for Legal Education – UKCLE 134
UK Centre for Materials Education 134
UK-Colleges 111
UK Data Archive 187
UKERNA *See* JANET UK
UK Film Council 187–188
UK Intellectual Property Office 188
UK MEDIA 188
UK Office for Library & Information Networking (UKOLN) 188
UKOLN *See* UK Office for Library & Information Networking
UKTV
Bright ideas 82, Documentary 82, Drama 82, Food 83, G2 83, Gold 83, History 83, Style 83
Ulster 83
Undercurrents 119
United Nations Association Film Festival 129
United Nations Centre for Human Settlements 119
United States Holocaust Memorial Museum 234
Universities Collaboration in E-Learning 188
Universities UK 188
University Channel 202
University College Falmouth: Media Centre 210
University College London: Media Resources 216
University Film and Video Association (UFVA) 196–197
University of Aberdeen: Department of Medical Illustration 205
University of Abertay Dundee: Information Services 205
University of Bath: Audio Visual Unit 205–206
University of Birmingham: Media Centre 206
University of Bradford: Learner Support Services 206
University of Brighton: Media Centres 206–207

University of Chester: Media Services 207–208

University of Dundee: Video Production Service 209

University of East Anglia: Audio Visual Services 209

University of East London: Learning Resource Centres 210

University of Essex: Audiovisual & Media Services 210

University of Exeter: IT Services 210

University of Glamorgan: Media Services 210

University of Glasgow: Learning & Teaching Centre 210

University of Hull: AudioVisual Service 210

University of Hull: Hull Immersive Visualization Environment (HIVE) 211

University of Keele: Media and Communications Centre 211

University of Kent: Audio Visual Services 211

University of Leeds: Media Services 211

University of Leicester: Audio Visual Services 212

University of Manchester: Media Centre 216–217

University of Newcastle – School of Neurology, Neurobiology and Psychiatry 234–235

University of Newcastle upon Tyne: Television Services 217

University of Oxford: Media Production Unit 218

University of Paisley: ICT Media Services 218

University of Plymouth: Television and Broadcast Services 219

University of Portsmouth: e-Learning Centre 219

University of Reading: Media Production 219

University of Salford: Audio Visual Services 220

University of Sheffield: Learning Development and Media Unit 119, 220

University of Southampton: e.media 220

University of Strathclyde: Learning Services 220

University of Sunderland: Audio Visual Team 220

University of Surrey: UniS Television 222

University of Sussex: Media Services Unit 222

University of Ulster Public Affairs Audio Archive 202

University of Ulster: Media Technology Support 222

University of Wales, Aberystwyth: See3D 222

University of Wales, Bangor: Media Centre 222–223

University of Wales Institute, Cardiff: Audio Visual Support 223

University of Wales, Newport: Audio Visual Services 223

University of Wales, Swansea: Media Resources 223

University of Warwick: Audio Visual Centre 223

University of Westminster: Computing and Audio Visual 223–224

University of Winchester: IT & Communication Services Department 224

University of Worcester: Digital Arts Centre 224

University of York: Audio-Visual Centre 224

Uniview Worldwide 119

V

Valleys Radio 101

Vega Science Trust 120, 189, 235

Vera Media 189

VET 107

VH1 83

Vibe 101 FM *See* Kiss 101

Video 111

Video Active 55, 197

Video Arts 120

Video Development Initiative 197

Video Performance Ltd 189

Video Standards Council 189

Videography for Educators 235
videolectures.net 235
Videomed 130
Videos for Patients 120
Videotel International 120
Viewtech Educational Media 120
Virgin Radio 87
Virgin Radio 105.8FM 89
Virtual Chemistry 235
Visual Cognition Lab 235
Visualisation Tools 111
VLE 111
Vlogdir 55
Voice of the Listener & Viewer 189

Wireless Telegraphy Act 2006 (c.36) 153
Wirral's Buzz 97.1 95
Wochenschau-Archive 236
Women Make Movies 120
Woodhead Publishing 120–121
World Association of Medical and Health Films (WAMHF) 197
World Intellectual Property Organisation 197
World Microfilms 121
World Wide Internet TV 236
World's Earliest Television Recordings 236
Writers & Scholars International 189
Writers Guild of Britain 189

W

Warwick Podcasts 202
Web sites 225–236
Wellcome Trust, Moving Image and Sound Collections 120
Wessex Film and Sound Archive 45
Westsound 100
Wildscreen Festival 130
Willingness to Pay for the BBC During the Next Charter Period 153

XYZ

XFM 104.9 89
XFM Scotland 100
York Films of England 121
Yorkshire *See* ITV1
Yorkshire Film Archive 45
Z-Axis: History of Animation in Court 202
Zee TV 85